WAR AND
EXISTENCE

WAR AND EXISTENCE

A Philosophical Inquiry

Michael Gelven

The Pennsylvania State University Press
University Park, Pennsylvania

Permission to reprint the four lines from W. H. Auden's poem "In Memory of W. B. Yeats" has been given by Random House, Inc., from *W. H. Auden: Collected Poems*, by W. H. Auden, edited by Edward Mendelson. Copyright 1940 and renewed 1968 by W. H. Auden.

Library of Congress Cataloging-in-Publication Data

Gelven, Michael.
    War and existence : a philosophical inquiry / Michael Gelven.
       p.   cm.
    ISBN 0-271-01052-5. — ISBN 0-271-01054-1 (pbk.)
    1. War — Philosophy.   I. Title.
    U21.2.G44   1993
    355.02'01 — dc20   92-41697
                                          CIP

Published by The Pennsylvania State University Press,
Barbara Building, Suite C, University Park, PA 16802-1003

It is the policy of The Pennsylvania State University Press to use acid-free paper for the first printing of all clothbound books. Publications on uncoated stock satisfy the minimum requirements of American National Standard for Information Sciences — Permanence of Paper for Printed Library Materials, ANSI Z39.48–1984.

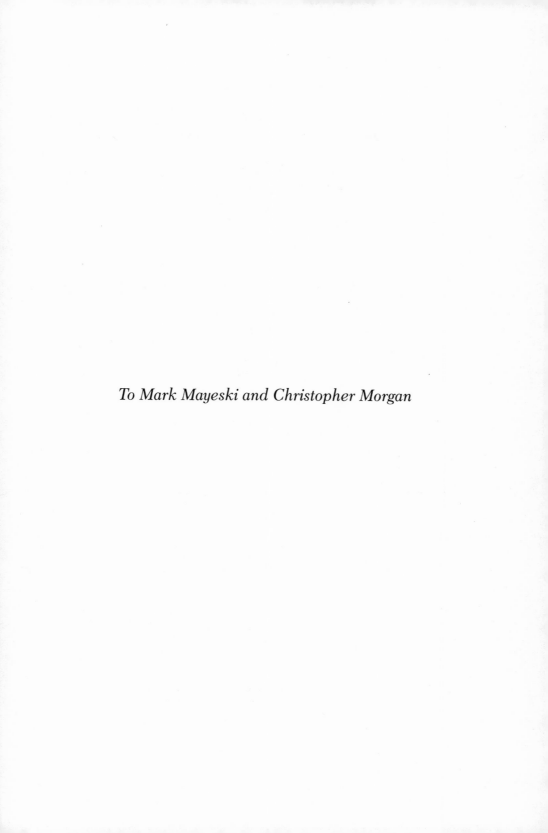

To Mark Mayeski and Christopher Morgan

Contents

Acknowledgments

It is the happy office of the grateful to number those in brief who sustained so long; it is a small but precious ticket to imprint their names as thanks, when what they gave was more: to Don Livingston, for patient and unstinting service, so long unacknowledged the debt seems unanswered; to Herman Stark, for enthusiasm and growing friendship through the dark days, reaching sunlight within a week of our triumphs; to my sister, Fran Mayeski, whose trust, as always, did not waver; to Craig Hulfachor, for reminding me often of the worth of these ideas; to Scott Sunquist, who gave them a French hearing; and to Debbie Sanderson, who did more than merely type the manuscript, she crafted it around my impatience and shortcomings. There were also others; they gave, and though unnamed, they are honored and remembered too.

Preface

This is a philosophical inquiry into the nature and meaning of war. It is not primarily concerned with the moral question whether war ought ever to be waged, and only indirectly concerned with the military question how war ought to be carried out. Rather it is solely concerned with what war is or what the truth about war is. In one sense, of course, we already know what war is, in the same way we already know what justice or love is; yet this does not stop philosophers from writing books about justice and love. We know enough about war to be able to identify it, spot it, define it, and even describe it. But one can still question how we think about it, and hence what the fundamental principles are and how it relates to the broader picture of our meaning and truth.

Because this is an inquiry and not a treatise, the procedure necessarily begins with a development of the question. It is important to understand why war is problematic at all and what the puzzles and paradoxes of this vast phenomenon might be, lest in providing overly quick answers one miss some vital and essential point. Being an inquiry, the approach is from darkness to light; that is, from a vague and generalized description of how we seem to think about war to the final isolation of principles and reasons; the argument traces backward from the phenomenon to what explains the phenomenon, as is revealed by a glance at the Contents.

Because this inquiry is philosophical, the sole purpose of the tortuous analyses is truth, truth for its own sake. The inquiry is carried out in order better to understand a seemingly puzzling, if not incoherent, occurrence, to make what is conceptual disorder into relatively ordered comprehension. Because it is truth alone that matters, the effects of such understanding, though important in many ways, cannot detract from the philosophical rigor required to illuminate what is otherwise a beguiling darkness. This focus on the nature of war places the inquiry somewhat outside the present mainstream of publications. There are countless articles and books on the moral-

ity of war, and fewer, though still many, ideas about how to wage war, but
only a handful on the nature, or fundamental meaning, of war. It may seem
strange that clever men and women should write so prodigiously on the
morality of a phenomenon before they understand what it is, but it is far
easier to indict than to understand.

In the fourth century B.C., Sun Tzu wrote *On the Art of War*, a taoist
interpretation of strategy in which the violence on the battlefield is integrated into a generalist understanding of all struggle, which is part of life
itself. It is thus a source of illumination not only of the mechanics of generals
on the battlefield but also of the workings of the spirit against the enemies
within us that threaten our personal tao, or harmony. Sun Tzu thus recognizes that war and human existence itself are intelligible by reference to the
same laws and principles. No philosophical account of war can restrict itself
to what occurs on the fields or in the war rooms of mighty nations. To
understand war requires that we understand ourselves, and the converse of
that proposition is likewise true.

In 1831 Carl von Clausewitz died, leaving his masterpiece *On War* to be
published posthumously. Clausewitz, like all German thinkers in the nineteenth century, was deeply inspired by the philosophy of Immanuel Kant;
and so in his single work one finds references to principles, categories, ideas,
and the important distinction between rational concepts and empirical
notions together making the world intelligible. Like Sun Tzu, Clausewitz
sought to understand the phenomenon of war, not as a single, isolated event,
but as a part of the social whole, recognizing that war is fundamentally
unintelligible unless it is examined in light of the totality of our existence.
War is coherent only as a part of who we are, but our being warriors in turn
illuminates who we are in the first place.

But it is Plato's reasoning in *The Republic* that most profoundly inte-
grates our understanding of the warrior with our comprehension of our own
reality. For Plato shows that the warrior's position in the emerging polis
corresponds to the same position of spirit within the human soul. In the
warrior's virtue of courage, we first recognize the autonomy of goodness
from personal interest; only through the education of the guardian in the
political arena, or the fostering of spirit within the development of the
human soul, is it possible to isolate goodness for its own sake. This discovery
makes the study of war necessary for a philosophically comprehensive view
of who we are. We learn from this the profound truth that life measured
solely by its length falls short, but a life shortened by honor reaches its
fullest measure.

Recent developments in the methodologies of philosophical inquiry have made analysis of many concepts more available to our contemporary prejudices; as a modern thinker, armed with these new techniques, I have endeavored to make modern war, by which I mean war since Frederick the Great, not merely the subject of moral debates but the object of a true philosophical inquiry. The approach taken was selected solely because it is the best, or at least most successful, way of integrating the vast contributions of thought from both Anglo-American and Continental traditions. It is a genuine inquiry into war; there is no attempt to persuade readers of a particular ideology or philosophical system. Because of this, I have avoided as much as possible all technical vocabulary and have taken the time and space to restate classical problems before giving traditional answers to them. I am convinced that the way one sets up a problem or even asks a question may distort or even forfeit any chance of meaningful comprehension. Thus, professional readers may find classical questions raised anew. This has the felicitous advantage of making the nonprofessional reader fully aware of what is going on. This may make the style of this work seem somewhat painstaking, but as long as the writing is clear, the force of the ideas should suffice. I do not consider it a liability to write clearly or to make ideas available to those outside certain cults of professional jargon.

It may seem odd that there are so few contemporary books that purport to provide a philosophical approach to the understanding of war itself. There are many, of course, who consider such an effort simply anachronistic, that since Wittgenstein such inquiries into the nature, or 'essence', of anything are ill advised and the authors in need of therapy to relieve them from asking unanswerable questions. But to indict before understanding has long been known as a form of prejudice, and all I ask is that this study be given the chance to reveal, if possible, a deeper understanding of one of the most baffling of human endeavors. Since the tags and labels of the ubiquitous isms of the academic ideologues are surely among the greatest impediments to truth, it should not, I hope, be held against me if I refrain from characterizing this work accordingly.

Part One

THE PARADOX

1

The Paradox of War

Some are only seventeen; many are even less than that. Their khaki
uniforms and steel helmets and high-laced boots appear as mockeries to
their innocence. In their young and skilled hands they hold terrible weapons
designed to send awesome destruction over great distances against targets
that are known as the enemy, often boys as young as they, boys whose
names they do not know. They kill and they die; and when they do, no one
assigns them felonious or capital charges, no one brings them before tribu-
nals of judgment, and few would even try to call them criminals. Their
counterparts, the enemy, are no less vulnerable, no less innocent, no less
loved by their mothers and sweethearts than they. The enemy, too, want to
live and expect to live, to grow and discover things and further the advance
of humanity at least by propagating their own kind, if nothing else. They are
always the young, possessing youthful virtues like valor and bravery and
great adaptability, but their curious vocation is death, taking and receiving
it, dying and killing. For the gathered host only one thing matters: victory.
That is how they see things: victory or defeat. No other value seems to

matter to them, not even their own. To achieve victory is everything; to suffer defeat is the only failure.

But if defeat is the only loss for the warrior, and victory the only triumph, it is not the same for those who seek to understand it. There is much that is puzzling in war, and the phenomenon itself seems totally incoherent. Men who do not even know one another are supremely dedicated to one another's annihilation. Good and honest soldiers on both sides seek to destroy one another with an almost universal approbation. Normally society cannot condone one person taking the life of another, but in war the question of legal censure against such acts does not even come up. This is what needs to be thought through if war is not to be judged an absurdity. If the warrior aches only for victory, the thinker aches for coherence. The general asks, How can we win? The philosopher asks, How can war be thought without contradiction?

It seems at first glance that war remains an absurdity, something that cannot be thought, something that contains contradictions, something that, when pressed, cannot stand the test of intelligibility. The spectacle of countless youths bent on mutual destruction certainly seems to qualify as something unintelligible. What could possibly justify the immeasurable suffering of a battlefield? What seems less important than the few yards of beaten ground that changes hands after a day's slaughter? What is the prize? Hamlet says it best: an eggshell. Thousands of men die for a mere eggshell. Surely that, if anything, is incomprehensible. Surely war, among all human activities, deserves the ultimate censure. Surely there is only a foolishness here, or a wickedness of a special sort, a wickedness of deceit and cruelty. Perhaps war is incomprehensible just because it is so thoroughly evil; it can no more be understood than it can be condoned.

There are many, of course, who are ready to condemn it accordingly. We are amply provided with eager condemnations, with censures absolute and terrible. War has been judged as wicked and barbaric, as evil and as insane, as unworthy of any thinker. It is the second horseman of the Apocalypse, the blight of greed, the offspring of power and corruption, the product of cunning and deception. And for anyone who has ever observed the brilliant carnage of a war, these indictments may seem pale and insufficient. Even the most hardened of observers cannot remain unmoved by the dreadful suffering of war and the exorbitant waste of what is beloved and precious. All who are thoughtful and sensitive, it seems, must abhor war. And indeed, for the most part, all who are sensitive and intelligent do abhor war.

But though they abhor war and condemn it and deeply regret its occurrence, few are pacifists. In spite of an almost universal antipathy to such costly belligerence, young men train for it, armies are still gathered and paid for, and governments prepare for military maneuvers. When there are wars, entire peoples support the cost of the belligerence with their labor, their voices, their sacrifices, and their pocketbooks. And the wars themselves go on. So the thinker must somehow try to make sense of what, as an event, seems to defy comprehension. It is a necessity for us to make sense of war, else we must assume a monstrous judgment against most of our fellow human beings. Unless we can make sense of war, we must assume that the millions and millions of men who fought were all quite mad. We must assume that all those who died believing they were making an honorable sacrifice were in fact beguiled, foolish, and hugely ignorant, for the logic is inescapable: if one argues that war is madness, then all the sacrifices were indeed in vain. It is difficult enough to think of men dying for their country; it is unspeakable to judge them fools as well.

The men who died did not always judge their sacrifice to be meaningless, nor do most of us. Yet, if we are to assume that war is not completely insane, we must somehow accommodate all the seeming contradictions. Sense must somehow be made of homicides that are not murder, of violence that is not wanton, and of values that can withstand the challenge of our sensibilities. In short, we must learn to think that what appears at first to be a contradiction is in fact a paradox.

If war is to be rendered susceptible of noncontradictory understanding, it must nevertheless remain a troubling notion just because it is impossible to forget completely the terrible price of suffering involved, just as it is impossible to deny the curious significance of war that makes us willing to endure its cost. Paradoxes, if they are genuine, are not resolved by rendering the problem untroubled; the best that can be done for a true paradox is to show that it is not self-contradictory and to isolate the various kinds of conflicting feelings or characteristics according to their own significance. One's sentiments may remain unsettled in confrontation with the paradox, then, but one's mind is at least saved from the ignominy of contradiction. In understanding war, one must continue to appreciate its inevitable sadness and grief, but one must also understand why we continue to fight in wars.

This is not to argue that all wars can be morally justified. It is quite possible that many wars can be judged immoral, though that is not the task of the present inquiry. It is enough to argue that war itself need not be immoral. Then, if one decides to judge a particular war immoral, it cannot be sufficient to give as reason simply that it is a war. Most people today, I believe, would argue that the Allies in World War II were morally correct in defending themselves against the Nazi tyranny. If this is so, then there must be some sense of what constitutes a morally justifiable war. But if that is so, then the idea that war per se is evil must be false. Fascinating as such considerations are, they do not constitute the present undertaking, which is concerned solely with the problem that war is a paradox: to be able to *think* about the meaning of war, one must somehow bring together the essentially negative instincts that one has against it with those principles, whatever they are, that explain why we do indeed fight regardless of war's grim and terrible costs.

War is a paradox. We go to war even as we hate it. Why? Is it because there is some dreadful mistake? Do we go to war because of ignorance? This is a view that some people suggest, of course, but even on the most cursory of analyses such an explanation will not stand. One of the more curious truths about war is that very often the men engaged in a war do not believe that the men they are fighting are in any way particularly wicked. Indeed, it is possible to refine this notion so as to bring out the true paradoxical character of men at war. One can imagine the following situation. A young man who lives on the western side of a river that divides two countries may, during a time of peace, visit and befriend a family on the eastern side. It is even possible that the young man could fall in love with the daughter of a family on the eastern shores. He visits them frequently; he grows to love them and appreciates their native goodness and their humanity. Then war is declared between the two countries, the young man is drafted into the army of his nation, and he is trained as a soldier. Perhaps it is with great reluctance, but the young man may find himself actually firing on the very village that is the home of his friends. He certainly does not believe his nominal enemy is wicked, nor is he ignorant of their own claims to a good and peaceful life. But one can imagine such a person actually fighting against those whom he loves. At the very least, this shows us that war is not dependent on simplistic notions of good and evil or that we go to war because of hate. Indeed, such stories need not be imagined; they are all too real in the history of warfare. Men have actually endured such agony; such human dramas have occurred on almost every border separating nations throughout the globe. There must be something compelling in a man's nature that will prompt him to destroy the very people he loves. However one describes this inspiration, it is paradoxical. It is a paradox because one does not forfeit the love one has for those of alien nations merely in going to war against them. In some way a person may feel an obligation and a reverence for both conflicting instincts; so to understand the phenomenon properly requires an understanding of how those values can conflict.

Like some sinister and dreaded fever in the blood that lies dormant for long periods, war seems an ever-looming possibility that generates anguish and strange excitement. The term "war fever" depicts this curious ambivalence toward the fearsome event. As a nation draws near to the hour of war, a quickening takes place in the pulse; the body politic trembles with cold and sweats with fever; a greater urgency to all things seems to take place. Life seems sweeter and yet more burdensome, an ache of huge longing grabs the sinews, and love is heightened. Few other experiences within a national life can be equated with this, and this too speaks of the profound paradoxical nature of the way we think of war. There is something so huge about its threat that it is almost sublime in proportion. It is almost as if the very realization that so much suffering is possible made us aware of unexpected dimensions of ourselves. Thus war, which seems to concern itself with death, becomes a curious quickener of life. This is a paradox.

How are we to understand the conflicting values that produce this paradoxical concept, war? What reasons are there that stimulate a heightened sense of life in the threat of awesome death? Why does the young man who loves the daughter of his enemy nevertheless find persuasion, if not justification, for donning the uniforms of his country and inflicting violent harm on his beloved? If the paradox is to make sense, the nature of these appeals must be made clear. Should we ask the youth why he is willing to war against the family he loves beyond the border, he might respond by pointing out the importance of his country. And should we reflect on our own excitement that seems to distort our moral sense like some strong and heavy wine, we might pinpoint the culprit as the value we place on our own nation. For the first time, perhaps, as the clouds of war eclipse the peace, we begin to think in terms of *them* and *us*. Victory we hope will be ours; defeat will be theirs. Victory, in fact, becomes intelligible as something profoundly ours, just as the threat of defeat undermines our entire sense of identity. War seems to underscore the difference between *them* and *us* almost to the point of equating war with the principle of we-they. Why does the boy accept the burden of fighting against his beloved? Because she is of *them*, because the appeal made is to *his* people. The possessive pronoun becomes a principle of thought. All of the normal and ethical values that support tranquillity are challenged by this curious authority of the *we* over the *they*.

Whatever the worth of peace, it is contrasted with the worth one places in preferring the we over the they. The paradox of war can thus be characterized in this way: the benefits of peace attract us, but so does the significance of what is ours. Value is placed on both ways of thinking. On the one hand, we treasure life and the respect for it: this is our instinct for peace. On the other, we esteem whatever is meant by the we as opposed to the they: this is our instinct for war. Only if there is genuine support for both sides can there be a true paradox. Whether such values are correct and whether such belligerence is justified, this is, at least, the fact. This is the way war is thought about.

The paradoxical nature of war is profoundly ingrained into our consciousness; we think the paradox often as a metaphor for other problems. It occurs almost naturally in our language, in our arts, and in our self-analysis. Perhaps war is an essential part of our own natures, and as it externalizes into actual feats of belligerence, the one becomes a source of understanding for the other. When we grasp the nature of war, we grasp ourselves. This is evidenced in the most sublime of our literature. In the fourth act of *Hamlet* the young prince comes across a huge army preparing to go to war. From the size and disposition of the troops, Hamlet assumes they are about to invade all of Poland, but a captain assures him that they fight "to gain a little patch of ground / That hath in it no profit but the name." The prince digests this curious information and compares it to his own anguish at not being able to act decisively. The sight of the army about to engage in bloody war provokes him to reflect:

> Witness this army of such mass and charge,
> Led by a delicate and tender prince,
> Whose spirit, with divine ambition puff'd,
> Makes mouths at the invisible event,
> Exposing what is mortal and unsure
> To all that fortune, death, and danger dare,
> Even for an eggshell. Rightly to be great
> Is not to stir without great argument,
> But greatly to find quarrel in a straw
> When honor's at the stake.

War may gain mere eggshells or straw, but to fight for them greatly seems to Hamlet to redeem what is otherwise supremely foolish. Terms like "honor" and "divine ambition" spring readily to our consciousness when we confront the paradox of war, for those are the kinds of terms that seem to constitute the value that mirrors the grief and lamentation of so much death. Surely it must be obvious to anyone that if we are to understand what war is, we must isolate and identify those values that prompt such costly quarrels. In calling these notions values, I do not intend to make a determinate, moral judgment for the rightness or wrongness of the act. Calling them values is merely a necessity if we are to see how we think about the meaning of war. The quotation from *Hamlet* shows that such thinking is a frequent and perhaps even necessary part of who we are. And from this quotation we also learn what seems to lie at the center of our willingness to cancel peace: Is that all we are? Surely there is more to me than what can be found in the behavior of animals — things, for example, like honor.

To argue that war is a paradox is to give philosophical significance to almost every artistic and critical attempt to depict war's nature. Even the most ambitious of pictorial endeavors finds both blood and triumph; even the most critical of artworks leaves a remnant of the nobility of sacrifice. It is perhaps a curiosity that those who would seek to deter us from war by depicting war's miseries rarely succeed in accomplishing a universal pacificism, for it is impossible to reveal suffering without likewise revealing sacrifice. Countless visions of twisted corpses make us weep, but they also leave us in awe of the sacrifice. Just as we are aghast at the loss of something supremely precious, like life, so are we impressed that such high and lofty price is paid for something that must be of enormous worth. Part of the paradox of war is that the more vivid and ghastly the depiction of its misery, the more it is treasured. And the paradox works the other way as well: the more triumphantly and gloriously war is depicted, the more grim and pitiful it becomes. This is not to decry such efforts but simply to show that war almost inevitably presents itself to us as paradoxical. Like love, it is a phenomenon that is at once dreadful and inspiring, and anyone who attempts to plunge its mysteries without realizing this dialectical tension is doomed to misrepresent and misunderstand.

Of course, not all warriors are self-sacrificing; some are grudging and reluctant combatants; some are forced through terror or conscription to engage in unwarranted slaughter for the aggrandizement of a despotic conqueror. War, like any other endeavor, can be debased by ignoble men and unworthy goals. So can love. That some men rape women does not indict carnality; that some women abuse their marriage does not indict the sacrament of matrimony. That powerful and ruthless leaders often terrorize or mislead their warriors into national pillage is an abuse of the meaning of war, just as rape is an abuse of sexual union, and infidelity an abuse of marriage. The present study is an inquiry into the meaning of a coherent, thinkable phenomenon known as war; it is not intended as a justification of all warlike behavior, nor need it account apologetically for these deviations.

The benefits of peace, however, seem far more obvious than the reasons for war. There does not seem to be any need to defend peace; the mere existence of tranquillity lends itself to our approval. War, on the other hand, appears to us as at least needing serious justification. If the nature of war is paradoxical, it is essential for us to isolate just what *kind* of reasoning justifies the disturbance of our serenity. Shakespeare, of course, points out the immediate justification, honor. He asks why we are created with such remarkable powers of thought if we are merely going to live as if our animal existence were our only concern. Instincts are far better instruments to guarantee our happiness; reason must have some other purpose. (It is of interest to note that Shakespeare seems to think that reason alone can justify honor; a similar argument is found in the ethical works of Immanuel Kant.) As noted above, there seems to be a kind of authority to the distinction between us and them. For even Fortinbras's warriors do not fight for honor by themselves; they are fighting for Norway. Honor comes to them because of who they are, Norwegians.

At the beginning of this chapter there is a description of the young warrior. If we ask, How do we understand this man? the answer must be that he is fighting for what is ours; he understands his own sacrifice and belligerence in terms of what is our *own*. The reason he may even go so far as to attack the village where his friends live is that the endeavor is his and ours. It is possible then to describe as a principle the kind of thought that makes sense of this conduct. A principle is a way of thinking that makes something intelligible. The acts of the warriors are rendered intelligible because of the principle that what belongs to them matters. And so it is possible to designate this kind of thinking the we-they principle. By this is meant that one acts in accordance with the worth that comes from the shared meaningfulness of existence, not because of egoistic principles, such as would be designated by the I, but because of mutual and shared meaning, which can only be designated by the we. Enmity, in this sense, is not determined by what is immoral or unjust but simply by the threat of something other — the they. War is made intelligible — meaning that we can *think* about it — by means of the we-they principle.

History itself provides ample demonstration of this principle. In the funeral oration of Pericles, the Greek leader points out that what makes the Athenian soldier so remarkable is his highly motivated sense that what he is fighting for is his own country. The Athenians had a more highly developed sense of this "ownness" because of their peculiar (to the ancients) notion of citizenship; they were free men, and their land and property were quite literally "theirs"; that is, it belonged to them and not merely to the sovereign. The early American patriots were likewise famous for their statements of a similar kind of loyalty. The naval officer Steven Decatur is known, if for no other reason, for his famous toast: "Our country! In her intercourse with foreign nations may she always be in the right; but our country, right or wrong." But it is not the patriotic toasts and orations of speakers but the remarkable courage on the battlefield that attests to the meaning of the we-they principle. It can be seen in the various kinds of wars that are fought.

In national wars, like the world wars in this century, to fight for what is ours against the hegemony of what is theirs is a paradigm of the principle. The United States and its Allies, especially England, saw the we as representing all the values and culture as they knew it. To them, the Allies were defending such noble sentiments as democracy in the First World War and western civilization itself in the Second World War. The British fought against the Germans for the simple reason that what was their own (Britain) mattered more than safety. To lose the war was to lose the importance of what this ownness meant. In the Second World War, when Britain was actually threatened with annihilation, the sense of the we over against the they was all-powerful. Nothing could be thought more dreadful than defeat by Nazi tyranny. But even if the moral support had not been so absolute, the British would have fought for what was her own. This is simply what is meant by a *national* war.

But the we-they principle is not always determined by nations. In the American Civil War, the South created a new sense of the we over against a new they, the union. This was more than mere geography; the South began to think of itself as representing a different sense of what is important, a new reference point to the primordial notion of "we." When a Southerner used the term "we" in 1800, he probably meant, "we, the United States"; but when he used the term "we" in 1861, he probably meant not the United but the Confederate States. How this shift of the we took place is the business of history to determine, but it is the essential and necessary principle that explains why we go to war. The same can be said for violent social disorders that alter history. Before 1776, good, honest Virginia gentlemen could not have understood by "we" anything other than "the British nation";

after July 4, the term "we" simply had a different meaning. Thus, there are wars of rebellion, wars of separation, and wars of foreign intrusion, but they all make sense only because the we-they principle determines what men hold dear and precious.

Decatur's famous toast is often criticized for being blindly chauvinistic. It sounds as if the appeal were made to back one's country regardless of the moral situation. "My country, right or wrong" sounds as if no moral restraints could be put on one's patriotic defense of one's country, which is not what Decatur meant at all. Suppose, however, we were to argue the converse. Suppose we were to suggest that one should defend one's country only when one's country was in fact doing the morally right thing. If, in a confrontation with another country, our country was in the wrong, apparently this would urge us to defend the other country and to abandon our own. If this is suggested, however, it seems that we are being urged only to do what is right. A country does not matter at all. It makes no difference whether we are French or German or English or American; just do what is right. Love America if it is in the right, but do not love it when it is in the wrong. This, of course, is to love the right, not to love the country. And although we should perhaps always love what is right, it does not follow that our love of right is the same as the love of country. If I only support my country when it is right, then I am saying that what matters is only the right; my country does not matter at all. It is this that Decatur rejects. My country has my affection because it is my country, not because it is always right. Decatur's toast does not endorse any and all violations of right my country might carry out, it simply says that being a native of my country *matters*. It matters independently of something being right. Otherwise, patriotism becomes the same as concern for righteousness, and that would eclipse an entire virtue by reducing it to another.

If we accept the validity of the value of what is ours, however, the nature of the paradox of war becomes clear. The value we place on the concerns of peace, such as happiness, compassion, and security, are challenged by those of war, which make up our communal meaning and allow us to posit the worth of what is ours against the challenge of what is alien. This is a paradox and not a contradiction, because the two appeals are not of the same order. It is a paradox and not a solvable problem, because regardless how one ranks these conflicting values, both sides are affirmed.

The paradox of war is not merely an abstract concern of philosophers seeking to identify the principles involved, it is a felt and passionate confrontation of our own natures being torn apart by conflicting demands. If we

THE PARADOX OF WAR

imagine a soldier, lying mangled by the horrors of war, facing a death that is far too early and too violent, our first impulse may be to protest that such a thing ought not to be. But valid as these feelings of repulsion may be, they do not exhaust our comprehension of the picture, for we would not lean forward and whisper into the dying man's ear that he had been foolish, that his death was in vain. Certainly, even if we were to lament his judgment, we would not gainsay his courage. Much as we would grieve his suffering, we might also commend his patriotism. He was not unaware of what he was doing, for if he were, we could only lament his death as supreme foolishness. He cared for something that he would have us understand, and his death burdens us with the need to understand. Our pity for his suffering clashes with the boldness of his sacrifice. His plea is the sacrifice of his life, which has a volume and an eloquence that we cannot insult or outshout by mere protest. Who are we to say he ought not to have died, when he himself, whose life it is, has said he should have risked it? He longed for victory and was willing to gamble his life for it. It may be that we must finally say the battle was ill conceived, but we cannot say that his daring was without meaning.

> Success is counted sweetest
> By those who ne'er succeed.
> To comprehend a nectar
> Requires sorest need.
>
> Not one of all the purple Host
> Who took the Flag today
> Can tell the definition
> So clear of Victory
>
> As he defeated—dying—
> On whose forbidden ear
> The distant strains of triumph
> Burst agonized the clear!

The poet here speaks of victory, not of justice. If the paradox is to be understood, we must realize that we do not fight primarily to achieve justice or to right a wrong but to achieve meaning. There are, in most wars, men on both sides who believe their cause is right, and there are some wars that must be judged perfectly legitimate. But these moral judgments are not what reveal the meaning of war. Emily Dickinson's poem speaks about the meaning of victory without any reference to a specific war; we do not know for whom the fallen soldier has fought, or even if his side won or lost. All we know is that in his death the meaning of victory is somehow more poignant than could ever be appreciated by those who lived to enjoy it. It is very often thus: we grasp the worth of something only when we have lost it, as when we have lost the trust of a friend. But the poet reveals even more: we know what victory means in part by how much it costs, and what is being paid in this poem is a life. But if the cost of victory is something so precious as a life, we must reflect on what victory means. The dying warrior tells us what victory means in part by showing us how much it means to him. The victory is precious not only because it is right but also because its price has been paid without regret, just as it is impossible to understand his sacrifice without appreciation. It is a paradox in which what is precious contrasts with what is valuable.

The we-they principle is not reserved exclusively for the understanding of war. It is present in our understanding of many things, including the satisfaction we take in reading history, the joy in poetry that depends on *our* language, the care we take in fostering our rituals and cultural celebrations. All the ills and joys that surround the value of hearth and home, from the anguish of homesickness to the instincts for visitation and return, depend on this distinction. The we-they principle is thus an essential way in which we think about the meaning of our own existence. We are therefore not speaking of a mere psychological fact that needs to be explained or justified. We are discussing a principle far more fundamental; it is a principle that illuminates the very meaning of the worth we place on what is our own. Because this principle is so fundamental, and because it articulates the very *meaning* of an existence that can be our *own,* it can properly be identified as an existential principle. Because the we-they principle is the basis of war, then, *war must be understood existentially.*

The analysis, however, does not depend on the moral superiority of the we over the they. Indeed, such an argument would sabotage the true significance of the present inquiry. If one were to argue that war is based on the we-they distinction, but then insisted that the we always be morally superior, the need for the we-they would simply vanish, and one would have reduced the meaning of war to the meaning of justice. But such an account in no way considers the paradox. The basis of war is the we-they distinction, but such a distinction is not itself based on moral superiority. What this means, then, is that it is enough for a community to be *mine,* and not necessarily *better,* to explain my fighting for it.

The point of this discussion is that the we-they distinction has autonomous significance; it establishes worth and meaning independently though not in disregard of moral distinctions. It is a *moral* point when I consider the worth of an action as either good or wicked, but it is an *existential* point when I consider the worth of something because it is mine or not mine.

The term "existential" may perhaps be unfortunate. It is sometimes associated with the works of Continental thinkers who in the last and present century espoused doctrines that are more accurately defined as nihilistic. The term, obviously, concerns itself with existence, so that if one were to be precise, an "existentialist" thinker would be one who reflects and thinks about the meaning of existence. Anyone who denies that this can be done—that is, anyone who claims that questions about the meaning of existence are wholly random and arbitrary—is strictly speaking a nihilist. Nihilism is the doctrine that existence as such has no meaning. The technique of the nihilist is to show that all seeming judgments of what it means to exist turn out to be either self-contradictory or simply without any meaning.

But one cannot battle against the popular usage of terms. Today we use the term "epicurean" in a sense completely opposite to its original meaning: Epicurus is about as far from epicureanism as can be imagined. The term "Platonic love" today means sexless love, but anyone reading Plato's dialogues *Symposium* and *Phaedrus* knows that these works are deeply carnal and manifestly and overtly sexual. But no amount of scholarly protest is going to change popular usage, and so the term "existentialism" will probably forever convey to the mind the works of Continental thinkers.

Thus, I avoid the academic term "existentialism," but retain the right to use the word "existential." I use this term because it says exactly what is meant: something about existence. To be absolutely strict, the term as I use it in this work refers to something about the *meaning* of existence. It is, then, exactly the opposite of the term "nihilistic."

What is one talking about when one makes an "existential judgment"? Perhaps the best way to focus on the proper meaning of this all-important term is to begin with an example. Suppose a father buys his young son a toy. If I were to ask the father why he had bought the toy for his son, I could imagine two meaningful and acceptable kinds of answers: he bought the toy because his son did well in school, or he bought the toy for his son simply because he is his son. We immediately recognize the distinction between these two responses. In the first case, the toy is a reward for what the boy has done; in the second, the toy is a gift, based not on what the boy has done but simply on who the boy is, the man's son. Rewards are earned; gifts are gracious. In my usage of the term, the gift is *existential* because it concerns who the boy *is*. The term "existential" often, though not always, is used in a sense that contrasts with the moral, as in the present case. It is morally right to give a boy a reward he has earned, but it is existentially significant to give a boy a gift. The gift celebrates the boy's existence; the reward celebrates the boy's good conduct. What is important about this example is that most of us readily accept both responses as coherent and understandable, yet everyone also immediately knows the difference.

Another example from ordinary language and experience may help. We are all acquainted with the phenomenon of forgiveness, but that to forgive is to rank the existential worth over the moral worth is obvious only after reflection and analysis. Suppose the son mentioned above commits a fault. The father realizes the boy deserves punishment. Indeed, let us allow that in this case the boy himself would readily admit that he deserves punishment. Now, suppose we say that the father, rather than punish the boy (which is what he *ought* to do), instead forgives him. This is not be confused with *excusing*, since to excuse is to argue for mitigating circumstances. To forgive is possible only if (1) the perpetrator is guilty of wrongdoing, (2) punishment ought to be meted out, and (3) there are no mitigating circumstances that might lessen either the guilt or the punishment. With this term clearly spelled out, it is obvious that forgiveness literally violates the moral law. Strictly speaking, it is a contradiction ever to say, "I ought to forgive," because the word "ought" establishes a moral imperative, whereas forgiveness cancels the grim necessity of the moral law.

On what basis, then, can the father forgive the son? One cannot argue that the basis of forgiveness is *moral,* since morality demands punishment. But one cannot simply forgive wantonly. There must be some ground, some basis, that outranks the authority of what is deserved. Again, the appeal is made to the existential worth. We say the father forgives the boy because the boy is his son. When we hear such a thing, it is completely intelligible. We understand it completely, because that is simply the way we think about fathers and sons. The worth of the boy's existence *as* son outranks the moral authority of the boy's deserving punishment.

In both cases the existential is contrasted with what is earned. The boy earns the toy because he excels in his schoolwork; the boy earns the punishment because of his wrongdoing. The boy does *not earn* the gift; that is given merely because of who he is. Nor does the boy earn forgiveness; that too is given merely because of who he is — it is part of what it means *to be* a son. We understand morality as the result of action; we understand existentiality as the result of who one is, not what one does.

These two examples may help in isolating the precise meaning of the notion "existential." In no way are these judgments to be reduced to emotions or feelings. To say, "I give a gift to this boy because he is my son," is not a statement about my feelings but about very real, objective relations. I may have emotional feelings when I say or think such things, but I may also have such feelings when I assert a fact: my friend is dead. The truth of the judgment is in no way altered because there is an emotional response to the realization of that truth. The claim that the gift is given because the boy is my son is also more than a mere assertion of biological fact. What it means to be a father is not exhausted by the biological accounts of fathering. This seeming subtlety about the uses of language must be emphasized. The judgment is not "I give the boy a gift because of how I feel about his being my son"; it is simply "because he *is* my son." Certain emotivists argue that the latter meaning is completely exhausted by the former. Such an argument is profoundly metaphysical and can be believed only if the entire metaphysical reductionist account is true. If one were to argue that what we are identifying as "existential claims" *really* are nothing else but dressed-up emotional utterances, the burden of proof would be on the emotivist. It is certainly not what most people mean when they say such things, and it is definitely not what is meant by this analysis.

So there are uniquely existential judgments that cannot be reduced either to factual assertions about the world or to emotive attitudes about the subject. One of these existential judgments is the principle that our meaning as a people (the we) is more fundamental than our ordinary concerns for peace. On the other hand, our sentiments for peace are well grounded. This is an intellectual paradox because we seem to have two differing and conflicting sets of principles that guide our thinking about war, but it is also an emotional paradox because we seem to feel in two totally different ways about our own warlikeness. Conflicts of this sort are either *mistakes* (one of our instincts is simply misguided or erroneous), or they are contradictory (the conflicting instincts simply cannot coexist, so that one must be sacrificed on behalf of rational coherence), or they are genuinely paradoxical, which means the conflicting sentiments are both valid, their coexistence does not produce a contradiction, and the task of inquiry is to ascertain exactly why and how the two conflicting instincts can coexist. War reveals itself as a genuine paradox in this philosophical sense; so, if we are to understand war, we must isolate those principles that make us go to war, analyze them in terms of their unique presuppositions and values, and test their validity.

The paradox of war is not only conceptual, it is also deeply existential. It is not merely an abstract problem for those who like to speculate about principles, it is a felt and endured agony of the soul that can be ignored only at the peril of self-defeat. The inquiry into war, initiated with a profound realization of its paradoxical nature, thus becomes an essential task for all honest self-knowledge. If we are to know ourselves, the supreme commandment for the philosopher, we must know how to think through this paradox. To understand war is thus to understand ourselves.

Part Two

THE DESCRIPTION

2

The Elements of War—I

War is a phenomenon that can be described by many marks, some more important than others. Since this is a peculiarly *philosophical* inquiry, the terms that should be used to characterize the major subject are those which help us think about it and which in turn can themselves be thought about. In anticipation of the developing argument, I designate these nine qualities the *existential marks* of war. Each of these nine marks is used to describe one facet of war's existential significance. In addition, each of these marks is itself illuminated by a classical philosophical argument taken from a wide variety of contemporary and historical figures. The point of this is to show that these descriptive ideas are not trivial or undisciplined in themselves. In the present chapter I consider the first three existential marks: (1) war as *vast*, (2) war as *organized*, and (3) war as *communal*. To support our understanding of the vastness of war, appeal is made to Kant's analysis of the sublime. As an aid to grasping the nature of war as organized, use is made of Nietzsche's aphorism "On Self-Overcoming" found in *Thus Spoke Zarathustra*. Finally, Heidegger's analysis of "being-with," as found in his

Being and Time, is used to support the idea of war as communal. These appeals to the philosophers are meant to support the independent worth of these marks.

In Chapter 3 the next three marks are analyzed: (4) war as *historical,* (5) war as *sacrificial,* and (6) war as *violent.* To support our understanding of war as historical, once again I make use of an existential analysis from Heidegger, this time employing his idea of historicality. To help us understand sacrifice, Plato's dialogue *Euthyphro* is analyzed; and to support the claim that war is violent, I consider the argumentation of Schopenhauer's *World as Will and Representation.*

The fourth chapter considers the final three marks: (7) war as a *game,* (8) war as *horrific,* and finally (9) war as *heroic.* War as a game, the seventh mark, is discussed in terms of Aristotle's notion of *skolē* in the *Nichomachean Ethics;* the eighth mark relies on the works of Edmund Burke and Carl von Clausewitz; and finally, war as heroic finds its philosophical roots in another Platonic dialogue, the *Symposium.* By this appeal to such a diverse background of authors, it is hoped, considerable breadth of understanding can be brought to these ways in which we think about war. It is hoped that it will be obvious not only that we *do* think about war in these ways but that we *ought* to think about war in these ways. However, the description must precede the argument.

It is, of course, possible to string these nine marks together as adjectives and establish some sort of loose existential description, and although such techniques are usually suspect, I will save readers the trouble of doing so on their own. I am provisionally describing war in the following way: a vast and violent struggle between the *we* and the *they* with historical significance and communal values, organized on rational principles and exacting sacrifice from its heroic participants in a horrific game whose goal is victory for what is ours and defeat for what is theirs. Each of the nine separate adjectives that modify the noun "war" requires special analysis and study before this somewhat inelegant and clumsy description can be rendered acceptable. When this analysis is completed, we will have an *existential description* of war, not an essentialist definition. In order to achieve a proper *definition,* the underlying principles must be revealed and analyzed. The definition of war, which requires an understanding of the *essence* of war, will be considered only later, in Chapter 6.

Whether these nine marks are necessary or even sufficient, at least few people would deny they are true. Not very many would deny that war is vast or violent, or that it is horrific. Some may think that terms like "sacrificial" or "heroic" speak of an attitude buried in earlier and more innocent times. Yet we are raising the question How do we think about war? and these nine concepts do play an essential role in responding to that question. However, since this inquiry self-consciously accepts the leitmotiv of *existence,* perhaps a few words should describe what is meant by an existential mark.

The term "mark" has dual significance; on the one hand, it has the function of designating a certain property, as when we say, "Speed is the mark of a good athlete," meaning that speed is a quality necessary for there to be a good athlete. On the other hand, the term can be used as a way of understanding something, a doorway through which we enter into a confrontation with a thing's essence: "His shyness marks him as a very private person." Here the term suggests that to understand his privacy one must study his shyness. The nine existential marks of war, therefore, are not only properties, or characteristics, of war, they are also avenues that an inquiry can take in order to enter into a direct confrontation with the existential judgments that make the truth of war available to us. Existential judgments must be contrasted with both factual and moral judgments. To say of a factual judgment that it is true is to assert a correspondence between what is said and what is the case. To say of a moral judgment that it is true is to assert that what is condoned or censured ought to be so condoned or censured.

What, then, is meant by saying of an existential judgment that it is true? To say that an existential judgment is true is to assert the rightness of how we think about the meaning of the subject. Hence, the reference is to the meaning and not the fact. Nor is an existential judgment the same as a moral one, because what ought to be does not correspond to what a thing means. In order to clarify this further, it may be helpful to consider an example. Suppose I claim that the *meaning* of motherhood entails the notion of maternal love. The fact there are obviously some mothers who do not love their children would factually invalidate the universality of that judgment. But such a fact (or counterfact) need not destroy the existential statement. What I mean when I say that maternal love is an essential mark of motherhood is that this is the way we do and must think about a mother's relation to a child. The "must" here is important. This is not an idle claim about the way I happen to feel toward mothers, or even about the way mothers *ought* to relate to their children. It is a claim about how we think, in which "we" refers to all thinkers. Existential predication is thus neither emotional nor subjective. My emotions cannot be false, although they may be unusual or improper. But to define mothers as those who have no concern for their children would not only be unusual or improper, it would be *false*. What makes it false is not the lack of correspondence between actual mothers and the way they are described, but simply that the *meaning* of the term contains more than the purely biological assertion of female parentage. It is because of this addition of meaning to the biological description that we can talk of some women being not "real" mothers or not "true" mothers; the term means more than what is factually the case.

Philosophers such as Friedrich Nietzsche and Martin Heidegger have succeeded in isolating those elements of our understanding that focus solely on the meaning of a term, separating this meaning from either fact or moral thought. These thinkers have also shown that such independent or isolated meanings not only are emotional utterances but also have an ontological significance and hence allow for universality. Since Heidegger pinpoints the peculiar range of these meanings as existential, it is fitting to characterize these judgments as existential judgments.

The definition of war that I am suggesting then is an existential definition, and the nine marks involved should not be seen as scientific, moral, or emotional, but as existential. What this means in each case will be obvious as the various terms of the definition are isolated and studied. Prior to a philosophical grounding of such judgments, it is necessary to see them in actual use. Thus, I turn now to a consideration of the first existential mark, war as vast.

WAR AS VAST

Perhaps the very first impression any given war has on its participants is the experience of utter hugeness and total enormity for all who observe it. Few, if any, endeavors of mankind can equal the sheer bigness of a national war. Not only are the statistics awesome, but the very language and conceptual metaphors of war reveal that one of the most essential ways we think about it is to think of it as overwhelming. War is vast. The very size of a warlike endeavor gives it the impression of inevitable power and irresistible magnitude. It is bigger than we; we not only fear it as a power that can destroy us, we also think about it as an event that has its own inevitable destiny. "War is coming," we say, rather in the same way we speak of winter coming. It is a vast and merciless reality that seems to eclipse all petty wills and endeavors to stop it.

The very words of war speak of its magnitude. A "legion" is a division of Caesar's troops with which he conquered the then known world. Yet today that term means anything that has a great number. "My name is Legion, for I am many," say the devils in Saint Mark's Gospel, and in ordinary conversation the term simply means a countless number. Or consider the term "dreadnought," which was used to designate the great battleships of the First World War, although Queen Elizabeth I had been the first to give that name to a man-of-war. The name contains such grim elements of meaning and sound. Dread is what we feel when we think of those enormous bulks lurking in the oceans; "nought" has a nihilistic sound, suggesting the overpowering enormity of the war machine. Modernity, however, is not the only epoch for which war implies bigness and power. From "the mighty shield of Achilles" to the dreaded and magical powers of Siegfried's sword, *Nothung,* the literature and language of war has ever resounded in the echoes of what is huge and vast.

There are, of course, quite mundane reasons for this. When war comes, the military has at its beck and call all the resources of an entire nation. It would be surprising indeed if the largest, the best, the most powerful, and the most impressive were not used in a war. Nor should the mind-staggering statistics really be so surprising once a life-and-death struggle has commenced. Should a nation possess some huge, destructive machine and *not* use it in its defense, we could only wonder why. Nevertheless, this purely practical and sensible reason for war's bigness does not eliminate the grander elements of this trait. There is a kind of awe and wonder at what is very large; there is a curious fascination at what is very powerful. The sleekest guns, the fastest ships, the strongest men, the smartest generals, the wealthiest states, the sharpest swords—all go to make up victory; and victory is the supreme goal. The need for excellence in war is critical, and it is therefore not surprising that what is most powerful and utterly huge should impress us as a necessary quality of Mars.

The supreme bigness and power of war becomes, of course, an important element in actually winning the victory. When a people become demoralized by the ubiquity of an invading army, they often capitulate. Morale among sagging troops may be revitalized at the sheer perception of their own enormity. The snowball effect has a tremendous psychological impact on both soldiers and citizens, so that the very notions of "big" and "powerful" play a role in conquest. There is a special kind of dread that one endures when having to face such a thing, just as there is a special kind of thrill and inspiration for those who participate in it. One aspect of the bigness of war is that bigness wins.

Even those who disdain war, or who hate it, recognize this characteristic of vastness. When war is criticized in cartoons, it is usually designated by some huge, wide-shouldered giant with a grim and ugly face, threatening a docile and fragile maiden, peace. Books on war should be big books; war memorials should be huge and expansive; poems on war should be long: there is no epic on peace. A small war seems a contradiction in terms, though a short one may be possible. Only a huge canvas is used for the pigments of war, and only the big and powerful instruments can play the music of the warrior. In all the arts, power and bigness are as essential in depicting war as these qualities are necessary for actually carrying out the battles themselves.

Nowhere is this power and magnitude more obvious than in the very terms of war. When we think of the belligerent terms, we think of them as either large or powerful. Consider the evocation of such words as army, host, phalanx, regiment, fortress, redoubt, bomb, rocket, battleship, artillery, squadron, destroyer, commander, attack, strategy, maneuver, rout, siege, flotilla, and blockbuster. These terms are more than descriptive, they intimidate. When Byron tells us, "The Assyran came down, like a wolf on the fold," we sense the enormous wash of endless power and strength. Wars do not just occur as do other disasters, they innundate us. So fundamental is this sense of overpowering bigness that it is perhaps the most dominant and pervasive of all of war's terrible marks. It is not only the actual invading armies that overwhelm us, it is the enormity of the concept itself: war just means bigness.

An important characteristic of war's vastness is its pervasiveness when the struggle is prolonged or pressing. To witness a nation at war is to see the *ubiquity* of its demands. Every department of government, every member of the society, every artist, student, worker, parent, and observer partakes of the war reality. At times, great wars, such as the world wars, seem almost to permeate the entire fabric of our social world. Very few experiences in the political or social order equal this pervasive involvement. Not all wars possess this extreme degree of public involvement, but it is a trait of war that it unites a people with spectacular glue when the war is favored, and disrupts dreadfully when it is not. It is therefore understood as a phenomenon with great quantified and qualified extension; war is vast.

What is the philosophical significance of this primary quality, vastness, which war seems to possess? There are many important aspects to this quality of bigness that affect such fields as art, history, and psychology, but the philosophical significance of this characteristic is best revealed in Immanuel Kant's account of the sublime. In *The Critique of Judgment,* Kant argues that our experience of the sublime is distinct from our experience of the beautiful (though both are aesthetic experiences) in that the latter provides us with mental pleasure, whereas the sublime offers both pleasure and pain to the mind. When the mind confronts the sublime, the faculty of understanding is simply inadequate to assimilate the enormity of the experience. Because of this inadequacy, the mind feels pain. But in the experience of the sublime, the mind is made aware of the loftier dimensions of reason that go beyond our mere understanding but nonetheless assure us of its authority and thereby provide us with a special kind of pleasure. In other words, according to Kant, the *beautiful* satisfies us because our faculties are in harmony, but the *sublime* excites us because the disharmony between our finite understanding and the experience of infinite hugeness or power reveals the awesome power of our minds. Kant's account of the sublime is impressive because he recognizes that we can appreciate precisely those experiences that go beyond our understanding. When the sublime confronts us, whether in terms of hugeness (what Kant calls mathematical sublime) or in terms of vast power (what he calls dynamical sublime), we suffer and rejoice at the same time. This wedding of opposites, pleasure and pain, gives the sublime its uniqueness.

To those who are careful in their language, the characterization of war as sublime is not a romantic violation of ethical restraint. J. Glenn Gray, in his important little book *The Warriors,* draws a similar comparison with the analyses of Kant. The difference between the beautiful and sublime predates the works of Kant, of course, having been examined by thinkers as diverse as G. W. Lessing and Edmund Burke. But Kant's analysis is of special interest because of his profound transcendental approach, in which he seeks to identify exactly what is going on in human consciousness itself when we experience the sublime. We are both pleased and terrified at once; the sheer bigness of the experience thrills us even as it frightens us; it is a kind of acceptable intimidation. According to Kant, only pure moral reason, the faculty of our consciousness that assures us of our ultimate *worth,* is capable of assimilating those experiences that are so huge and powerful as to surpass our categories of identification and assimilation.

The very vastness of war, therefore, awakens in us a lofty sense of our own worth as rational beings. Yet no one can deny that the hugeness and power of war is also intimidating. What Kant has done with his analysis is to show that such conflicting experiences are not misological; that is, they do not lead us to despair of reason; rather they excite us by showing hitherto unrealized dimensions of our rational consciousness. It should be noted, however, that this heading speaks of the "vastness" of war, not the "sublimity" of war. Kant's analysis is not completely adequate for the phenomenon of war for several reasons, chief of which is that he speaks exclusively of *aesthetic* experience, whereas war is not always merely that. Granted few honest observers would deny that war has aesthetic qualities, and that perhaps the sublime is among them, but the vastness of war is more pervasive than that. Nonetheless, the Kantian analysis of the sublime is extremely helpful in our attempt to understand the vastness of war because it shows how we can think about this characteristic of the we-they principle as it confronts us both quantitatively and aesthetically. The first impression one often gets of war is of its vastness; by this analysis we see how such an experience has aesthetic significance. The emerging interpretation of war reveals the we-they principle in terms of Kant's analysis of the sublime.

The thrill of seeing one's *own* being revealed in such sublime dimensions is then an essential part of the we-they conflict.

WAR AS ORGANIZED

On June 6, 1944, General Dwight David Eisenhower gave the command to launch the greatest sea invasion the world had ever seen. The number of deaths on that single day reached the many tens of thousands, and more organized human effort went forward on that day to accomplish a single goal than any other sea-launched invasion in history. Few men have ever had their words obeyed to such effect. Who or what gave Eisenhower such awesome authority? The political forces at work that isolated this American general are less significant than the deeper question why all the men under him obeyed that command. The only answer that truly responds to that question is that the nature of war demands such obedience. If vastness impresses itself as the primary existential mark, surely this awesome peculiarity of men at arms willing to obey the command of their leader is second. What is it about war that prompts such obedience? But even before that question is asked, it is perhaps necessary to dwell on the question of meaning: What is the *nature* of such obedience?

The phenomenological presentation of an army affords us the first clue to this problem. Armies are divided into two essential groups of men: officers and soldiers. No matter how "democratic" an army might be, or how informal, the mind thinks of these two groups differently. The officers give the orders, the men obey them. At times, to be sure, this obedience fills us with chagrin, as when the object of the exercise is wanton savagery or when the men are treated merely as cannon fodder for a meaningless slaughter. At other times, however, the relation satisfies our deepest respect, as when a brilliant maneuver saves countless lives and achieves bold success. But whether for good or ill, the notion of army cannot be thought without the division between command and troops.

History does not unequivocally favor the well-disciplined and obedient army over the gathered ragtag individualist army. Sometimes, as in the Battles of Lexington and Concord during the American Revolutionary War, for example, the privately brave colonial sharpshooter proved himself a match for the rigidly disciplined troops of the British army. Far more frequently, however, the discipline tells, as when the British defeated armies many times their own number in India and Africa. Even the American Revolutionary army, after Bunker Hill, needed to organize itself along the lines of officers and troops. (For this reason Washington put his army at Valley Forge under the direction of the remarkable Baron Von Steuben, who drilled the American individualists into an effective fighting force. Von Steuben therefore signifies much of what is meant by this mark, and perhaps this section should be dedicated to him.) The point is, in spite of some contrary evidence like Lexington and Concord, we *think* of an army in terms of the discipline of its troops and the spirit of command among its officers. An essential way, therefore, of grasping this important idea is to realize the phenomenological meaning of officers and troops.

The picture is almost universal. The troops grumble and complain; they are rough, unshaven, courageous, and strangely loyal. Among them are saucy corporals and seasoned sergeants; they possess a cynical exterior, and a sullen, mutinous resentment steams just beneath the surface. They are unafraid to fight but are contemptuous of the grand strategies of their leaders. Yet when the time comes, almost inexplicably, they perform as they are told. This fact is truly remarkable; throughout the modern history of warfare, genuine rebellion in the ranks and outright refusal to fight because of cowardice are rare indeed. Perhaps it is because of the training, but if so, the teachers are better than they know. Perhaps it is because most men secretly love to fight. At the moment, it does not concern us here what the true reason is; it is enough to appreciate the fact. Under command most men will face astonishing odds and spectacular violence, and what is even more remarkable, they will return on another day and repeat the performance. These men do not usually have much affection for a commanding officer, and only if he is competent do they have respect for him. Often, indeed, they sneer at the inexperience of green officers, or they wax in amused and cynical contempt at the grand strategists. Only in rare cases do the men both love and admire their leaders, and in such cases great things can happen, but usually only a grudging respect or scarcely veiled contempt defines their view of officers. Of their own sergeants, however, they probably experience more fear than anything else. Most of them seem to have a healthy skepticism about the grander elements of war.

In literature there are many resources from which to draw a fairly universal picture of how we think of the fighting men who doggedly go about their grim business. I have selected two widely divergent sources to complement this phenomenological description: Bill Mauldin's *Up Front* and Shakespeare's *Henry V.* Although Bill Mauldin is a simple political cartoonist and Shakespeare the greatest poet of the language, they both present a similar picture of the ordinary fighting man. And if two artists, so broadly separated by time, space, and culture, provide us with equally profound and similar descriptions, there must be some universality to what they reveal.

When Mauldin was only twenty-three years old, he found himself with the American army during the invasion of Europe. He drew cartoons for the army newspaper *Stars and Stripes.* Later, in 1944, he gathered together a number of his best cartoons and wrote a sympathetic little text that was published as *Up Front.* Mauldin was a GI's cartoonist: he drew for them and about them, he called them dogfaces, and he was one of them. Because he drew them as they were, with humor and affection, they seemed to like him a great deal, and his drawings were enormously popular. What they show is that a quiet, dignified, unpretentious courage can be represented in an often painful and usually winsome humor. His created heroes were known as Willie and Joe, two irreverent and scruffy men who in spite of their toughness and naïveté managed to represent the dogface GI. In one drawing, for example, Willie and Joe crouch behind an embankment with rifles ready. The caption reads, "Must be a tough objective. Th' old man says we're gonna have the honor of liberatin' it." They know that what passes for "glory" is often simply danger; yet they are there, and they do their duty. Another drawing shows two GIs peering out of a tent designated the officer's mess;

they are witnessing the arrival of an important general. The caption reads, "Another dang mouth to feed." Respect, perhaps, for the brass, but no reverence. An even more revealing drawing shows several GIs with somber faces standing around a jeep carrying an officer. The vehicle is deeply mired in mud. The driver is saying, " . . . I'll never splash mud on a dogface again (999) . . . I'll never splash mud on a dogface again (1000) . . . *Now* will ya help us push?" And finally, there is the simple drawing of Willie standing tiredly before a seated officer saying, "I'll just take two aspirin. I already gotta purple heart."

These drawings show us the GI as he sees himself. There is a truth in them that cannot be achieved by more elaborate and sophisticated art. In many ways Mauldin's cartoons provide us with an indelible and universal picture of what it means to fight in a war. More important, they show us how we think about obeying commands. There is nothing inferior or undignified about military obedience; its abuses are the abuses of individuals and not of the system itself. One of Mauldin's better drawings represents this rather cleverly: Two officers are seen on top of a hill, watching a glorious sunset. The caption reads, "Beautiful view. Is there one for the enlisted men?"

In an earlier century, and with a supreme master's touch, Shakespeare draws us a picture of the Elizabethan version of the dogface GI. In his *Henry V,* on the eve of the great battle of Agincourt, the king, disguised as a common soldier, makes rounds of the campfires and confronts the soldiers Bates, Court, and Williams. These tough, loyal, and direct young men express in universal terms the sentiments of most troops. They are not overly sanguine about their chances: "We see yonder the beginning of the day, but I think we shall never see the end of it." When prodded by the disguised king, the men express a healthy dubiety about the royal courage: "He may show what outward courage he will; but I believe, as cold a night as 'tis, he could wish himself in Thames up to the neck; and so I would he were, and I by him, at all adventures, so we were quit here." And they similarly express doubts about the royal wisdom, suggesting that perhaps the king should simply be ransomed, thereby saving many lives. They are not even sure that their cause is right. The disguised king suggests, "Methinks I could not die anywhere so contented as in the king's company, his cause being just and his quarrel honorable." To which Williams replies simply, "That's more than we know." But Bates quickly inserts the redemptive remark: "Ay, or more than we should seek after; for we know enough if we know we are the king's subjects. If his cause be wrong, our obedience to the king wipes the crime of it out of us." This is not an appeal to the license of ignorance, but a grumbling acceptance of what it means to be a soldier.

These two images, from Shakespeare and Mauldin, reveal a fairly universal picture of the common soldier. What is of importance for us in this inquiry is to recognize how these representations distinguish the special kind of obedience to command that characterizes the military personality. Obedience, even when it is grounded in considerable doubt about the wisdom, efficacy, and even righteousness of the enterprise, is here not the same as the obedience of a slave. A slave must submit his will, and hence his autonomy, to that of his master, but a soldier obeys because it is his duty. Henry V makes it clear, in the speech just following the above quote, that in obeying the king the men do not forfeit their moral autonomy.

Every subject's duty is the king's, but every subject's soul is his own. The grumbling, the doubt, the fear, and the scorn heaped upon the glory of the army are all a part of the serving and obedient soldier because in this guise he manages to disjoin his own private worth from the success or failure of the battle. Obedience, therefore, for the soldier does not cancel out his own independence any more than obedience by a single musician to a conductor's direction in any way cancels out the musician's musicality. Unlike the slave, whose condition we think of in terms of a complete lack of autonomy, the obeying soldier establishes his own worth in his willingness to fight for what is his own. After the somewhat lengthy speech by Henry, the sour and reluctant Bates assures us, referring to the king, "I do not desire he should answer for me, and yet I determine to fight lustily for him." This is not mere obedience, it is valor. It does not stem from the well-educated or the noble personage, but from a simple soldier, a complaining soldier, a grumpy soldier. But it reveals a great deal.

In contrast to this rough simplicity of the soldier, the officer does not usually fare as well in our imagination, unless he is truly outstanding. We often think of the officers as young, arrogant, unfeeling, high-spirited, and inexperienced. They have learned the theories of their trade in schools and lack practical wisdom. Many remain distant from their men throughout an entire campaign. Yet their knowledge, however flawed, can determine the success or failure of a military endeavor. Their bungling costs the lives of the troops they do not personally know, just as their adherence to the science of warfare can extricate these same men from disaster. And their authority rests solely in the phenomenon of the spoken command.

Yet, should any of these officers possess any talent or spirit at all, a wondrous thing occurs: there is the magic of a successful command. Respect is developed, an enviable esprit de corps takes place, and the unit can function with impressive effectiveness. It is precisely because both kinds of men, officers and troops, know this can happen that the relationship is so important. Among officers is a further distinction between field and staff officers, and another between the great generals and the middle officers who are as subject to command as the troops. In some cultures, the officers either come from an upper class or try to imitate those who do; in other cultures, the officers come from universities and special training schools. In either case, the officers, particularly the younger ones, are thought of as smart, sophisticated, would-be gentlemen. That many do not ever reach this pinnacle only heightens the image. Their essence is to give orders. It does not matter if the orders are intelligent, sensible, or even coherent; they must shout something. There is an amused disdain when a young officer gives a command that has his unit march directly into a wall or bump into another unit on the drill field. But such glorious embarrassment strangely is all part of the notion of obedience and command.

What does this picture of the officer, presented here from the perspective of the ordinary soldier, tell us about the nature of command? How we think about officers should reveal how we think about orders and organization. First, the aloofness, often foolish and even cruel, is apparently necessary for our understanding of the spirit that gives commands. Mauldin's denuding humor and Shakespeare's artistic genius show us that the aloofness and arrogance of officers do not depend on a lessening of the moral worth of the soldier; yet neither artist suggests that the separation is improper. We separate the one who gives orders from the one who obeys, for many practical and militaristic reasons, but the existential meaning is clear: the authority of mind must not only be obeyed but respected as well. The officer is known by his office; he accepts the guilt and responsibility; it is his knowledge or genius that makes the organization work. Even the most truculent and independent soldier, chafing under the yoke of command, realizes that his struggle depends on working together and that this unity depends on authority. Without this authority, the vision of the warrior is simply of the jungle beast.

One reason why successful armies insist on a sharp division between officers and troops is that one who can order another to place his life in jeopardy cannot be a friend. J. Glenn Gray, in his *Warriors,* for example, makes a telling distinction between *comrades,* those for whom one is willing to die, and *friends,* those for whom one is willing to live. I do not want to be intimate with someone who can tell me to hazard my life on the front line.

Conversely, I do not want to become friendly with one whom I may have to order to take such dreadful chances. A soldier does not address an officer by his first name because he will have to obey that man when told to take horrific chances or to do unseemly acts. Nor does a commander desire intimacy from a person he may have to sacrifice. This is simply psychologically sound. If the separation is not respected, the capability of the army is undermined. History shows us too many instances in which the fraternization of an officer with his troops has undermined the fighting ability of the corps. The Red Army under Stalin had imposed its Communistic ideology on the men early in the Second World War, and the ensuing debacle of the huge Russian forces being stymied by the much smaller Finnish army was the result. Stalin quickly reversed himself after the Russo-Finnish war and the effect was startling. In just a few months the ridiculous Red Army became one of the most formidable military institutions in the world. Those who must execute a policy cannot be integrated with those who formulate it.

Even within the individual, we think differently about our reason than about our bodies, despite the persuasion of the identity theorists. The metaphysical significance of this distinction need not concern us here; it is enough to recognize the fact. Illness of the body affects us in quite a different way than illness of the mind, so much so that some question the propriety of the metaphor entirely. We think of illness as an imbalance of nature, as something gone awry with the system, as something that can be righted by medicine or therapy. But to think of the mind besieged by an alien substance brings a deeper terror. I can easily distinguish my body's misadventures from myself, but I equate my mind with who I am. We revere the mind as the seat of our identity. We would rather lose a limb than memory. Indeed, when confronted by misery, we seek solace in the separation, convincing ourselves that our worth remains intact throughout the fiercest agonies of our senses. In the same way, those who represent our commanding, the officers, are thought of as *apart* just because equating them with the troops threatens both.

They are thought of as spoiled, as arrogant, and as privileged, because that is how we think about authority. In the huge existential struggle for meaning, the source of command must be not only isolated but also set apart as special and precious. In the more successful armies, even such mundane matters as eating, sleeping, and ridding our bodily wastes are separated in accordance with rank. The sillier the separation seems to a civilian mind the more important it becomes for the military. This is because the army is a profoundly symbolic institution; meaning is everything, since that is what men fight for above all else. Thus, the picture we have of officers fits our self-understanding: command entails privilege.

Ideally, the officer is revered because it is his *knowledge* that molds the fierce powers of angry violence into a successful unit. But the officer's knowledge and skill of the craft of war is useless without that ability to give commands. For this reason the entire institutional structure of the army is designed to emphasize the mystery of command. Whatever it takes to produce this impression will be utilized, whether it is sitting on a white charger or wearing a ceremonial sword or being saluted. By nature, we do not want to obey anyone, but if we must obey someone, it should not be merely one of us who perform and execute the grim duties on the battlefield. We think about officers the way we do because that is how we think about the remarkable phenomenon of obeying and commanding.

From the officer class a few emerge as genuine commanders, and it is these people whose names are found in history books. Alexander, Caesar, Napoleon, Moltke, R. E. Lee, Frederick the Great, Ludendorff, Rommel, Patton, Eisenhower, Yamamoto—the names remind us that there is such a thing as military genius, perhaps as ephemeral and elusive as artistic genius, perhaps even a subdivision of that category, but something with which one must contend. What is it that gives a Hannibal the leadership to bring his unwieldy army across a seemingly impossible barrier? Or Rommel the imagination to build the silhouettes of tanks on top of Volkswagens in order to fool the British? Or the Greeks the inspiration to turn the burnished shields to catch the sun and blind the invaders? Whatever it is, it deserves the name of genius, and history follows from the result. However, it is the enormous influence that such men have on the notion of *command* that is of importance here. Perhaps part of this can be understood as a willingness to participate in great historical events, or perhaps it is because in some way these giants of military history incorporate a profound sense of we-they in those who follow. In any event, these men were able to give commands in a way that produced astonishing responses. The soldiers who followed such leaders performed acts of supreme heroism and greatness, almost as if it were an expected and daily affair. One's normal understanding and appreciation of command and obedience pales before these rarer phenomena, but their rarity does not make them irrelevant. Obedience to military commands is not merely the result of training or the grim mechanism of fear; there is something more. It is present even in the ordinary commands of common officers, but it is evident in the obedience given to the great military leaders. There is a respect for the institution itself, which is usually remarkably high even in the worst of armies, and there is a strong sense of a participation in greatness. What makes this so effective is that the sense of participation is not in some abstract sense of greatness but in a very powerful sense of *our own* greatness. The meaning of one's existence is celebrated in the participation of military command. The I is not here subjugated under another's will, rather the I achieves its deepest meaning by the realization of its being of the we; indeed, when properly conceived, under these special events the I literally becomes the we. There is, in the minds of those participating, no real difference. Meaning is thereby established of a special sort: that the I is never fully realized alone, that it reaches its fullest significance in the we, and indeed through the medium of sacrifice. This is what we understand by the obedience to a great command.

How, though, are we to understand such commanding and such obedience? If Kant's theory of the sublime illuminates our understanding of war's vastness, to whom must we turn for philosophical support in understanding the question of command? In his great work, *Thus Spoke Zarathustra,* Nietzsche provides some remarkable insights into the nature of this question. In the section entitled "On Self-Overcoming," he writes:

> Wherever I found the living, there I heard also the speech on obedience. Whatever lives, obeys.
>
> And this is the second point: he who cannot obey himself is commanded. That is the nature of the living.
>
> This however, is the third point that I heard: that commanding is harder than obeying; and not only because he who commands must carry the burden of all who obey, and because this burden may easily crush him. An experiment and hazard appeared to me to be in all commanding; and whenever the living commands, it hazards itself. Indeed, even when it commands *itself,* it must still pay for its commanding. It must become the judge, and avenger, and the victim of its own law. How does this happen? I asked myself. What persuades the living to obey and command, and to practice obedience even when it commands? (226; Kaufmann translation)

Nietzsche has here pierced to the very core of his inquiry into the meaning of existence. Why should laws and commands so fascinate Nietzsche, or any philosopher? A close interpretation of this text will show us a great deal about our own natures as well as about the meaning of war.

"Whatever lives, obeys," Nietzsche says. What does this mean? In all that I do, even when such "doing" is nothing else but reflecting, I am governed by laws. There are laws of reason, without which I could not even think; there are laws of nature, by which I make sense of the events that happen within my experience; there are moral laws that govern my responsibility and guilt; there are also local or provincial laws, set up by society, which govern my activities in relations with others. And finally there are specific laws of specific institutions that I may or may not accept. But in all the modes of my existence, sense is made of my own being by reference to the laws that govern that particular modality. Quite literally, then, "Whatever lives, obeys."

But, one asks, where do these laws come from? Who is it that gives commands that must be followed? In the case of the first three kinds of laws, we give the laws ourselves. That is, my being reasonable is sufficient for my understanding the rules, or principles (laws), of reason. I do not need to ask someone else whether the law of contradiction is valid, or whether *modus ponens* always holds: to reason is to establish and hence to follow these laws. It is the same with the basic laws of nature (every event has a cause) and the laws of morality (treat every rational being as an end in itself and never as a means only). These commands can be figured out as stemming from our own minds. Yet just because we are the source of such laws, it does not follow that such laws are capricious, relative, or variable. I *must* follow my own laws; that is the nature of a law. A law governs universally; that is what distinguishes it from a whim or a discrete experience. Perhaps only a few have ever experienced the taste of Dom Perignon, but given the fact that the bottle of champagne exists, it follows that someone or something had to have made it. The general principle that every event must have a cause is universal, though the experience of that particular effect, the champagne, is particular. Thus, we accept the lawlikeness of our own reasoning and feel bound by it. It is this that so disturbs and excites Nietzsche. "What persuades the living to obey and command?" he asks. And his question is by no means intended to dispute the *fact:* men do make laws and accept them. But why?

Suppose a king passes a law that all men shall be clean-shaven. The first man who must shave is the king himself. It is not merely the case that the king does shave, it is rather that the king must shave. Now, this is peculiar, since it was the king who passed the law in the first place, and he is capable of changing the law and passing another requiring that all men grow beards. But the point is, as long as the king has made it a *law,* he himself must obey it. (He could, of course, pass a law saying that all men except the king must shave, but that is not to the point.) How, then, are we to understand the giving and obeying of laws? And why is this the source of such astonishment for Nietzsche?

In the first place, even the most cursory of reflections will reveal the truth that laws, by their nature, are universal. This is what is *meant* by law. Second, the fact that a man makes a law, or discovers one, or reasons one out, does not deny or remove its claim as universally valid. This reveals that a man's nature is indeed capable of *producing* laws and commands that are greater than himself, even though they generate from himself as a rational being. Thus, in one man I can see the reflection of all men: insofar as one man discovers universal laws, the persuasion is to all men. It is therefore in commanding that reason finds itself manifest in the particular. This understanding of the power to universalize is known as respect. For Nietzsche, who is seeking the meaning of human existence, the power of law giving is indeed awesome and wonderful, for through it we transcend our simple particularity; we become no longer merely men but are now able to go beyond such limits, to go beyond ourselves, to be 'beyond-people', or overmen, supermen, *Übermenschen.*

Now, not all commands are universally valid; but as Kant had pointed out earlier, the command (or the imperative) is the *form* by which reason establishes itself as the principle for our guidance. Hence, the command itself is important for self-understanding and for achieving authenticity. Without commands there would be no transcendence, and without transcendence there would be no authenticity. Thus, it is in recognition of the power of command that one comes to realize the ability to succeed or fail simply at existing; it is possible to affirm the meaning of one's existence or to be a nihilist.

In war, of course, the commands of an officer are rarely seen as having the same rational imperative as the moral law. But two things must be pointed out with regard to a military command: the nature of command as such and the oath taken by the soldier to obey. In the first case, commanding itself is the source of existential authenticity, for without commands there would be no universality. The oath, on the other hand, is taken freely and boldly and binds the oath taker to his word. For Kant, to break one's word is the supreme wrong, since it undermines the very consistency and hence rationality of language; for Nietzsche, to keep one's word is the surest sign of the nobleman, for to be true to one's word is to rank who one is over what one does. The antimilitary critic, of course, sees in obedience to orders a loss of individuality and a sheeplike, uncritical existence. Such obedience is also seen as an eclipse of oneself, a submission to another's will and hence a capitulation of responsibility. Yet it is clear that in the absence of any orders whatsoever, the entire edifice of social reality would collapse. It does not demean a person or belittle his spirit to cooperate with others in a joint effort to achieve a common good. Indeed, if one is willing to accept the input of experience and history, it is obvious that most of those whom one calls great, in any field, were not without their own periods of obedience to commands and orders. It is simply naïve and silly to argue that a person can succeed in this life without rules, orders, commands, and laws. It is, to be sure, possible and regrettable that for some the adherence to rules is all there is to life, and the subsequent automaton that follows such mean-spiritedness is unseemly and unsavory. But such poor fish no more constitute an indictment of commands than rapists constitute an indictment of sexual love.

Nevertheless, it is important for this inquiry to point out how the organizational structure of the army reflects the importance and meaning of human existence. What are we doing when we take an oath to obey military commands? It *is* true that to some extent we are removing our own will and independence for the sake of the whole or the group, and this, to some extent, cannot help but de-emphasize the individual. In fact, what participation in the organized violence of warfare amounts to is the existential shift from the I to the we. In submitting to the right of others to give command, the notion of authenticity shifts from *mine* to *ours,* and what begins as a simple distinction between myself and others now becomes a distinction between a we and a they. In other words, it is because of the lawlikeness of military commands and one's acceptance of them that authenticity no longer needs to be characterized as mine and not mine but as ours and theirs. And as such, the realization of the importance of a military command and obedience to it establishes a profound understanding of the we-they distinction.

There are, of course, many ways to describe this participation within a community and the identification of one's central values with what is commonly shared and defended against outsiders. One speaks of such things as patriotism, pride in one's culture, a love of heritage, tradition, and history. The annals of our history abound in instances of this togetherness, manifested in the triumph of the we-they over misfortune, distress, and suffering. The point is, human beings by nature are organizational; they prefer to have an order to their suffering rather than disordered wantonness. If war is the *organized* violence that sustains the we-they distinction, then this organization must reflect that dependence on the we-they. By taking an oath to obey commands, a soldier ceases to be a mere I and becomes instead a part of the we; but furthermore, the way in which one understands the we-they is revealed in the way the soldier relates to the officer.

The critic of war who points out that the individual soldier is jeopardizing his own well-being has missed the point altogether. Of course the soldier has sacrificed his personal comforts, but he has done so in order to find meaning in the new level of consciousness, the we, which can be established only by the curious form of military organization known as the command. To obey a command is hence not belittling but elevating. It is exactly as Nietzsche points out in *Beyond Good and Evil:* the identification of one's meaning in terms of one's own personal satisfaction gives way to a higher, sacrificial level. Silenus, the hedonist par excellence, has no meaning for his existence. To surrender the I for the we is, then, a *necessary* though painful transition. No mere protest that the soldier is being treated unfairly or inhumanely will ever deter the warrior, for the simple reason that he has long known the truth of it. Soldiers have known their lot was a painful one long before the scholars and the professors began to wring their hands over the plight of the sufferers. The chain of command, however, is contingent upon that stunning quality of human reality, the capacity to obey and to command, which Nietzsche found to be the keystone for understanding the meaning of human existence.

I have used as the central theme of this section on organization that simple phenomenon of command, the giving and obeying of orders. In a command, the formal elegance of an imperative outranks mere personal interests, just as in the categorical imperative of the moral law. The sacrifice of individual wants for the sake of the wider community, under the authority of a command, allows the soldier to shift the basis of his authenticity from the I to the we, and in this way the simple, observable phenomenon of how armies are organized—the division into officers and men—serves as a principle for understanding the existential meaning of war as the violent establishment of the priority of the we-they. However, to ask someone to forgo the authority of his own personal "I-ness" and replace it with a sense of "we-ness" requires that all valid wars be fought on behalf of and with reference to an institution, like a nation, that can provide meaning for one's sense of we-ness.

We have considered Nietzsche's remarks on the nature of commanding and obeying as a source for understanding the organizational character of war. Before turning to the next mark, however, it is fitting that we consider briefly the sense of war as organized in another sense. Often when we speak of something being organized, we mean it permits of being articulated in scientific terms. War is surely a rule-governed discipline in this sense; it is possible to carry out an inquiry into the way in which war works. This was actually done by Carl von Clausewitz (1780–1831), whose famous book, *On War,* established him as the supreme analyst of the nature of war. This book has been used in military schools throughout the world. In it, Clausewitz gives clear and explicit descriptions of the major notions involved in war, such as tactics, strategy, intelligence, the use of weapons, the difference between total and limited war, and the relation of war to policy. It is not, however, merely a guide for the military strategist; it is a genuinely philosophical work, in which the problem of the relation between theory and practice is deeply analyzed, along with the troublesome question how it is possible to have a theory of war at all. War, therefore, is not only an organized belligerence, it is also objectively measurable; it has principles and rules and patterns.

We can see this order in a number of ways. There is something both awesome and beautiful about the fierce jet fighters flying in precise formation as they roar overhead, or in a crack drill team performing their dazzling displays of choreography. We see it in the study of historical battles as we plot on a map with arrows and lines the maneuvers of a great general; it is even possible to discern something of a grand pattern in the film clips of actual military events. It is especially awesome when one personally experiences the shock of defeat as one's own group disintegrates before a more organized assault. There can be no doubt that through the blood and torn bodies of slaughter, mind is there. Confusion, however, if not chaos, is also a major part of the war experience, but this in no way repudiates the basic doctrine of organization.

A word should perhaps be said here about clothing. The uniform is an essential accoutrement we associate with war. There are, of course, quite practical reasons for dressing one's soldiers in the same outfit. It gives them a sense of unity and camaraderie; it allows one to identify friend from foe in the heat of battle; it emphasizes the concept of regulation and obedience. Apparently, one of the more important historical reasons for dressing soldiers in bright and attractive wear was to keep the desertion rate low, for a brightly clad deserter is more easily spotted among the citizenry. But there is obviously an existential reason as well. In addition to the practical concerns of modesty and warmth, we wear clothes as part of our being-in-the-world. From the sloppy T-shirts and blue jeans of our rebellious youth to the stern black robes of a judge, clothes tell us who we are. In this sense, it is almost impossible to avoid wearing a uniform of some sort. Military uniforms, then, are not only serviceable and psychologically important, they also play a role in how we understand ourselves. The uniform establishes a manifestation of belonging; its sharp, catchy, precise lines and colors present us with a sense of what it means to be a soldier. And part of what it means to be a soldier is to be organized, or uni-form, of one form. We not only live under rules, we actually wear them. As Nietzsche says: whatever lives, obeys.

WAR AS COMMUNAL

One of Clausewitz's most famous claims about war is that it is "the continuation of policy by other means." By this he means that we do not conceive of war as happening in a vacuum; wars have goals and reasons. The very kind of war being fought is often determined by the political situation. This may seem an obvious and even commonplace thought, but many overlook it. Not only do philosophical theorists on the nature of war often overlook it, but so do commanders and politicians. At times in our history, warriors have battled each other with great vehemence without having a very clear idea why. After the first month of the First World War—that is, after August 1914—two huge, spectacular armies settled down to growl and claw savagely at each other for almost four years without having any clear idea what they wanted from each other. That was almost a war without policy, or rather, policies had completely been absorbed into senseless attrition.

On the other hand, history provides ample evidence of wars that are fought with a clear adherence to Clausewitz's famous doctrine. Hitler's invasion of Poland, though criminal, was clear and precise in its political goal. Germany wanted *Lebensraum,* and they were prepared to take it. The Allies also had a clear policy, articulated by Churchill: wipe the Nazis off the map. The wars that were fought in these cases make sense only as extensions of political policies; we understand the war if we understand the policy.

However, it is the other side of Clausewitz's famous dictum that annoys many thinkers, the notion that political reality presupposes the necessity of military institutions, that there can be no policy without war or the threat of it. This suggests that there is no such thing as a nation without an army, and that the execution of policy through war is no less legitimate than through the normal channels of diplomacy. It is indeed difficult to imagine how a nation of any size could carry on diplomacy without some military strength to back it up, but this is not the full import of Clausewitz's statement. A nation is more than a geographical location or a sociological accident; it is also a cluster of values, a source of meaning and life. If one cares about these things — and it is almost inevitable that people do care about them — one must defend them against threat and aggression. Indeed, if one does *not* defend a state or a country, it must be doubted whether one really does care about them at all. If the interests of a state can be articulated in terms of policy, it seems obvious that the importance of these interests, including the willingness to defend them with violence, must be a part of that policy. We cannot separate the warrior from his fellow citizen as if they belonged to two separate worlds. Indeed, the distinction between citizen and soldier, though necessary in many ways, cannot be overstressed. If I fight, it is for my country and those citizens who share, with me, its values; if I do not fight, I share with the soldier my concerns for the well-being of the state we share.

Thus, this sharing of values makes the soldier part of the state's essence and also makes the noncombatant a part of the military effort. What is necessary now is to understand this sharing and interdependence of values existentially.

During the Second World War various cities were under siege or attack. Leningrad endured one of the most bitter assaults on any city, and for a time it threatened to become like Troy, a city erased. Stalingrad ceased to be a city altogether; it became a simple fort whose sole existence was determined by the armies in and around it. London, though not as severely threatened, suffered through the blitz and, remarkably, continued as the seat of government even through this terrible assault. Moscow was not quite besieged, but the German army was within sight of its towers; the people were out digging antitank ditches, and as in London, the government stayed. What is impressive about Leningrad, Moscow, and London is the uncommon valor and lofty spirit manifested by the people themselves. Their own suffering became a part of the war effort. In London, even at the height of the blitz, the daily affairs went on with almost stoic disregard for the horror around them. The theaters continued to put on plays, libraries continued to accept patrons, nonessential commerce continued in almost charming ways, and restaurants continued with service that was impeccable even if the food was not. This indomitable spirit seemed to be saying to the world, "This is London and you will not deter us from being what we are;

we, the people of London, are participants in this war, as are our sons on the battlefield, and we shall never surrender our involvement. The war is ours."

In Moscow, the archvillain and atheist Stalin came openly before the people and spoke, not of the revolution or of communism or of Marx, but of Mother Russia; the churches were opened and in this atheistic state there were public prayers for the homeland. The people did not disappoint him. Although the Russian capital did not manifest those charming characteristics of capitalism, the spirit of unity and devotion to what was their own showed the close relation that exists between citizenry and military in a modern war. Although Paris, in the First World War, was not under siege, Parisians thought it would be, and taxicab drivers bravely drove the soldiers stationed to defend the city to the exposed right flank facing the south-turning Germans. Paris in the Second World War, of course, for fear of destruction, became an open city. Some think the city sold its soul.

The point of these stories is that these cities became a part of the war effort in ways both actual and symbolic that undermine any sharp distinction between combatant and noncombatant. In these warm and charming and, indeed, heroic stories of personal bravery and stalwart pride, one can see that we think of a *people* at war, not merely *armies* at war. The poet John Milton assures us that "they also serve who only stand and wait," but the contribution of the citizen in cases like the noble besieged cities is far more than the passivity of the anxious parent waiting the return of the boy gone off to the wars. This picture, of the brave, enduring cities, is not meant to prove anything but to present a concrete image of the fact that wars are communal in a profound sense; they are not some meaningless game played out on some vast playground known as the battlefield.

The second phenomenological picture that may be used to help us with this idea is that achieved by contrasting the way we think about the soldier and the way we think about the police officer. Both are members of noble professions that demand our respect and that involve dangers requiring courage. But there is a special kind of affection we have for the soldier that is not so universally felt for the police officer. The latter protects us from criminals within our system, the former from the enemy without our system. The police officer works on behalf of justice, but the soldier on behalf of what is our own. For this reason we have not only respect for him but love as well. Consider how we send him off to war. There are parades and tears and bands playing and handkerchiefs waved by all, as if each one were a son to each of us. We weep and wave and care, not merely because they are in danger (for a policeman may well be in greater danger than his military counterpart) or even because they are young and hence beloved; no, it is because of the nobility and beauty of their meaning to us. A part of us goes with them to the front. Or, if we are the soldiers, we take with us a clod of our own earth; we accept the joyful sadness of our leave-taking because we realize that it is not only stern duty that sends us away, but also affection and love.

The difference between how we feel toward a police officer and how we feel toward a soldier corresponds to the respective virtues they serve. The police officer serves the law and, through that, justice. We respect and admire the law and justice. Their defense is important and usually tedious, often grim. The soldier serves what is our own, and for this virtue we feel for the warrior that which cannot easily be transferred to the constable. Perhaps in part this is due to the fact that the police and their concern for justice are ordinary, but the warrior is extraordinary. But in any event, there can be no doubt that such a difference really exists; we simply *do* feel differently about the two people, the warrior and the police officer, however unfair this may be. I am suggesting that this difference reveals much about the shared meaning we enjoy with the warrior's protection of what is our own, that the soldier is a part of our understanding of the we against the they and that therefore we have a sense of pride, affection, and bittersweet anxiety that tells us what is at stake is very much our own.

If these two pictures are successful, they should pinpoint the kind of thinking that judges war as a communal rather than a professional effort. The struggles of the embattled cities show us rather poignantly that the ordinary citizens are often a deep and integral part of the war effort, that peoples and not merely armies go to war. The rather specialized contrast between the police officer and the soldier also reveals an important way in which we idealize the warrior and incidentally shows us the hierarchy of the existential over the moral once again. It may be objected that the image of the cities is unfair, since such universal warring against whole populaces is fairly recent and true only of modern wars and not war as such. Such remarks show little grasp of history or of philosophical meaning. There have been periods of fairly clinical wars, but the question is, Which represents the reality? There is something rather artificial about such purely professional wars. Furthermore, the historical fact is that most wars have been fairly savage to the populace as well as to the combatants. Troy, after all, was completely destroyed. Rome was sacked and routed by the invading hordes. Sherman devastated Georgia and burned Atlanta. There is a strong similarity between the people of Vicksburg enduring the brutal siege by Grant and the peoples of Moscow and London enduring the assaults by the

Germans. Past wars are not as neat and digital as some would have us believe.

But even if we grant that the images of the great cities and the difference between police officer and soldier provide us with rich and suggestive insights into what this concept of the communal war means, it is still necessary to focus on principles and philosophical arguments to help us complete the task. With the assistance of these two phenomenological images, it is now possible to turn to some comments by Martin Heidegger to find out how a major philosopher has provided us with even better tools.

In his description of what he calls the 'existential analytic,' that is, the analysis of the ways we exist, Heidegger argues that there are certain categories of explanation that are a priori and that apply only to the question of our existence. He calls these existentials, and among them are being-in-the-world and being-with. To say that being-in-the-world is an a priori existential is to claim that one does not first know oneself privately and then later discover an "external" world that somehow provides a landscape for the individual; rather one understands oneself *already* (a priori) within the world, so that the notion of "world" is not the result of external experience at all but is a precondition for making any sense of existence whatsoever. In characterizing this mode of existence, being-in-the-world, we see that *one* way in which being-in-the-world happens is to be *with*. Again, we must see that being-with is a priori; it is a necessary way we think about ourselves: it predates any particular experience.

In order to grasp the nature of this being-with, it must be contrasted with being-next-to. I can only be with another person; I can be next to a thing. However, I can also be next to another person, but I cannot be with a thing. An example of how we use ordinary language may show what this means. Suppose I visit a movie theater and I enter the auditorium alone. I sit down next to another person. We would not say I am "with" that person. However, if I enter the theater with a friend and we sit down together, we would say that I am with that person. What this shows is that there is a simple but profound difference in the way we think about being-with and being-next-to. Should I enter a theater and sit next to a post, there would be no *existential* difference between that and my sitting next to another person. I may indeed even be physically closer to the person I am next to than the person I am with (my friend's chair may be several inches further away from me than the chair of the stranger). Indeed, I may even be *next to* a friend and *with* a nonfriend, so that how I *feel* about the person next to me cannot be said to determine the existential meaning. There is nothing spectacular about this; it is manifested in the way we use language, and as soon as we see the point of the distinctions, the mind grasps the difference as meaningful and important. But I cannot adequately account for the distinction between being-with and being-next-to merely by appealing to physical predicates; the difference concerns how we *think* and, specifically, how we think about the meaning of our existence.

Recognizing that being-with, therefore, is an a priori existential, not a mere accidental property of physical objects, we can now see that being-with is one of the ways we can be said to be-in-the-world (also an existential a priori). Thus, being-with is an essential part of how I understand myself. If we allow ourselves to leap ahead in Heidegger's analysis, we will also see that in his description of our temporality, he shows that our *historicality* is also an existential a priori and, further, that an essential dimension of our historicality is our heritage, fate, and destiny. If we put together the notion of our heritage and our being-with, we have the basis for communal existence. It is not merely that as a matter of fact we happen to live with others who share our heritage; it is rather that being-with-others and sharing a heritage are essential to our self-understanding.

Heidegger develops a simple expedient for making sense out of the various modalities of our existence. We are either authentic or inauthentic in our modalities. Authenticity is the way in which our meaning is manifest in the ways in which we exist; inauthenticity is the way in which that meaning does not occur. To put it simply, each and every one of the various a priori existentials, such as being-in-the-world and being-with, can be either authentic or inauthentic.

Authentic being-with and authentic heritage require that one's historical and one's communal existence be made meaningful. In other words, I cannot remain indifferent to who I am or what my history is and remain true to myself. Who I am is determined in part by who I am *with*. Thus, my American historicality and my American being-with provide their inevitable destiny. It is on the basis of this that we recognize the primordial right of every man and woman to his and her own meaningfulness. Since this meaningfulness is *necessarily* historical and communal, it explains why war is accepted as a grim but undeniable right. Not to sacrifice on behalf of what is mine is to discredit the very authenticity of being at all.

What Heidegger has done is to show the philosophical legitimacy of judgments about meaning. He has shown that being who I am *matters,* and if being who I am is characterized by both heritage and being-with, then it can be shown that a supreme and existential value can be placed on one's nation and tradition. War is the violent defense of these rights, these special existential rights, and since the existential awareness of self-worth must be assumed if any other value whatsoever is possible, the right to war is fundamental. It is the persuasion of the present argument that this self-worth includes a sense of we-self-worth, that is, that the worth of the self required for any and all values understands the self as shared, as we as well as I.

When we imagine the people of London bravely going about their business during the blitz, we can explain this philosophically as their presenting themselves as beings whose collective self-worth matters. Theirs is a statement of the sort, "This is who we are, and who we are matters." Similarly, when we reflect that soldiers are thought of with a kind of affection lacking in our image of police, we can explain the presence of this affection in terms of what the soldier means to us, a protection of what is ours. Again, the philosophical basis of this attitude is the worth of the we-self over against the threat of something not belonging to what is our own, the they.

This, of course, is going far beyond what Clausewitz says in *On War*. His point is merely that in our attempt to understand the phenomenon of war, we must see that it is rooted in the political order. Nevertheless, this suggestion has many consequences, among which are these existential observations about war as communal. It is perhaps sometimes difficult to identify with a far-flung and distant war, particularly when things at home are going well or when the reports of the war focus solely on the suffering, confusion, and grief of the combatants and their families, but it is simply inauthentic not to associate oneself with these vast endeavors.

Of all the existential marks, this one most reflects the basic principle of the we-they. If wars are essentially communal, it is easy to see that men fight for the communal we against the threatening other, the they. However, the existential priority of this principle influences not only the content of the description but the method as well. *War* must be distinguished from other forms of conflict in that it is fought *because of* the communal sense of being-with-others and not merely fought *by* groups. This leads us to the consideration of a genealogical account of war.

We can imagine our primitive ancestors engaging in various forms of violence for almost any reason. Perhaps a family group, living in truculent and suspicious togetherness, suddenly confronts unfamiliar others. Then, because of simple fear or distrust of what is unfamiliar, the two groups begin to fight. Given our own natures and our own instincts to rely on physical force even when protected and gentled by millennia of civilization, it is quite natural to suppose that our early ancestors were similarly inclined. Such outbreaks of savagery probably erupted millions of times. However, claiming such fracases are the origins of war would be mistaken. It is impossible to generate an acceptable account of war by means of a genealogy rooted in rude struggles between primitives. War is organized violence rooted in a profound sense of communal meaning articulated in the difference between the we and the they; in the absence of such meaning, all forms of human violence would be prewar or even nonwar events.

It is tempting to speculate on a possible genealogy of war rooted in natural events, like one district's having insufficient game, leading to its members' crossing over into another's territory in order to acquire food. By such an account, any decision as to which comes first, the feeling of community or the happenstance of success achieved by working together, would be highly subjective and arbitrary. There is no way of determining such matters, and even if we were somehow able to discover what actually happened, the temporal development would not guarantee the formal hierarchy. Philosophically, the first war happened only when a community, self-consciously recognizing its own existence as precious, willfully accepted the sacrifices necessary to sustain it. The group may have fought many times before without this realization, and the struggles may not have been externally much different from that in which genuine warlike consciousness takes place, but until and unless it did, there was not a real war. No mere genealogy, then, would be able to spot or determine that point.

The genealogical account sketched out in the previous paragraph begins with the recognition of one group as alien or foreign to another. From this account it might seem as if strangeness, or alienation, would be a central cause of wars. There is, however, a recurrent and powerful theme of human history that rejects this assumption. Wars more often than not occur between groups that are quite familiar with one another; rarely are wars fought between complete and total strangers. The history of wars shows that the most savage are usually civil wars or wars between close neighbors. The sovereigns of three of the major belligerents in World War I were first cousins. Rather than strangeness, it seems that too much familiarity can cause wars.

But if the most savage wars are civil wars, and if national wars occur with far greater frequency between close neighbors, how does this fit in with the basic principle of we versus them? Surely the observations about intimacy causing more wars than xenophobia provide an argument against the we-they principle. But if we look closely, we shall see that civil wars and wars between close neighbors are *about* the meaning of the "we." Just exactly how a nation or a people should characterize themselves as a we over and against a they is what causes civil war. Thus, we must learn from this that the notion of "they" is not to be understood as "strange." The we-they distinction is not between the familiar and the alien but between that which provides an understanding of our meaning versus that which challenges it. Why should I want to fight against a completely foreign and unfamiliar enemy? It is better simply to leave them alone. The further away one culture is from the other, the less likely it is they will go to war. The only reason why the North invaded the South was because the Yankees felt the Rebels were *of their own.* Lincoln's passion was for a Union he felt preexisted the war. France and Germany were both Christian states sharing religious and cultural similarities; yet between 1870 and 1945 they went to war in most savage violence against each other three times. In these cases the wars were fought because of what constituted one's sense of a we versus a they. Distant and foreign peoples do not *threaten* what is our own.

It is sometimes argued that greater familiarity should be established between any two powers that may go to war. Potential enemies should send each other representatives of their cultures; artistic exchanges should be encouraged; student exchange programs should be fostered; tourists should visit each other's country. There may be excellent reasons for saying this, but one reason that is *not* very persuasive is that such ties of familiarity will lessen the likelihood of war. It is far more likely that they will bring war about. If the two powers remain distant, glowering at each other suspiciously from afar, they are likely to remain afar. For there becomes little reason to go to war. Of course, there are independent reasons for sharing cultures, students, artists, and tourists, and they might outweigh the dangers. But it is simply an observable fact to anyone who has read much history that closeness, far more than distance, provokes belligerence. In the first place, I am more likely to be disturbed or upset if my friends are doing something I feel is wrong than if perfect strangers are doing so. Among nations, familiarity breeds contempt. Thus, an idea generated from a genealogy (that strangeness causes war and familiarity provokes peace) turns out to be false and misleading. Lack of familiarity may have caused a few fracases among our early ancestors, but the cause cannot be carried over to a principle. Indeed, it is far more likely that if one group met another, they both would simply have run away. Such accounts of war as are generated from a purely speculative genealogy are always suspect.

There is a further danger. The ease with which we can spin speculative genealogies out of the empty air makes one account just as valid as another. Not much is learned from tracing things back to some original and simple event. That it is possible now to reflect on our own principles and to ask what rules govern these actions does not, in and of itself, allow us to know when this reflection first occurred or even whether it occurs in others today when they do not express themselves in this way. There obviously was once the first war, and there might be much that we could learn from knowing about it. But we could not derive anything about the nature of war from it, since we derive these ideas from our own war making and judge the past event by these criteria. All effective philosophical genealogies, such as Plato's account of the state in *The Republic* or Nietzsche's remarkable account of the genealogy of morals in the book that goes by that title, are formally a priori in this sense. They illuminate without having to be historically accurate. The priorities are formal ones, not necessarily derived from chronicles.

For these reasons, one must resist the temptation to speculate about the natural history of nonnatural ideas like war. This is not to deny that our understanding of war is historical. It is merely a remark about method. The historicality of our understanding of war indeed is essential, and it is to the discussion of this idea that the inquiry now must turn.

3

The Elements of War—II

In this chapter I consider the next three marks, war as *historical,* war as *sacrificial,* and finally war as *violent.*

WAR AS HISTORICAL

As I write these pages, it is significant that the language used is English. To some extent I owe the privilege and honor of speaking English to the military skills of Braddock, Wolfe, Forbes, and Washington, who in the French and Indian War of 1754–63 established this tongue as the prevalent language on the continent. That my home and person are protected by the rights of free people is due to the wars against repression that my ancestors and forefathers fought. That I am not a slave, or that I do not own slaves, I owe to the nameless dead who fought in the Civil War. That I am able freely to inquire philosophically into this subject is possible only because more recently our grandparents fought in Europe to defeat the oppressive, world-dominating ideologies inimical to freedom and dignity. Very simply, then, most, if not all, of the values I hold dear were defended and possibly even saved through wars fought in the past. Of wars yet to come, the same things will be true: they will establish values and alter the way people see and do things. Sometimes, of course, the wars bring about results that are regrettable. The good and the right do not always win, and one of the reasons they do not always win is that they do not possess the better soldiers. Things would have been much better had Poland been able to defeat Germany in 1939. The Allies were finally able to accomplish that defeat six years later not because they had the superior ethical position but simply because they had better guns and tanks and, finally, better armies. There simply cannot be any denial of the basic truth: wars alter history. Wars change humankind. Wars determine who we are.

It might be argued that it is less the wars and more the thoughts that determine who we are. To be sure, Patton helped defeat the Germans, but Plato, Christ, John Locke, and Thomas Jefferson provided the ideas to make him an American. There is no need to trivialize the import of such thinkers in order to establish the value of the men who fight for the ideas. There is a happy though often contentious marriage between the thinker and the warrior, but as in all marriages, offspring require two parents. The ethical ideas of a Socrates, of a Christ, of a Kant, are not beneficial without the spirit to defend them against those who would eliminate them. On the other hand, militarism by itself brings about nothing of worth. The fact remains, however: who I am is determined as much by those who have fought for the ideas as by those who have thought the ideas.

It might further be objected that many things determine who I am, things that happened in the past but are not warlike. The Black Death and the Lisbon earthquake certainly affected human history, perhaps even more than some wars. Why not think of human belligerence in the same way we think of natural events, simply as phenomena that can be regretted or lauded but that have no special existential meaning? The answer to this lies in the fact that even though many natural events do affect history they are not thereby rendered historical. The human enterprise of war includes not only the will and reason but also the understanding that one's fate and destiny are involved. A violent storm may sink a ship as well as a submarine, but the latter event is thought with entirely different predicates than the former. There is much that goes to make up the phenomenon of historicality, but it is insufficient for something merely to have happened in the past for it to be a part of this existential meaning.

When one visits the site of a famous battle, such as Waterloo or Gettysburg, it is possible to feel the poignancy of historical meaning mingled with the blood-stained earth. Were it not for the courage of the British soldiers and the brilliance of their commander, the tyranny of Bonaparte would have risen unchecked, and the current of human affairs would have been radically altered. Had Meade not persisted in his movements, Lee may well have triumphed, and there may have been two American republics today instead of one. The British and French, Northern and Southern soldiers who banged away at each other on those fateful days may not have realized the full range of their toil and valor, but they certainly felt something of their historicality; and what is even more relevant, when we think of those distant battles, we cannot disjoin the history from the sacrifice. Built into our very *concept* of war is its historical significance. Just as in the previous existential mark, we cannot think of a war without understanding it as part of a concerned community, so we cannot think of war without the mark of historicality. This does not mean only that military events are *datable;* it means rather that the entire way in which we think of war is deeply influenced by our historical natures. To fight in a war is to engage in a decisive, historical act.

One consequence of this realization is that certain wars make sense in terms of their position within a certain historical development. It has often been pointed out, for example, that among the reasons for World War II were those which emanated from World War I, that the spirit of the American Revolution helped and influenced the French Revolution, that certain wars could have happened only at certain, precise times in history. This means that the flow of history is part and parcel of our understanding of the wars that take place in the current of that muse. Precisely because human beings are historical animals, they are, then, warring animals; and to some extent the converse of that sentence is likewise true. Just as no specific war makes sense without reference to its history, so the general, existential understanding of what it means to *be* warriors cannot be disjoined from our understanding of what it means to *be* historical.

Two remarks may help elicit the full import of this truth. Travel the world over, and you will find countless war memorials, from the grand and spectacular to the modest and provincial. A place is made sacred by these memories. Sometimes the memorial is dedicated to "those of the small town of —— who fought in the Great War"; others are dedicated to the place itself: "Here, on this spot, Alexander defeated the Persian Army." Scarcely anywhere on earth is there a land without some such citadel to memory. And why? Because without these monuments to remind us of our history, we may forget not only the events of the past but who we are. It is, however, the purpose of a culture to remind us of who we are, from the language we speak and the clothes we wear to the food we eat and the values we inherit.

It is this emphasis on who we are that prizes history. Human beings do not hatch in incubators devoid of culture and then set out to make up all their own preferences into a scheme of values. Moral and social beliefs are inherited from our first waking; we flourish precisely because a wonderfully rich source of meaning is already there. To deprive a child of such spiritual nourishment, even if it were possible, would be a cruelty beyond the most severe corporeal savagery. To be sure, the child grows to adulthood in a protective environment of surety, and then new ideas and original challenges open the way for a dialectic between the inherited and the achieved, the old and the new. But the mass of accepted beliefs finds its roots in our inherited culture, and this same concern for what is ours prompts us to pass on to our offspring the same wealth of meaning. That our forefathers may have died to protect what is ours needs to be transferred to the next generation in order to retain the value of what was fought for. This is more than mere affection for those who have died; it is a desperate need to remind ourselves that meanings bought at such a terrible price must be retained. The monuments to battles and to those who fought in wars past are an essential part of our historicality.

It is, of course, possible to educate youth without due reverence for their history. However, the impoverishment of spirit that results from such poor education can only serve as a warning to would-be educators. A child unsupported by a historical education is a spiritually crippled child. Emphasis on the immediate gratification of pleasures, coupled with the ahistorical focus on the present, produces an atmosphere that can only breed nihilism. Though indifferent, perhaps, to any structural institution of culture, such parents who dismiss these traditions are punishing their children with the worst possible form of spiritual agony, the grinding misery of not knowing who they are.

This is not to rank the historical scholar above the rest of us. Indeed, a *reverence* for history, rather than a mere knowledge of it, may speak of a deeper historicality. History and religion share a common strain in our existential consciousness—perhaps, in some, even to the point where the two are absorbed into a single resource. But like religion, history can be enhanced by rite and ritual as well as scholarship. A boy awash with high spirit at the explosions on the Fourth of July may well be planting this spirit of historical meaning more deeply than the history major who knows the highly arbitrary assignment of that date. We manage to transfer this sense of our tradition and culture through many public events and places, and war memorials of both place and time are an essential part of this.

We are, in our deepest existential nature, historical beings. The dialectical conflict between this tradition and the yearning for new achievements in no way reduces the power and importance of this historicality. Since we are remembering beings, to celebrate the past is to celebrate ourselves. But conversely (and for my purpose here, perhaps even more important), to achieve meaning is to invoke the muse of history. When we engage in some great enterprise, it is almost impossible for us not to wonder at its historical significance. In Shakespeare's *Julius Caesar,* after the assassins have done their bloody deed, Brutus bids them wash their hands in the carnage. Cassius says, "How many ages hence / Shall this our lofty scene be acted over / In states unborn and accents yet unknown!" This remark reveals much about our natures. We appeal to a future history to underscore the importance of what we do. This is not some idle hope for immortality or fame; it is associated with one of our most profound existential instincts: that history and importance belong together. Since what is ultimately important can be appreciated by the costs involved and by the sacrifice endured, the great battles of history become saturated with this existential flood of meaning.

The English word "history" is etymologically connected to the word "story." In French, *l'histoire* can mean either a tale or a history, and the same is true of the German *Geschichte.* One of the more interesting things about the discipline of history is its form. History tells a story. Indeed, without the fundamental structure of a story, there would be no history at all, there would only be rude chronology. If we are to understand war as essentially historical, then we must first understand what it means to tell a story.

A story gives meaning to events. By its form it provides intelligibility as truly as the structure of science provides intelligibility to isolated data or as the structure of law gives meaning to political acts. Indeed, storytelling may well be more fundamental than either science or law as a source of comprehension. Civilization may well have begun with the telling of the first story. Yet, remarkably, philosophers have been derelict in providing an account of the presuppositions that make stories possible. We know as little about the form of a story as we know about a distant galaxy, as far as professional philosophers are concerned. Yet, many sciences, including biology, anthropology, and history (if history is a science), are structured on stories. In the present inquiry, only the briefest of examinations of this all-important form is possible.

When children hear a story, they instinctively know that the first part of what they hear will have a significance for the remainder. The very notion of telling a story assumes that what occurs at one time is connected to what happens at another. Suppose, for instance, we begin a children's tale, "Once upon a time a certain woman had a little dog whom she loved very much." When children hear this they know immediately that if the story is going to be any good, the dog will get into trouble, the woman will lose the dog for a while, and then, after some adventure, the dog will be returned. They know this because there would be no sense in saying that the woman loved the dog unless it *mattered.* The subsequent adventures of the woman searching for the lost dog make sense only because of the first statement, that she loves the dog. The past is made intelligible by its pregnancy with the future; the future makes sense only because it is rooted in the past. So, at the very least, coherence in stories presupposes the interconnectedness in time. Perhaps it is even the case that time itself is rendered understandable only because something like the interconnectedness of meaning that we find in a story is an a priori form of thinking about time.

Stories are developed in terms of three essential elements: character, plot, and theme. Each of these serves to reveal a kind of importance or significance to the unfolding of time. Whether the story told is fictive or true, the telling of it gives meaning to otherwise unrelated events. It seems an inevitable prejudice of all peoples that who they are requires an ancient tale of their origins. The past is nothing without a story to make it coherent, but the present similarly requires a storylike link to what has gone before. It is important for us to realize that without stories our past is sundered from our present, and that tends to make the present as well as the future simply without meaning. Thus, telling stories is a weapon against the threat of nihilism. In the development of character, the idea of a person is rendered worthy of attention; in the unfolding of the plot, the temporal significance of our existence is spotted; and in the revelation of a theme, a special meaning is given to what happens. In history, we tell the story of a people, a nation, or a movement. When we tell our own history, then, we seek out the story of our roots, our development, and our place in the world.

A mere chronicle of events is not history. We all recognize this as an important truth, but it is not obvious just what this means or why it is so important. However, it is obvious that history is not merely about the past but about the *meaningful* past. What makes some events in the past meaningful and others not? The answer must lie in the nature of a story. If the series of events makes a story, it is history; if the event is merely an event in the past, it is not a part of history.

We tell stories in part to celebrate our own temporal nature. Even a fictive story represents how we are in time, that is, how we are as temporal beings whose past provides a structure of meaning for our present and whose projection into the future is not without connection to what has gone before. When we turn our attention not to mere fictions but to actual events, the telling of the story reveals who we are. In the great and intense business of our humanity—namely, coming to understand what we are—stories, and particularly true stories about our past, serve to illuminate the darkness. If one asks even the most primitive of people who they are, inevitably they will answer in some sort of story or myth that explains their origins. This is not due to some primitive simplicity; it is due to the very real persuasion of human consciousness that who we are must be understood in terms of its unfolding. Man has been defined in many ways, but one of the most revealing is that he is the storytelling animal. This definition is not completely removed from the Aristotelian definition, for the rational animal may well be the animal that thinks in storied sequences. To tell these stories about our past as a people is to "do" history.

By "doing" history, as opposed to "making" it, I mean reading, writing, and critically thinking about major events in the past; reflecting on the meaning of epochs, periods, and eras; discussing such issues, celebrating certain days, and visiting certain places for the sake of cultural memory; and indeed reflecting about one's own personal heritage and nature as a temporal being. To "make" history is to cause or participate in events that alter or affect the course of the human story. Doing and making may, on occasion, overlap, as when Herodotus not only wrote and thought about the story of his people but, in so doing, initiated a new discipline.

To say that war is historical, therefore, is not a mere casual remark about the past. It is not only that wars *change* history or that history is made up of wars. It is the deeper point that both war and history stem from the same primeval origin, that the current of life matters. If we are seeking to understand the warrior in all of us, if we are asking what it means to war at all, we must also ask what it is about us that makes us tell stories, particularly stories about our own. To plunge to the depths of our warlikeness is to ask, What does it mean to be historical? To throw light on this profound question, I now turn to the philosopher whose analysis of our own historicality will support this capital quest.

In the previous section Heidegger's analysis of being-with was used to probe the meaning of communality. With the present focus on history, however, we are concerned with one of the fundamental and essential ideas in Heidegger's philosophy. The very title of his major work, *Being and Time,* reveals the profound importance that time, and particularly time as history, plays in the existential understanding of human nature. History, for Heidegger, is not the study of past events; rather it has its origin in the simple, given reality of how we exist. The inquiry into the nature of history, then, begins neither with a concern for what is no longer the case (the past) nor with the unique problems of how it is possible to carry out the science of history. Rather the inquiry begins with an inquiry into our historical natures. What must be presupposed about human beings in order to account for their doing history? Heidegger's answer to this question is found in his analysis of what he calls *historicality,* which refers to the existential modality that explains our being concerned with the past. For Heidegger, historicality consists of our heritage, destiny, and fate. History, then, *happens* because we, as beings conscious of the meaning of our existence, have a heritage.

In the previous section it was pointed out that Heidegger develops what he calls a priori existentials, that is, categories that explain the meaning of existence. Heritage is seen as an a priori existential. Like all existentials, it can be understood in terms of authenticity or inauthenticity. In section 74 of *Being and Time,* he writes, "The resoluteness in which Dasein comes back to itself, discloses factical possibilities of authentic existing, and discloses them *in terms of the heritage* which that resoluteness, as thrown, *takes over*" (BT 435). Dasein is Heidegger's term for the human being conscious of the meaning of his existence. According to Heidegger, Dasein is thrown into a world that is already meaningful and already characterized by values and traditions. Each of us has certain qualities that we were given and that we cannot alter, such as our sex, our nation, our age, and our position in society. This thrownness is contrasted with the fact that we also have a certain amount of freedom, in which what we do is our own responsibility. These two elements, the one given, the other free, are equiprimordial. An authentic existence is one, therefore, in which we accept and affirm both our freedom and the guilt that ensues from it, as well as the givenness (thrownness). When I claim that I am free, the I is already set in a certain way; freedom itself presupposes a given. Thus, I am responsible not only for the things I choose to do, but also for the kind of being I am, which is, in part, determined by circumstances beyond my control. What is so important about this analysis is that responsibility is no longer restricted merely to free acts but applies to the entire structure of existence. I must accept not only what I determine but also who I am.

A crucial term in understanding this notion of heritage is "resoluteness." Heidegger defines it as "this reticent self-projection upon one's ownmost being-guilty in which one is ready for anxiety" (BT 343). Thus guilt is built into the very understanding of Dasein. But guilt requires a sense of the past as meaningful. I cannot be guilty if the past is cut off from me in some irretrievable nothingness. To be resolute, which for Heidegger is the ground of authenticity, one must embrace not only the past that includes one's own actions but also the past that was formulated by our predecessors, those who have come before and so characterized the world that in being born we are already thrown into it. Thus, I can accept the glory of my nation's past, I can feel its guilt, and I can suffer the ignominy of its failures, because, as part of my heritage, they are a part of me. If Heidegger is correct, it would be inauthentic for me to disjoin my meaning from the past that gives me meaning.

The notion of thrownness as a characteristic of free Dasein is highly significant. It means that an essential part of who I am is that which is given to me by my heritage. I did not choose to be American, but to be authentic I must accept both the glory and the shame of the name. All true freedom is thus seen to be grounded in a thrownness that is inherited, not earned. It may be an "accident of birth" that I am who I am, but to be authentic I cannot forget my origins. I am no longer thought of solely in terms of my chosen actions; I am also thought of as being meaningful because of what is given me in my heritage. By making both the free and the given equal forces in my self-understanding, Heidegger has shown how history is possible. It is possible because of who I am, a being who must confront his freedom from his heritage and his heritage from his freedom. What is it that accounts for human beings doing history at all? It is done because, as authentic, humans *care* about the past as part of who they are. Thus, this caring itself must be analyzed. Heidegger unpacks this "caring about time" in terms of our dual nature as free and given. This duality between what is inherited and what is chosen is characterized by guilt and anxiety; that is, I see myself as the ground of actions and as a being who confronts nothingness. The existential character of Dasein provides, on analysis, not only the epistemic qualities by which it reaches back into the past to *find out* what happened, but also the reason why it even cares about the past, namely, that it is guilty and resolute about its existence.

This analysis puts our historical nature on firm foundation, for it is seen as an essential part of our authentic existence. It is not that history is one among many disciplines that we can do; rather we discover that we do history (that is, we read about the past, we wonder about it, we think historically about what we do now, and we also carry out historical inquiries) because we *are* historical. We do not become historical by doing history; rather we do history by becoming historical.

It may seem strange to a reader familiar only with the Anglo-American tradition that we are expected to be "free" both for what we do and for what we are. It is frequently argued in this tradition that one can be held responsible only for what one chooses; emphasis in life should be placed on the open and the free. But Heidegger challenges this tradition at its deepest roots and suggests that in a very real sense we are responsible for who we are as well as what we do. This does not mean that we have chosen to be who we are (I cannot choose to have been born an American), but it can mean that we accept or embrace the tradition, that to deny it would be inauthentic. One might argue, in defense of Heidegger, that whoever performs a free act must be more than the mere perpetrator of an act; he or she must be a person *already* meaningful in order to be held responsible. What Heidegger is saying is that this idea of being already responsible is provided by one's heritage. One cannot imagine a "free act" done by a purely abstract entity. We are *first* meaningful beings before we can *do* what is meaningful. What I do as morally meaningful is done by someone with a heritage, a heritage I must either accept or reject. But to reject all that has gone to make me who I am is to reject myself.

To be sensitive to history is therefore an essential part of an authentic existence. It is formally nihilistic to see oneself as ahistorical. And this becomes a crucial point in understanding history: to embrace history is to reject the nihilistic idea that we can be worthwhile without a tradition and a heritage.

By placing the central focus of history in the understanding of our meaning, Heidegger has shown the existential necessity of historicality. When we realize that war is historical, then, we must also realize that war is a part of our resistance to nihilism. History is the page on which we make the marks of meaning. This reinforces the central thesis: we do not fight primarily for justice or right; we fight for meaning. I do not fight only because I believe America is in the right; I fight because I am an American and to continue being an American. The justification of this lies in the realization that unless I do, I have no meaning.

WAR AS SACRIFICIAL

In the Book of Genesis we are told the world's first children, Cain and Abel, were asked to give sacrifice to the Lord God. According to the scriptural story, Cain's sacrifice of fruit and grain was not acceptable, but Abel's, of his own calves, was acceptable. Chagrined by this disfavor, Cain grew jealous of and venomous toward his brother, and slew him. Much has been made of the fact that the first homicide was a fratricide, that perhaps the expression "brotherly love" is overrated, that enmity usually occurs between the familiar rather than the strange. But far more fundamental than the world's first murder is the cause of that event: the world's first sacrifice. Not only does the story of Cain and Abel tell us that brothers can kill and that murderers have "the mark of Cain" on them, it also tells us of unfavored and favored sacrifices.

What is it about human consciousness that seems to find a profound need to sacrifice? Why does a God, whether actually existing and loving or invented as loving, accept costly sacrifices? Such things occur not only in our own testaments, they proliferate throughout all of theological literature, regardless of tradition or custom. Even godless traditions hold the idea of a true sacrifice as a noble and lofty endeavor. And surely, of all the marks assigned to reveal the meaning of war, this is doubtlessly the least controversial: we all accept the fact that young men sacrifice their very lives for what they honor and love. What, however, is sacrifice? What does it mean?

Etymologies are notoriously uncertain resources for the philosopher. The word "October" means "eighth month," but this never convinced anyone that Halloween comes in August. Furthermore, many terms simply change their meanings through usage, and the etymological roots may often be at variance with a prevalent definition. Nevertheless, when there is independent support for an original meaning, often it is beneficial to isolate the deeper significance of a term through its etymology. This is the case with the term "sacrifice," which means "to make holy." For it is that elusive, antimodern notion of "holiness" that really supports our understanding of the word "sacrifice." The point here is not the tired anthropological one that the modern mind has grown incapable of mythical profundity; rather it is the more startling notion that the sacred is somehow tied up with the surrender of something precious.

Consider the following critique.

Who thought up the idea of sacrifice, anyway? Is it not the meanest, most antihedonistic, antiutilitarian sentiment ever to be squeezed out of a bigot's brain? Imagine suggesting that one can show depth of feeling only by *hurting!* It is a perverse notion, a carrion-thought fit only for jackals to snap at. Surely I do not need to *sacrifice* something to manifest affection; surely it is better all around simply to share the good things together. Sacrifice is a remnant, along with hairshirts and flagellation cords, of medieval asceticism. I might well feel that should anyone want to make a sacrifice on my behalf, that person should be disabused of the notion. Such a practice is like dentistry without anesthesia, something our grandparents did to make themselves feel gutsy. For the point cannot be escaped. Sacrifice, if it means anything, *hurts.* Now it might be a virtue to be *able* to endure pain for the sake of a greater good, but it must surely be only perverse actually to *prefer* to surrender what is dear as an essential part of one's affection or reverence for another being.

Yet, in spite of the critique's sentiment, this is exactly what sacrifice means, and most people revere it. Certainly the *pious* revere it, and to that extent the sons of Mars are pious. It can be seen in the eyes of the parents who greet only a wooden box covered with a flag instead of their warm, living son. Behind the tears and the awesome grief, there is that glimmer of pride that their son has done not only a good thing, an admirable thing, a noble thing, but indeed a *holy* thing. And it is this sentiment, when rightly anchored, that will lead us to this tragic idea. For when we honor the sacrifice of the fallen, we are praising not only their courage but also that which makes of their slaughter-place not merely a battlefield but an altar.

We know what we mean when we speak of sacrifice in the normal way. We mean surrendering what is precious, giving up something that is dear to us or that cost us something, either in labor or in assets. We say a friend sacrificed her time to come and help us when we were alone, or that a father had sacrificed his own advantages for the sake of his children. We also know the etymology, and so we say that to make something holy requires this sense of deprivation. When we speak of the soldier's supreme sacrifice, we mean he has given up his life, which was precious, for our benefit; and this is so close an approximation to holiness within the purely mortal sphere of human endeavors that it seems to endow the race with a touch of divinity.

These ordinary meanings are quite sound, but as usual they leave more thought provoked than settled.

Furthermore, we do not wish merely to say that the individual soldiers sacrificed their lives; we also want to say that war itself is sacrificial: it makes things holy. This requires some digging.

Let us return to Cain and Abel. Before the famous murder the drama on those early fields was even more compelling than the violence that followed. God apparently was displeased with the sacrifices of Cain but accepted those of Abel. Why? Careful reading of the admittedly uncertain text does not entirely rule out that the sacrifice of living cattle was preferable to that of grain. If this seems somewhat unfair to post-Enlightenment thinkers, it should be remembered that the symbolic meaning was as important as the literal. Perhaps if Cain had given the best of his grain, his sacrifice would also have been accepted, but the text does not say so. Animals are closer to us in nature than is grain; perhaps they are more costly. In any event, Cain did not give enough. But he did *give,* so the point cannot be entirely symbolic. In some way, however, either by the mercantile value of the goods offered or by the meanspiritedness of the bestowal, the offering was rejected.

On the aesthetic or artistic level, however, one thing obviously stands out. In Abel's sacrifice blood was spilled, but in Cain's it was not. Perhaps Cain's offering actually cost more than Abel's, but it seems an essential part of sacrifice that blood must be spilled. The animal killed by Abel shed its blood, not Abel's. However, since the animal was his, he offered not his own but what was of his own. Blood is surely a symbol of life, and since Abel offers what is his own, as living, it symbolizes the offering of life itself. And it is this willingness to offer life that makes something holy.

The suggestion is that only bloody offerings are genuine sacrifices. This is not only in the biblical image but also in our ordinary usage of the term; sacrifice means pain, and even ultimate pain—death. The supreme offering is life. Why, however, are offerings made at all? One must first consider a purely practical meaning to an offering. Perhaps it is merely appeasement: buy off the gods, and they will not get angry with you. In this sense, sacrifice to the gods ranks with tribute money given by inner-city schoolchildren to the youth gangs in order to keep from being beaten or even killed. There is nothing wrong with this, particularly if it works. Reverence, after all, can often be accomplished through fear, and mythical consciousness is often fairly direct in such matters. But even if such appeasement was a part of the original sacrifice, it cannot be all there is to it. If God had simply wanted more, Cain would have provided it. But we must try to understand why

Cain felt so personally abused by the refusal of his offering, why he should be so moved that he would commit the first murder. Sacrifices are to be distinguished from mere gifts, in that they come as a part of us and represent us. We have already seen that a reward is different from a gift, in that the former is given because of what is done or earned, whereas the latter is given because of who one is. A sacrifice is a gift, but one in which the bestowal speaks not only to who the receiver is but to who the giver is as well. Sacrifices must cost us something in a way that a gift need not, because with the sacrifice we send a part of ourselves. If a gift is *given* because of who one is, the sacrifice is *received* because of who one is. God, therefore, in rejecting Cain's offering, was not only rejecting what he was giving but was also rejecting Cain, and the eldest son of Adam knew this. Hence his distress.

This is the first key in seeking to understand why we sacrifice. Even if a part of sacrifice is expiation, another part is the bestowal of one's own worth as a part of what is given. Instinctively, perhaps, people seek to abuse what is their own, in sacrifice, to make it worthy and thereby make themselves worthy of the gods' approval. This transcends mere appeasement because it resounds off the deep well of human longing to participate in the divine. Since it is obvious that I should value my own life, to offer it is the bestowal of the supreme value I possess. This is true when what is offered partakes of that life, when, for example, I shed blood as a symbol of life.

Consider a gift given by a young boy. For some reason we seem to appreciate what is given if it cost the child some time, labor, or money that was dear to him. The child seems to realize this as well, for he is ready to inform us how much he had to work or pay or suffer to be able to give it. This certainly does not imply that we want the child to suffer; it merely means that the nature of the bestowal is more highly honored when the gift costs something. The intrinsic value of the gift itself may be negligible, but the value in the giving itself is highly prized.

In the Genesis story, God refuses the offering from Cain but receives that from Abel. Why? One answer may be, of course, that Cain's offering was inadequate. But another reason may be that the offerer was inadequate. Perhaps even if Cain had offered the prime cattle of the herd, his gift would have been rejected because it came from Cain. Contemporary theologians often try to convince us that if Cain had more sincerely offered his sacrifice, it would have been accepted, for they are convinced of the moral vision of God: a man cannot give more than he has. But the texts do not say this specifically, and it may be that the author of the testament sensed more profoundly than the contemporary theologian the importance of the difference between who one is and what one does. Perhaps no matter how fervently and devoutly Cain offered up his best stores, they would have been rejected. Why? Because a sacrifice makes things holy, and Cain simply was not a holy man; he was not a man willing to shed blood. Although, as murderer, he shed Abel's.

The image of sacrifice as a kind of payment to avoid divine wrath is, in this interpretation, no longer adequate. For if there is a market price for salvation, then any sincere offering is accepted, a view well fitting contemporary egalitarianism. But Cain's offering was rejected. If the offering simply had not been adequate, Cain could have offered an even larger amount next time, and apparently this, by the egalitarian's interpretation, would have been accepted. But he gets so angry he kills his brother. He must have been either very hotheaded or very profound. Perhaps he sensed that it was not his offering but he that was inadequate. To be rejected on *that* level may well inspire the outrage that accounts for the first murder. When you offer *yourself* and the recipient turns you down, then what worth have you?

This offering of the self distinguishes a sacrifice from another gift. Furthermore, the sacrificer's need to endure suffering purifies the giving and renders it holy. Both of these elements, that one's own self is given and that the pain produces the holy, are essential for sacrifice. Neither of these qualities is reducible to moral goodness, nor do they imply such goodness. I can be perfectly moral and not be holy, and I can be holy and not always be moral.

The notion that things can be cleansed or purified through suffering is an ancient and deep persuasion. In the attempt to separate the various ways in which we think about our values, our early consciousness focuses on the twin notions of purity and purgation to isolate what is holy from what is merely good or right. Sacred objects should not be touched by ordinary hands; virgins should be revered as attendants to the shrines; ritualistic bathing or at least washing of hands should precede any solemn event. At certain profound rites, only the pure and unsullied, such as innocent children or virgins, may perform the ceremonies. This is not based on a naïve belief in the moral superiority of innocence; this shows the significance of another kind of value, holiness. Those who are not naturally pure like children and virgins can achieve a kind of redeemed holiness through suffering. For in our understanding of holiness is a kind of spiritual radiance, a light that shines through the murky confusion of the profane. This metaphor of light reveals much of how we think of the holy: in order to let the light shine through, the panes must be clean, and the most thorough cleaning is done by fire. When all the grime has been burned away, the brilliance can radiate through and illumine who we are.

The holy can be distinguished from the morally good insofar as moral principles tell us how to act, but the rites of the sacred simply show us who we are. It is for this reason that religious communities put so much emphasis on the giving of names. To name is a sacrament; it is to baptize. We sprinkle with water or even immerse in water the one to be named, and names tell us who we are. In some cultures, the "true" name of a person is hidden from the populace and is known only to a select few. At certain important events, such as entering a convent, monastery, or marriage, names are changed, implying that a new person now exists. The reason for this emphasis on names is that the *holy* functions as a source of light, a radiance, in whose glow alone we find who we are. In Wagner's *Parsifal,* for example, the young, innocent, and simple fool, *wer guter Tat sich freut,* does not know his name. That he is called Parsifal, the foolish, pure one, is an essential step in the self-realization of his special calling. All of these curious attributes of naming, purity, holiness, and suffering seem to belong together almost necessarily.

Natural purity may, of course, be of ritualistic significance for the ceremonial necessities of our spirit, but it is, of itself, not an absolute virtue. Realism, strength, and the richness of experience bring us beyond the simple and pure fool of Parsifal. But *achieved purity,* through purgation, is something quite distinct and much more highly ranked. Never to have sinned has a certain charm about it, but to have sinned and then to have had the sins burned away provides spiritual stature. It is this that is provided by sacrifice. Sacrifice makes us holy because the suffering cauterizes the wounds and makes them clean. It is this kind of holiness that is achieved by the warrior in the crucible of battle. War, for all its savagery, is a deeply ritualistic thing, with ceremonies and rites and rituals; but its truest celebrations are not on the parade ground but on the battleground. Dedication is provided by those who battle and only imitated by those who perform ceremonies, as Abraham Lincoln so profoundly teaches us in the Gettysburg Address. It should perhaps be emphasized here that sacrifice should never be seen as a symbol of something else more real. Sacrifice does not show something other than itself; it *establishes* its meaning. After all, sacrifice is a harsh and cruel word. The young bodies are actually maimed and torn, very real bullets pierce very real flesh, and the screaming heat of shrapnel destroys with completely unsymbolic pain. There is nothing metaphoric about this all too real agony. These young men are really dead, and it is real blood that pours out upon the ground. The realist's objection that these points may sound abstract or romantic misses the significance of this truth. There is nothing symbolic, romantic, or abstract about such intense agony. *Real* suffering makes the holy, and that is why it is sacrificial.

We cannot understand war, then, without understanding what is holy. The phenomenon of sacrifice has shown us that it cannot be understood except as manifesting the holy, so the question now must be, How do we think about the holy? To answer this question adequately is beyond the scope of this book, perhaps any book, but a meaningful response can be given, and no one has done as well as Plato, in a little dialogue subtitled *On Holiness* (or piety), known as the *Euthyphro.* As usual in these annoying little Socratic dialogues, Plato does not give us a precise definition of piety, or holiness; indeed, he seems to be intent on making things more difficult rather than easier. Nevertheless, I know of no resource as rich as the *Euthyphro* for understanding the virtue of piety, and so in what follows, I shall try to focus on what Plato reveals in that dialogue.

First, the term "virtue" here needs some preliminary discussion. The English term is based on a Latin etymology and stems from the word *vir* meaning "man" in the gender sense. So "virtue" means "manly"; it is very far from the contemporary usage that suggests modesty in sexual behavior. The Greek term is *aretē,* which seems to come from the god of war, *Arēs.* By it, the Greeks meant something like "excellence" or "that which makes life worth living." Again, no sense of prudery or delicacy is implied in the word at all. *Aretē* is that which allows a man fully to realize his own worth. Perhaps the best way to get at this all-important term is by way of negative examples. Let us consider drunkenness and miserliness. An alcoholic is a slave to one of his passions; under the influence of this weakness, the alcoholic is simply not free. Not only does he become an object of scorn from others and pity from his friends, he even recognizes in himself his own dependence and begins to hate himself or to wallow in self-pity. Such a man is not manly; he is lacking in virtue, or *aretē.* The same can be said for the miser. One for whom money and the achievement of it is the supreme guide to activity becomes less of a man than one not enslaved by this vice. Greed for money is not considered evil because of its ill effects on others so much as its ill effects on oneself. A miser cannot enjoy the fullness of life when pinched by his own crippling lust for wealth. Thus, it is a *virtue* to be generous, or "liberal," without being foolish. It is a virtue to be independent of wine's bondage. There is nothing wrong with drinking wine, indeed, with drinking it fully, as long as the effects are not demeaning. Abstinence, therefore, is not in itself a virtue; it would be virtuous to abstain only if one drink would start you on a binge of self-destructive inebriation.

From these two examples it can be seen that the operating principle behind *aretē* is freedom from self-enslavement. To most Greek thinkers, life could be lived well or badly, and here "well" means "in as excellent a manner as possible." If one does not possess the virtues, then one is foolishly depriving oneself of an important dimension to life. And here the adverb is crucial. How could you be so stupid as to be a miser? This seems to be the question. And if it is the question, then obviously the essence of vice is foolishness, or ignorance.

When we put the question in this way, we may find the Greek approach somewhat different from our contemporary approach to ethical questions. Socrates asks, How could you be so stupid as to be unjust? or, How could you be so stupid as to be impious? Most modern people would perhaps wonder if it is intelligible *at all* to be pious. And yet, Plato has deep and powerful reasons for making piety intelligible and for assuring us that it is indeed a virtue. Piety (*ousiou*) is a fairly broad concept that reveres not only the gods but such "holy" institutions as the family as well. Patriotism too is a form of piety; it is, indeed, that virtue by which the holiness of one's nation is served as appropriate to one's own.

In the dialogue, the young man Euthyphro is about to bring his father before the court on a charge of manslaughter. He considers this act to be one of piety, but Socrates questions whether it is proper filial piety to bring one's own father to court. Do family ties and affections mean nothing? Yet, the father has indeed violated the law and perhaps should be punished. Socrates himself never reveals whether such an act, in his view, is morally right, but he does *question* (not to be confused with *deny*) the piety of the act. Perhaps it is right or just to turn the father in, but not pious. This, then, emphasizes the acuteness and anguish of the dialogue: Can one serve piety and justice equally? Is there no difference between turning in one's father and turning in one's neighbor or fellow citizen? If one argues that there is no difference, then one seems to be saying that family ties simply do not matter. But normally, having family ties *matter* is what one means by familial piety.

Perhaps, then, one might say that when justice is concerned, piety does not count. That is, the concerns of justice should outweigh the concerns of piety. But unless piety can dissuade the simple matter of justice, then piety is rendered unimportant. And even if this were the proper answer, it would have nevertheless been wrong of Euthyphro to characterize his suit against his father as pious. It might be just, but not pious.

Euthyphro, at one point, defines piety as that which is loved by the gods. Socrates then asks, Are things made holy because the gods love them, or do the gods love them because they are holy? This question is, in itself, a profound interrogation of how we think. If I were to assume that God gave us the Ten Commandments because the commandments were good, I would thereby entertain the notion that the goodness of the commandments was independent of God giving them to us. Thus, if I could imagine men learning of the goodness of the commandments independently, there really would be no need of God at all. On the other hand, if I said the commandments were good because God gave them to us, I could imagine God giving any set of ten precepts; and should God have given Moses a commandment to torture all blue-eyed children, he would have done so. But both of these conclusions seem highly unlikely. The first makes God into a mere messenger of what is good independent of God; the second equates what is good with what is given by God, and that renders the meaning of "good" empty. What then does this question reveal?

The question itself shows that the way we think about what is holy is different from the way we think about what is good. One's feeling toward one's father is not rendered complete by a mere adherence to the civil laws. If one believes in a God, it is not because that belief provides one with what is moral and right, for many can reason about what is moral and right without the idea of God. Such things as forgiveness and gift giving, however, are made sense of by an appeal to meaning beyond the good.

The dilemma of poor Euthyphro deserves our attention and concentration. If he turns his father in, he offends piety but supports justice; if he does not turn his father in, he offends justice but supports the notion of piety. It must be emphasized that Plato, through his description of Socrates, never fully develops a response to the question What ought Euthyphro to do? For if that were the form of the question, the answer would immediately be seen in terms of ethical or even moral principles, and the virtue of justice would be triumphant. Euthyphro probably should, under the influence of this question, turn his father in. But the brilliance of Plato consists in this: we all recognize that such an act would be impious. (For if piety is nothing else but doing what one ought to do with regard to the state, then piety is reduced to justice, and an entire virtue is lost.)

In many ways, to recognize the *autonomy* of piety is to focus on its essence. Holiness cannot be approached by any other notion, for holiness is unapproachable. When we read the *Euthyphro,* however, we sense two things at once: that Socrates has not provided us with a very good definition of the virtue of piety—but then, he never does—and that we nevertheless sense in Socrates a profound embodiment of the holy that is lacking in Euthyphro. One reason the arrogant young man lacks piety is, oddly, that he is too legalistic; one might almost say too just. This is what holiness seems to mean: that not everything of value can be weighed, counted, analyzed, and measured in terms of human good. Socrates, on the other hand, impresses us as holy, or pious, just because he is struck by the incongruity of sending one's own father to jail. There is more to life than we can accomplish; our reality is determined by more than our wills and our fortunes. Reverence toward the forces that keep this world from computerized dominance is a part of piety, but it is not merely an empty appeal to the irrational. It can be worshiped.

Piety is the reverence for the forces beyond us that make up who we are as much as what we do. When this is a unifying force, as in a family or a nation, it is revered as sacred; and the modality necessary to approach it is one of purity, either natural, as with children, or achieved, as with sufferers. Those who suffer on behalf of a sacred institution, therefore, are seen as holy, and it is profoundly true to speak of warriors as sacrificial.

Individual soldiers may be godless. The single, tough-minded warrior may be neither pious nor holy, and certainly he may not be sacrificial. Nevertheless, when we think of war, we think of sacrifice, an offering of what is precious and a suffering that is purgative and hence purifying. Some soldiers do indeed sacrifice their lives willingly for the sake of their friends or even for their country, and when these extraordinary heroes are thought about, the normal predicates of praise fail us. Such acts are beyond the simple moral law; they appeal to a higher kind of worth, that expressed in love. Sacrifice, of course, makes sense to us especially in love, for in love the emphasis is placed on the worth of being rather than doing. Romeo loves Juliet not for what she does but for who she is, not because she is good but because she is beautiful.

A word here must be said about the mystery of suffering. It deserves to be called a mystery because it seems to be revered without any acceptable reason. Inexplicably we seem to honor and esteem those who have suffered much. The ethical theory of utilitarianism claims that people see the good as happiness, and under this notion the intrinsic worth of suffering simply makes no sense at all. The ethical theory of deontology maintains that the morally good is the adherence of one's will to one's duty. Under this theory it is somewhat easier to see that one might have to endure suffering because it is one's duty, but even the deontologist fails to isolate the worth put on the value of suffering itself. Nevertheless, experience provides us with an instinctive respect for it. If two people are introduced who are fairly identical in all attributes (equally good, equally intelligent, equally beautiful), but one has suffered greatly, there is an almost inevitable respect and reverence for the sufferer. We seem to gravitate toward the sufferers as if they were, by dint of their suffering, endowed with greater wisdom, greater humanity, and greater profundity. On stage, tragedies have an almost inexplicable appeal. Those who have suffered greatly are just more *interesting* than those who have not.

Stoicism, particularly its Roman advocates, went so far as to make pain a positive good. Epictetus is said to have told a youth, who had boasted of never having suffered, that he was "unfortunate never to have had a misfortune." Only a Roman could appreciate Brutus's wife, Portia, stabbing herself in the leg in order to impress her husband. The trouble with the Romans and the Stoics is that we simply cannot accept their ethical position, but at the same time we cannot but admire their inner strength. There does seem to be a kind of *triviality* about hedonism, a giddiness about a gaggle of pleasure worshipers. The reason for this anomaly may be that the Stoics speak, not to an ethical or moral worth, but to a spiritual worth. There simply cannot be any moral good in suffering, but there may be a spiritual value in it. Suffering focuses on who we are; happiness, on how we feel. What is so impressive about having suffered is that one's intrinsic worth has not been lessened; indeed, it may have been increased, and that just means that we are more than our pleasures. There are countless stories, dramas from throughout history, that attest to the profundity of suffering, and many people who may have been distracted from their existential meaning in fortuity have found a deep resource of self-understanding in adversity. This makes sense, it seems to me, only if we sharply distinguish the two kinds of worth: the worth of the existential from the worth of the moral. The realm accessed by suffering shows a kind of worth that is separate from the calculus of happiness and goodness. This realm is the holy.

All wars, then, are holy wars, but this does not mean that all wars are fanatical. If one's homeland is sacred, to fight for it is to participate in the holiness of the place. Even the most sullied can be purged by the scouring suffering of martial sacrifice. The contemporary usage of the term "holy war" does not signify the same thing, of course. Today when we use the term "holy war," we mean a war fought for religious and indeed fanatical reasons, a war that cannot be restrained by humanistic limits or practical urgency. The holiness that is purchased by the willingness to sacrifice is of quite a different order. It means that the way in which we think about the sacrifices in war cannot be exhausted by moral or political meaning but is instead understood in terms of what is sacred.

In Muslim traditions the death of a warrior is considered to have a special theological meaning that guarantees salvation. Even a scarlet sinner, who otherwise would be headed straight for hell, is promised immediate redemption should he die on the battlefield. Some contemporary critics lament such teaching as an inspiration for radical militarism among such believers. The fact that history has not shown this to be the inevitable result does not deter these critics. The doctrine of battlefield salvation is not meant as a spur to militarism as one might expect; rather it is a simple realization of the profundity of martial sacrifice. The doctrine represents how we think about those willing to give their lives for their country: they are sacred.

The sacrificial character of war, then, depends on our understanding of the elusive but powerful notion of the holy.

A disturbing phenomenon in the history of modern warfare should perhaps be mentioned in this context. Often the side defending the more questionable morality nevertheless seems to possess a greater spirituality. The success of the villains in these confrontations puts a lie to the naïve belief that the gods favor the just. It is today almost universally accepted that slavery is a morally ignominious institution, and few, if any, contemporary thinkers would argue for the return of such an ignoble practice. But few historians or military observers deny that during the American Civil War the South outfought the North, especially in the eastern theater. The Southern soldier did not universally support slavery, but he did support the South, and his support was spiritually greater than the Northern soldier's support of the North. More recently, in the horrific magnitude of the Second World War, the hated Nazis were grudgingly admired as superior fighters. In most of the vaunted campaigns, the Germans were victorious against greater numbers. Even in the later campaigns where they lost, the Germans fought with remarkable valor and spirit. Certainly Kesselring's spirited struggle in Italy and Rommel's brilliant maneuvers in Africa reveal no lack of dedication or willingness to sacrifice. Even in the Pacific theater, the morally flawed Japanese outfought the morally superior Allies. Is there any reason for this, aside from luck?

There seems to be an almost inexplicable equation that suggests the less one's cause is supported by ethical ideas, the greater is the spiritual enthusiasm.

It is almost as if the more morally questionable one felt about one's country, the more emphasis one would put on the sacredness of it. In countless stories of the Confederate soldiers, one hears of Johnny Reb's belief in the "sacredness of his cause," whereas the Yankees believed in the moral rightness of their endeavor. Perhaps when we can no longer rely on righteousness, we turn to the sacredness of what is our own. It is certainly an uncomfortable suggestion, of course, but there does seem to be sufficient historical evidence for it to mention it here, for it must be emphasized that the holy and the good are not equivalent notions. Holiness, like beauty and being loved, is not achieved by doing what is proper or right. Rather it seems to be understood in terms of purity or reverence and in its highest form is conceived in terms of being favored by God. Warriors who sacrifice their lives are often thought of as completely redeemed, and hence achieve a kind of holiness by the purgation of their sacrifice. From the story of Cain and Abel we learn that holiness has no market price, that in bestowing oneself, a sacrifice is distinguished from goodness, and that this oddly is an essential way in which we understand the holy: it is unapproachable.

This point, however, is more firmly shown: young men do indeed sacrifice their lives, and do so willingly and knowingly. We cannot escape the significance of our understanding this — namely, that such sacrifice is valued as something transcending our normal evaluations. In trying to characterize this special kind of evaluation, we must not lose sight of the primordial reality: these sacrifices do indeed matter; they are true; and unless we accept the ignominy of unspeakable insult, we must recognize the autonomy of their worth.

WAR AS VIOLENT

That war is violent may seem a most futile statement of the obvious. Are oceans wet? Yet, for all its seeming redundancy, the claim that war is violent needs not only to be said but to be probed deeply so as to reveal its meaning. One reason it must be reiterated that war is violent is that, surprisingly, many fail to bear this truth in mind. Not only do the hotheaded and overeager fame seekers sometimes make this mistake, but so, often, do the pacifist critics of war. Many act *surprised* to discover that in war real human beings actually die, and many die horribly. They die because of the deliberate and self-conscious will of one nation to use violence against another. Not all the pious praises or empty slogans can eradicate their unwanted deaths. A true understanding of war, however, would seek not to disguise this dreadful truth but to embrace it. Clausewitz, for example, makes the following observation: "We are not interested in generals who win victories without bloodshed. The fact that slaughter is a horrifying spectacle must make us take war more seriously, but not provide an excuse for gradually blunting our swords in the name of humanity. Sooner or later someone will come along with a sharp sword and hack off our arms" (260; Howard and Pavet translation). Within the memory of a few great-grandfathers, still living, an event occurred that bears repetition and reminding. At the battle of the Somme, during the First World War, there were almost a million casualties. One million casualties. That is twenty times the number of casualties from the atomic bomb at Hiroshima. It was achieved without the benefit of contemporary weapons, without the use of nuclear armament, without even the use of bombs dropped from airplanes. These dead and wounded were destroyed by intimate, immediate weapons held in the hand or by artillery. That is violence. That is violence in the supreme, and to forget it is to trivialize those who endured it. It is this that we are seeking to understand in the analysis of this sixth existential mark of war.

The term "violence" is often used with its dogged modifier "senseless." However, in spite of the fondness with which many contemporary critics seem to link the two words, there is really very little violence that is senseless. Unless one were to adopt a peculiarly somnolent metaphysics, most human violence is indeed quite intelligible, if by that one means that there is a reason for the use of physical coercion. Many may disagree with the efficiency of the reasons given, but they do exist. Every violent crime is perpetrated for a reason; every familial quarrel that erupts into physical severity is based on a reason; every contest between forces of strength has a reason. When the hungry lion leaps on the back of the gazelle and breaks its spine, there is a reason. And indeed, throughout human history, every time one host has drawn up its numbers against another, there has been a reason. It is admittedly often difficult to isolate a reason sufficient to justify the extent of the violence on a legalistic or moralistic basis, but even in such cases it is always possible to focus on a goal, an end, a purpose, and say that here is the reason these men fought. Thus, it is not senseless violence with which we must contend, but sensible violence.

The reality of violence itself is one reason for being violent. Physically to push one willful being from a position that being does not want to relinquish requires sufficient power and strength to carry it out, as well as the will to use these resources. Not all the abstract analysis, the legal maneuvers, the political wranglings, and the official reports can equal one overt act. If a man takes from me an item of my property (say a stereo) and I sue him to get it back, I will not be able to use my stereo again until someone actually takes it from the thief. If the thief resists, violence must be used. The judge's order will not do it; the writs of my lawyer will not do it; the urgings of his cleric will not do it. Perhaps, however, the physical strength of the arresting police officer may do it. To be sure, the police officer is acting under the order of the judge, the persuasion of the attorney, the moral conviction of the cleric, perhaps; but the fact is that as long as the thief is determined to hold my property by dint of physical possession, no formal maneuver can divest him of my property. The police officer must physically enter his abode and physically take up the stereo and physically resist the thief. Because of this ultimate reliance on the use of corporeal strength, there is a satisfying feeling that accompanies the cessation of quarreling and the reliance on action. There can be no doubt that this satisfaction is often too readily used without due regard for procedure, but the point here is not that such reliance on action may never be unwarranted but simply that it is often seen as final, and hence as ultimate.

In the contest between formal maneuvering and overt violence, the latter will always succeed if adhered to. It is for this reason that violence and the threat of violence become inevitable once it is *possible* to use violence. In this purely material sense, then, no power outranks the physically violent. And it is for this reason that it demands our respect. People do violent things. Under civil agreement, the uses of violence are restricted and organized. But as long as it is possible for an uncivil person to violate the property and peace of a civil person, the latter must rely on some ultimate arsenal of violence if civility is to be maintained. Thus, the ultimate use of violence is not to be seen as the breakdown of civility but as the ground of it. It may be that military power should never be used except as a last resort, but such a truth does not imply the impropriety or lawlessness of military power.

As long as there are different views concerning the ultimate values (which is not much different from saying that as long as there are human beings), there will be contests of prowess and withal the ultimate depend-ence on force. How one *thinks* about such reliance on power often deter-mines the very worth of a nation. But that there can be both meaningful differences about the ultimate values and a mutual suspension of any reliance on force or violence is impossible. One must guard not only against actual and imminent threat but also against possible and distant threat, particularly if what is threatened is of ultimate worth. Therefore, the greatest insurance against violence is the overt determination to use it if necessary.

This is not only speculatively true, it is also historically true. Honorable and self-respecting nations throughout history have not shied away from this need for an army. There have been neutral countries, to be sure; the United States was officially neutral in 1915 and again in 1940, no less than Switzerland or Sweden. But neutral countries are not pacifist countries, and neutrality itself is no guarantee of nonbelligerence unless all other powers respect that neutrality, as Belgium so tragically discovered in 1914.

But violence, whether national or personal, hurts. Indeed, that is why men are violent, because it hurts. Napoleon and Hitler were, of course, against war; they were selective pacifists. They did not want to go to war. What they wanted was for their enemies to make concessions *without* resistance. In order to force the other nations to bend to their wills, they brought about *pain,* hoping that the pain would be sufficiently demanding as to wrest capitulation. If not, the amount of pain was increased until the body politic simply succumbed to the will of the invader. In this sense, pain becomes the method of violence. Once it is admitted that there can be a clash of wills, it is ridiculous to assume there can be an accommodation without pain. Honor will, of course, restrict one's use of violence to what *ought* to be done rather than to what one *wants* to be done, but if the disagreement is sufficiently deep, the imposition of pain and suffering cannot be avoided. This, however, except for the squeamish, is not unacceptable. As human we are suffering beings, and we do not expect an entirely pain-free existence. What we do hope for is that our suffering is not without meaning. We distinguish our wants from our wills, and are prepared to sacrifice the former for the latter. To forgo all violence whatsoever is to capitulate the autonomy of our wills and hence our meaningfulness. Although within a society there may be a few who forgo personal violence for religious or spiritual reasons, such dedication presupposes the willingness of others to support their independence. Further, such meekness cannot be universalized, and even among its most ardent supporters, such as Christ and Gandhi, it was never absolute.

Violence has its aesthetic meaning as well. I have already spoken of Kant's analysis of the sublime in my consideration of vastness; a similar respect is often given to violence per se. There is often huge satisfaction taken when a simple but forthright man casts aside the effeminate restrictions against action and boldly asserts his rights and claims to the world. Huge violence often exerts a sinister fascination on even the most reluctant observer. In the *Poetics* Aristotle speaks of the importance of spectacle, and few experiences are as spectacular as great violence. The dullest plot and most uninspired characters can always be enlivened by a few awesome explosions or energetic displays of power. There is something fascinating, awe inspiring, riveting, and demanding about spectacular violence. Some of what is satisfying in our experience of the violent is similar to what delights us in our experience of the sublime, and Kant's analysis would cover those similarities. But in addition to being sublime, huge violence has its own attraction. Primarily, this satisfaction in the aesthetic realm is due to the complete and total dominance by the artistic medium. When violence occurs on the stage or screen, the mind need only watch, perhaps can only watch. Violence is also often the end of suspense, and the titillating discomfort caused by suspense increases the delight we take in its resolution. At least something *happens* in violence.

The aesthetic characteristics of violence carry over to the spiritual. Violence is wonderfully *decisive*. It cuts short the agony of uncertainty and fearsome expectation. We read in Matthew: " . . . the kingdom of heaven suffereth violence, and only the violent will bear it away." We understand this as a spiritual recognition of the importance of commitment and boldness, twin defenses against the nihilism that strangles souls. The spirit cannot abide an entirely passive and tranquil existence, for things of spirit are too important and too serious to await indifferently and without urgency. Violence, of course, means more than mere action and even more than mere commitment. By violence we mean the final step of the will, the ultimate surrender to the demands of a project or enterprise. It means the acceptance of pain and the bringing about of pain. At times violence entails complete destruction or even total creation. Whether an original act by a willful God or a chance explosion of the highest order, the start of things, the beginning of the universe, is an act of enormous violence, no less so than its spectacular end.

In addition to the aesthetic and spiritual meaning of violence, it is important to focus on the metaphysical meaning of this notion as well. The metaphysician is required to render an adequate account of all the levels of beings and meaning. Where he begins, of course, will to some extent determine his overall ontological outlook, but it is possible at least to consider the possible range of his inquiry. First, then, there are what might be called *things,* or, possibly, entities. By this is meant not only physical things like rocks and oceans but the possibility of other kinds of things as well, such as souls, God, minds, and processes. To assert the existence of a mind or a God is no less a metaphysical claim than to deny the existence of such things. However, it is obvious that no matter how broadly one describes or defines things, there are also *events*. Thus, in addition to rocks, there are also rockslides; in addition to oceans, there are also tides. Any adequate metaphysics cannot be satisfied with a complete listing of all things; it must also include the principles by which we understand events.

There are purely natural things, or entities, that undergo events. The spring mousetrap is a thing; when the trigger is loosed, the bar slams shut. This is an event. The event is understood in terms of the physics of the spring. In the case of the mouse that nibbles at the cheese, its actions may perhaps be explicated in similar or even identical terms: the natural laws governing such things as animal instincts and hunger. Since there *may* be more going on in the case of the mouse, however, we may perhaps want to distinguish between the purely natural phenomenon of the spring and animal behavior of the mouse. Instinct may be thought with different predicates and principles than the laws of physics. It is possible to speak of the mouse wanting the cheese, but we consider it somewhat odd to speak of the spring wanting to return to its unwound position. However, when we turn to the man who sets the trap, there is a further complication. Here we speak not only of the following of natural laws governing springs and animal behavior, we also speak of a will. It is the introduction of human will that complicates the metaphysics, for the act of the man is often judged as one that could have been otherwise; it is an act that permits of responsibility. We say the man is responsible for setting the trap, and in saying this we introduce an entirely different way of thinking than when we, by recourse to natural laws, account for the mouse eating the cheese or for the trap springing shut.

Since some events seem to happen solely because of natural laws and other events seem to happen because of the intervention of a human will, any adequate metaphysics must either reduce the latter to the former or establish a metaphysical autonomy for the will. Human acts are events no less so than natural occurrences, so they cannot be discarded. But they seem to possess a special kind of meaning that prima facie at least cannot be explicated merely as another event propelled by the laws of physics. The notion of a will is engendered by this difference. It is the acceptance of the metaphysical autonomy of the will that generates the idea of violence. When one man's will conflicts with another's, and when one of the men is not reluctant to use physical force to establish his preference, there is violence.

Violence forces us to weigh the pain we endure from the violence, against the value we place on having our own way in the contest between wills. If the pain is too great, we will yield, and the will of the other triumphs. If the desire for our own way is greater, we will endure the pain and possibly inflict counterpain on the other until we or the other eventually yields. If the pain is sufficiently enormous, the capitulation may be unavoidable; or if the violence is sufficiently effective, death may ensue, and the contest ceases. Although there may be enormous eruptions of power within nature, such as storms and earthquakes, the uniquely human significance of violence is here considered a necessary condition for our understanding of the term. Thus, the will becomes, in such a metaphysical description, an essential part of human violence.

We do indeed describe natural events as violent, as when we speak of a violent storm or eruption. Since the noun *violence,* however, seems to be derived from the prior form of the verb *violate,* such uses may be seen as metaphorical. To violate something implies human volition, and in this context violence almost always implies a human will. The verb form suggests impropriety, as when one violates a trust or denies a right, and the usage usually connotes some sense of guilt or wrongdoing, hence a free or willful act. Will is usually distinguished from want; I may not be free from my wants, but I am thought of as free for my will. (I may not want to pay my taxes, but I may be willing to do so.) There are some philosophers, of course, who would deny any distinction between wanting and willing, except perhaps as a matter of degree; and indeed, there are some who attempt to define both willful and desired acts as purely natural phenomena no different from the spring on the mousetrap closing. But such metaphysical reductionism does some violence to our normal usage of terms.

Violence, then, usually suggests the use of physical force in the contest of wills. Resistance to the influence of another is therefore just as much an instance of violence as the threat to influence beyond acceptable means. Not only is the will usually thought of as an essential part of violence, the two terms "willful" and "violent" are often used almost interchangeably. To claim that war is violent is to characterize the warrior as willful and war as an overt contest between wills.

It is possible, of course, to question the distinction between nature and will in the explanation of events. Some would reduce all seemingly willful acts to nature, but others reverse the reduction and describe all *natural* acts as some kind of world will. In 1818, Arthur Schopenhauer published his great work, *The World as Will and Representation,* and in it he argues for such a metaphysical view. Because of the wealth of ideas that Schopenhauer provides for our understanding of the will, he shall be used as the philosopher whose analyses support this notion of war as violent.

Schopenhauer, strongly influenced by Kant, recognized that the principles and rules that govern our understanding of nature cannot come from the external world—for then they would not be a priori—but come rather from our own minds. Thus, the world is our representation. The various senses are means by which we represent the world to ourselves, but such representations are necessarily limited to how we see the world, not necessarily how it is. Indeed, "we see the world as we see the world" seems for Schopenhauer analytic and hence necessarily true; "we see the world as it really is" is a metaphysical claim that requires nonexperiential verification, which we do not have. However, this seeming idealism is not complete, for in addition to the world, we also have access to an independent notion of the metaphysically real, which is not dependent on the faculties of our representation. This idea of the world as it "really" is comes to us in two ways: one, internally, in the recognition of our own will; the other, by means of an argument based on the idealistic character of our knowing. The first source of the world as will follows the Kantian insight that our free acts must be governed by principles that are separate from the ways in which we interpret the world. We are aware of ourselves as wills directly, not filtered through the interpretative functions of the categories. When I perform an act of my free will, I am directly aware of myself as the source of that agency. The moment, however, I attempt to reflect on the cause and nature of my will, I do so by representing the phenomenon, and thus it once again becomes appearance. However, in the awareness of my will I go beyond mere appearance to reality.

It is the second way in which the mind can know reality, however, that is so remarkable. Our understanding of the world of appearance requires the use of categories: space, time, and cause. (In this, Schopenhauer disagrees with Kant, who analyzed space and time as forms of intuition, and who held there are twelve categories instead of three.) Because these categories are provided by the mind, they cannot be attributed to the extramental reality, which, by dint of the argument, must be timeless, spaceless, and uncaused. Since order is brought *to* our experience by the mind, that which is interpreted by experience, namely, the external reality, is disordered. Will therefore does not originally refer to the human volitional faculty but to blind and feral power. So radically different is the world as we understand it through our categories from the world as it is in reality that Schopenhauer insists we see them as two basic "worlds": the world as will and the world as representation.

How are we to understand the relation between mind and world-will? It is possible to imagine a kind of metaphysical genealogy. In the beginning there was only will; it was blind, destructive, ruthless, and powerful. Ultimate reality is therefore savage and raw. The study of nature reveals this primitive violence. Everything that occurs in nature is simply a manifestation of primeval violence: the thrust of the newborn plant can crack stone, the wailing infant is violent hunger, the tumbling of the old is but the ruthless conquest of the new. Shakespeare's sonnet 64 represents this grim picture:

> When I have seen by Time's fell hand defaced
> The rich proud cost of outworn buried age,
> When sometime lofty towers I see down-razed,
> And brass eternal slave to mortal rage;
> When I have seen the hungry ocean gain
> Advantage on the kingdom of the shore
> And the firm soil win of the watery main,
> Increasing store with loss and loss with store . . .

In the midst of this black and sinister metaphysics, the will, which seeks only conquest and destruction, even against itself, devises a new method or new tool with which to wreak devastation on itself. This tool is the intellect. The mind originally, therefore, is little else than the weapon of the will. It is an effective weapon because, under the influence of mind, power is increased and the ability to destroy, devour, rape, and pillage is enhanced. The calculative function of mind multiplies the primordial savagery of reality, from the first crude weapons to the holocausts of the nuclear age. Our very bodies are nothing else than external manifestation of the world-will. If we look at our hands, we see instruments of possession: the hand is merely a manifestation of *grasping;* teeth are nothing else but embodiments of *devouring;* the sexual organs are mere externalizations of the will to rape (male) or seduce (female). Birth itself is savage, violent, painful, and terrible. With the mind as its instrument, the eternal world-will expands its reign of terror. There are not several wills, for plurality and magnitude are due to the mind's imposition of its forms on experience; there is only one world-will, and it wreaks its devastation on itself, embodied into parts, each of which exists only for a brief and hopeless span.

The mind, however, begins to develop a slow and painful autonomy from its parent, the will. Like all children, the mind rejects the character and nature of its parent. It establishes reasons that no longer merely serve the will, ideas that are no longer merely useful but that have their own significance. To escape from the relentless authority of the will, the intellect establishes ideas that have no purpose, no use, no utilitarian value: mathematics, art, philosophy. In this way, the mind creates a new "will," one that opposes the world-will. It is distinguished from its parent by the nonpurposive nature of its highest achievements. In art, things are no longer perceived in terms of their utility, but merely as sources of delight in being seen at all. Philosophy does not seek to establish control or to change the world; it seeks knowledge merely for its own sake. In this, art and philosophy are inimical to the world-will, for they seek to establish autonomous values.

This rebellion from the will cannot succeed forever, though. Soon, the intellect, which is individual, must always succumb, in death, to the will. The individual can therefore achieve at best a fleeting independence from the cavernous emptiness of the will. For Schopenhauer, this fleeting autonomy is the essence of our meaning, and hence, to capitulate to the self-destructiveness of the will, as in suicide, is unworthy of the mind. The belief in ultimate defeat of the individual, and the characterization of reality as fundamentally savage, have earned Schopenhauer the title of pessimist. But his profound isolation of true value consisting in overcoming the will is not completely dark. According to this theory, one should strive to overcome the simple will to live in order to achieve the independence of the savage world-will. To overcome the will to live does not entail suicide or even a pessimistic attitude; it is, rather, a realization that our true values must be those of the autonomous mind, things like truth, beauty, love, and saintliness. As long as we hold on to life, we are little more than any other manifestation of the will, like the sea washing away the shore or the sheer fecundity of the jungle eclipsing the light of the sun. But to embrace precisely those truths that are self-contained, like beauty or philosophy, is to outrank the senseless lust for life at all costs. The love of life must be changed to a life of love.

Schopenhauer's philosophy had an enormous effect on nineteenth-century European thought. When the composer Richard Wagner read of the doctrine of overcoming the will to live, he embraced it as his own and wrote the opera *Tristan und Isolde* as a concretization of the teaching. Tristan and Isolde could only realize the fullness of their love in death, and the two lovers greeted their deaths with a spectacular joy. Indeed, the great musical motif of the opera is known as *Liebestod,* the love-death, in which the ecstasy of love is taken literally, a "stepping out of"; and life is sundered in order to achieve a unity that only death can offer. The philosopher Nietzsche also recognizes great indebtedness to Schopenhauer, and the writer Thomas Mann wrote most of his great masterpieces as concretizations of his philosophy. At first glance, however, it may seem that Schopenhauer is the last person one would appeal to in seeking to understand war. After all, he sees the achievement of peace as the highest good; he attributes all cruelty and savagery in man, *homo homine lupis,* to the world-will, which must be overcome. For Schopenhauer, the more we can overcome the influences of the will and the satisfactions of our baser appetites, the closer we can approach true goodness, which is profoundly pacific and calm. With such lofty views of peace, how can Schopenhauer play a role in our comprehension of war?

To overcome the will to live is, of course, what is achieved by anyone who sacrifices his or her life. The soldier does not want to die, but his willingness to live in such a way that the mere *length* of his life is offered as price payable for the *meaning* reveals his virtue as courageous. Schopenhauer's philosophy supports the notion that human life itself is not the supreme value (which is what the pacifist maintains); indeed, life is seen as a part of the natural thrust of the world-will. What matters is not how long we live but how well we live. But Schopenhauer goes beyond that. He also shows that what constitutes the worth of existence (how "well" we live) is the autonomy of the "unnatural" will, the independence of the spirit that judges our worth in terms of nonpurposive values like truth and art. The sublimation of our natural and powerful desires (the will) to the service of nonpurposive values requires a huge spiritual effort and, indeed, the creation of a totally new nonnatural will.

War, then, can be seen in Schopenhauerian terms as stemming from both worlds. In the breakdown of order, war is like the original world-will: violent, dark, and savage. But in the willingness of the combatants to sacrifice their lives and to risk their continued participation in their bodily existence, there is a celebration of the autonomous values of the mind. The warrior overcomes his will to live by the recognition of his service to others; in this, the warrior is not unlike the saint. Furthermore, it must be underscored that the notion of the *individual* is, in this metaphysical scheme, achieved only at the cost of overcoming the will. It is from this new violence against our natures that the sense of uniqueness and individuality can arise. From individuals, of course, one can derive the sense of *ownness,* and from this the we-they principle can be understood.

From Schopenhauer we learn the important doctrine that violence is not merely something we do; it is an essential part of our very nature. We are bound, in death, to submit to the supreme violence of the world-will, which is the loss of individuality. But in resisting the influence of the world-will, there is also a new violence, a violence that boldly denies the hegemony and reality of world-will and establishes the values that cannot be found in nature. War, of course, speaks of both of these meanings. The paradoxical nature of war, which began this inquiry, is here restated in remarkable terms. War is at once the supreme realization of both the will as primeval reality and the overcoming of the will to live as long as possible. After Schopenhauer it is no longer possible to imagine the origin of war as some foreign notion intruding on the naturally peaceful and tranquil man. Under his influence, there is no such thing as a noble savage corrupted by society; rather, "natural" man is as savage and brutal as can be imagined. But civilized man's willingness to go to war cannot be seen merely as a regression to this native savage, since its inspiration is the willingness to sacrifice one's life.

Few would deny, I think, that war is essentially violent. But Schopenhauer has shown that there are profound elements at work in the warrior that embody both worlds, and that the violence in war thus pierces us to the very core of our paradoxical nature. There is, however, a further meaning to this existential mark that brings us beyond the strict metaphysical vision of Schopenhauer's philosophy. Indeed, it may even deserve to be treated as a separate notion altogether, and that is the observation that war is *passionate*. Of course, passion is admittedly a kind of violence, but our understanding of the former cannot be completely accounted for by an understanding of the latter. There is little to be gained by unrestricted lengthening of our list of marks, however, and if it is possible to include what has to be said about the passionate under this heading, it shall be done.

Huge passions are provoked by war; indeed, war itself is a deeply passionate undertaking. So essential is passion for our understanding of war that it actually becomes a necessary ingredient for the *success* of a war. A nation that undertakes as dangerous a mission as a war, without high and sustaining morale and spirit, embarks on the enterprise at its peril. There is something refreshing about witnessing a release of violent passions, whether in an individual or a state. Somehow there is a purity about it, a clarity in the experience. Particularly in our staid and almost dandified atmospheres of dreary and lackluster civility, the notion of releasing these giant forces of spirit can produce a fascination for the passionate that is hard to resist. Since in many engagements the side with the most spirit may often defeat a foe with superior technology and numbers, it is important for us to understand just what is meant by this term.

Passions are not the same as emotions. The latter are thought of as characteristics of the body, feelings that can be controlled by discipline and analyzed by the psychologists. The former are of the spirit, and are the province of character. We ordinarily distinguish between the emotion of desire and the passion of love, the emotion of fear and the passion of overcoming it in courage. Passion also implies intensity, a heightening of feeling and spirit to hot and lofty levels of meaning. Our existence becomes *operatic:* the gestures are wide and generous; the sentiments, exaggerated and underscored; the pace and pulse, quickened and stirred. What is it about these bold and daring characteristics that not only attracts us but also *reveals* much of our nature that remains hidden in the sedate? Why is there this persuasion that passions, in spite of — or perhaps even because of — the dangers they present, are nevertheless precious? Surely one reason the passionate is favored over the tranquil is that we regard the passions as indications of *caring.* The passionate man cares about what is important. His demeanor reveals that his concerns are serious, untrivial, vital, urgent, and weighty. The evocation of the passions by war and of war by the passions reveals a deep level of human understanding that certain things *matter.*

And herein lies a significant point. What does it mean to value something if I am not going to exert myself on its behalf? Does not my holding something as valuable imply that I shall be moved to some expenditure of energy because the thing exists? Let us test this suggestion in our minds. Suppose we claim that I value the institution of free speech. Suppose a tyranny takes over the government, banishes all free presses, and burns all books. Now, suppose that I accept tranquilly all this usurpation and do not even suffer the slightest unease; nevertheless, I affirm that I value a free press. Such a scenario is not intelligible, because to value something means to care, and care implies a willingness to act. It cannot be argued that care implies one *will* in fact do something, since there may be other restrictions on my behavior, such as fear or physical restraint or even indecision. But care is inconsistent with indifference. We do experience frequent conflicts in our values, and if I value privacy as well as a free press, the conflict may arrest my instinct to support one over the other. But to remain totally unmoved by a complete usurpation of a highly held value is totally inconsistent. In his analysis of the various modes of human existence, Heidegger argues that all modes eventually are reduced to the fundamental modality of care; this is a doctrine that attracts many readers because of our fundamental appreciation of the importance of caring. In the absence of caring, of course, nothing matters. For nothing to matter requires nihilism. As I have suggested above, men do not fight for justice or goodness so much as they fight for meaning.

Passion is appreciated because it emphasizes that things matter; it embodies the fundamental ontological modality of care. There are risks in passion, and most people are willing to admit that an entirely risk-free existence threatens us with a destructive boredom and indifference. Passion is a form of violence, though, and all violence brings with it pain. But although the mind cannot accept pain as a thing to be desired, it does not reject pain as an evil in and of itself. In the last analysis, we would rather die in a blaze of glory than die of boredom.

4

The Elements of War—III

In this chapter I consider the final three marks of war: (7) war as a *game*, (8) war as *horrific*, and (9) war as *heroic*.

WAR AS A GAME

Man is the playful animal. In many ways, his games are far more important to him than his security, his sustenance, and even his life. In the modern world, there is almost a continuous uninterrupted series of sports available to us at the flick of a television switch. The dream of almost every young man at some time in his education is to become a famous athlete, and even those who do not aspire to such achievements often either play or watch others play. So ubiquitous is this phenomenon that to imagine a culture without play seems almost unnatural and definitely oppressive.

Play is often contrasted to work, such that we think of work as providing what is necessary, whereas we play only when we are free from necessity. By this declension we think of play as gratuitous, contingent, free, or even privileged. One of the more persistent reasons for rejecting Marxism is that it is difficult to accept one's description as a worker. Nevertheless, even the most leisurely of people give lip service to the grim necessity of work, even as they celebrate the pleasure of play and fun.

We often associate the idea of "games" with that which is not serious or unimportant. Games are also seen as the province of the young, whereas the realm of the adult is work. Because of this sense of unimportance or even triviality, games often suggest some kind of cruelty, as when we speak of someone "playing games with us," meaning they are deceptive. A game is therefore deceitful and untrue. When Brutus says in Shakespeare's play, "I am not gamesome like Antony," he is not merely stating a fact, he is expressing his contempt for the devious and menacing player. To be "gamesome" for the stern Roman was a fault, for it suggested unseriousness, wantonness, and, in Antony's case, sycophancy. Thus, the term "game" often bears with it a certain pejorative meaning. Even when not so debased, it still implies something unequal to the more serious and more important affairs.

To describe war as a kind of game is therefore often seen as a kind of indictment of the entire enterprise. The warrior is seen as a child playing with lethal toys. The qualities of the soldier are spotted as childish and immature; these are grown men who refuse to grow up, immature Peter Pans unwilling to accept the responsibilities of adulthood. The implication of this judgment is that these infantile adults playing with their dreadful toys will bring about fulsome destruction for no worthy reason. To say that war is a game is to say it is unnecessary. Alter the battlefields into playing fields, take away the weapons and give the soldiers footballs and baseball bats, and the world will be much better off. Indeed, the parallel with sport is so often made that one wonders which is the more fundamental. Is war merely an extension of the gamelike spirit in our natures, or are sports merely an extension of the warlike spirit within us?

Even if we do not go quite so far as to accuse the warrior of childishness, there is an important, though troubling, similarity between games, especially in sport, and the business of war. Among history's most successful warriors we often find the same qualities as those found in the most successful athletes. If a man does not thrill to the challenge of the fight, if there is not an almost wanton sense of excitement in engagement, if indeed an almost ruthless and merry attitude toward danger cannot be found, the man will probably not succeed. There must be an instinct for the throat, a native sense of aggressiveness and high spirit if one is to achieve success on either field, the playing field or the battlefield. The point is, we do not applaud tennis stars or football heroes because of their gentle ways or their kindness, but because they win; and we think the same way about the warrior. We are thrilled by the victorious, and for the man who brings home the trophy, there is almost unlimited forgiveness of his other faults.

This analogy with games is not only true of the athletic contests but also true, and perhaps even more so, of the intellectual challenges of a mental struggle like chess. The brilliant moves of a chess master seem remarkably similar in many ways to the tricks, feints, and moves of a star general. Certainly cleverness and intelligence, if not wisdom, often determine the victor in both games and wars, so that the comparison between the two cannot be totally unwarranted. Few people, I think, would deny that war *is* like a game, and whatever deeper meaning can be analyzed from this isomorphism, it should not distract us from the obvious truth that playing games and fighting wars have much in common. It is the character of that deeper meaning that must be tested and examined.

Not all the comparisons of war with play are invidious, however. It has often been said, for example, that the true greatness of Greek civilization is that they knew how to play. Although it is possible to take the terms "play" and "game" as indications of frivolity and unimportance, it is also possible to recognize their utmost seriousness. The Athenian contributions to our self-understanding are best embodied in their playing: the dramas, the poetry, the sculpture, and even their philosophy were due to their achievement of leisure. Great cultures take play seriously. The creation of leisure is coincident with the establishment of human excellence, and leisure is surely judged as necessary for the quality of life. It is in this special and rather profound sense that war *is* a game. We understand war by means of the same ways of thinking that are present in our understanding of art, culture, and philosophy itself. Although we share with the animals a native instinct to preserve and extend our lives, only when that instinct is surpassed by a preference for quality does reflective thinking become possible. Games, in this qualitative self-reflection, become very serious indeed.

It is perhaps helpful here to consider the teachings about ends and means, or about service and the served. Ordinarily we rank the ends above the means; we consider the one served more important than the server. If medicine is seen as a means to health, we recognize that health is the true value, and medicine a mere utility to achieve that end. The cabinet member who serves a sovereign cannot be more important than the sovereign, at least formally. The question then becomes, Is life an end or a means? If all of the achievements of humankind are but means to life itself, one way of thinking is established; but if life itself is a means to achieve the end of quality, then a totally different way of thinking follows. The argument that in the absence of life one cannot achieve any quality is not sufficient to distract those dedicated to achieving a most meaningful life. This becomes especially true when one is willing to sacrifice life in order to achieve that meaning. If life itself is seen as the end, of course, leisure and all of its products, such as art and culture, become mere asides, important only as enhancing and promoting a longer existence. But if life itself is but a means for the achievement of excellence, then the attraction of longevity must take second place to the dedication to a life worth living. For the gourmet, it is sensible to live in order to eat; but for the unreflective, one eats merely to live. An artist who dedicates his life to beauty, a philosopher who dedicates his life to truth, or a saint who dedicates his life to God's will—all repudiate the ranking of life itself as the highest goal. The warrior also rejects such hierarchy. Not only is he willing to forfeit his own life for the sake of his country, he is willing to forfeit the lives of the enemy to ensure that this institution is not eclipsed by foreign control. Leisure concerns itself with raising the quality of life; its meaning focuses on that which is not necessary for life.

In most advanced societies, this ranking of values is often manifest in the ways the basic tasks and endeavors are judged. Farmers, husbanders, carpenters, merchants of foodstuffs, physicians, and health officials are not as highly regarded as artists, musicians, poets, thinkers, and religious teachers. Even the much-maligned struggle for the almighty dollar is a recognition of this ranking: wealth is not a guarantee of longevity, but rather a means for achieving a life of leisure, in which the quality of life is important. The notion of a game presupposes the importance of leisure. If games are seen as mere distractions—and note the implication here, distraction *from* the truly serious matter of living—they can be ranked as sustaining or refreshing endeavors, valuable only to the extent that they do not disturb the basic health of the individual. The playing of games may provide essential recreational therapy, but as such the playing of games is a means only. Or games can be seen as serious. In that case, life itself is seen merely as the background from which one can focus on the worthy existence achieved by leisure and games.

There can be no doubt that the warrior belongs to the leisured modality. Unless such cultural values are esteemed beyond the value of vital duration, it makes no sense to hazard so many young lives. The Greek warrior is not judged by how long he lives but by how well his struggles support and defend the Greek way of life. Anyone who appreciates a Greek tragedy must be grateful for the countless Greek soldiers who fell protecting the leisure of Greece wherein Sophocles and Aeschylus could bring forth their art. The Greek warrior participates in that accomplishment directly, whereas the Greek farmer, whose labor helps feed the warrior, is seen only as an indirect and merely servicing participant. This may seem ungrateful or even unfair to the farmer, but it is how we think about these rankings.

If games constitute an essential part of what we understand by leisure, we must now focus more directly on what games provoke and provide. Games provide two important ideas: (1) they offer a special kind of delight or pleasure to the mind; and (2) they establish the disjunction between victory and defeat. These two ideas are closely interconnected, of course; one reason we take delight in games is the triumphant feeling we receive when we are victorious. But in spite of the overlapping, these two notions should be kept separate in our analysis because of the considerable richness to be garnered from each.

1. One of the more important distinctions between "game" and "sport" is that the former possesses to a greater degree this sense of mental challenge. The more a contest depends on sheer brute strength, the less it is a game, although such struggles of physical prowess may still be designated sport. War is therefore more of a game than it is a sport. Indeed, when war itself becomes bogged down to the level of sheer attrition, it is thought of as *less* warlike; it becomes mere slaughter. World War I at times became just that; there was no soldierly skill or possibility of military genius; it became a mere slaughter in which the determining factor was the sheer number of corpses. In such a case, the world might well hope that war were more gamelike, since the spectacle of two powerful forces simply spilling each other's energy or blood benefits no one. This is why generals fear the notions of stalemate and deadlock so greatly. Deadlock does not imply a cessation of belligerence; instead it conjures up the picture of two giant animals with their horns locked together in fruitless struggle, with no way to bring the destruction to an end.

Games, whether on the playing field, on the parlor table, or in the war room, delight the mind. The very idea that there can be such a thing as mental pleasure deserves reflection. The body takes pleasure in the satisfaction of its wants and needs, as in food, sleep, warmth, sex, and comfort. The mind also takes similar satisfaction, as in the solving of puzzles, the challenge of wits, the bringing about of order from chaos, and, if Aristotle can be believed, in the pure contemplation of its own coherent nature. Some things delight both body and mind together, as when sex not only satisfies our carnal hunger but brings us closer to another person. But it is this ability to isolate the pleasures of the mind that is so fascinating. What must we presuppose about a mind in order for it to be pleasured? Certainly the mind cannot be conceived merely as an instrument or calculative machine if it can have its own pleasures. Machines do not take delight in their performance. Neither do machines suffer, but minds can. Whatever can take delight can also take pain, and it is no less remarkable that we should speak of a mind's pleasure than that we should speak of a mind's suffering.

Disorder and chaos are the source of mental anguish, whereas the achievement of system and order produces mental delight. For this reason, many intellectual types take inordinate delight in mystery stories, which begin with disorder and confusion and conclude with clarity and light. This is also the form of comedy, which similarly begins in darkness and confusion and leads to light and order. (Which is why the best mysteries are written as comedies.) In other words, we take delight in the establishment of order for its own sake. The mental satisfaction in finishing a complex crossword puzzle has as much to do with the neatness and cleverness of the parts fitting together as it does with the satisfaction of our erudition. Kant has argued, in the *Critique of Judgment*, that the proper realm for the pleasure of the mind is aesthetic, and he defines the beautiful as the harmony among the faculties. Whether this is an adequate account, at least it shows the rather special meaning given to the idea that the mind can enjoy its own pleasures.

The institutional program for the mind's own autonomous delight is known as leisure. Games are an essential part of leisure because they give independent delight to the mind. The essence of leisure is the nonpurposive character of its interests. Thus, it is often recognized that games are games just because they serve no external function. From this it is mistakenly argued that games are therefore unserious or unimportant. Indeed, it could be argued, following Schopenhauer's suggestion, that the *importance* of games consists in their nonpurposiveness. If there is to be autonomous worth to the mind, it must be independent of the body's interests, and nonpurposiveness achieves such independence. Although wars are decidedly purposive, they are nevertheless gamelike, and to this extent they belong to the institution of leisure.

It may seem both shocking and counterintuitive to locate war within the broader concept of leisure. *War is leisure?* Surely this is as false as the earlier claim that war is violent is vacuously true. This may indeed be our first response to this suggestion, but such a reaction cannot becloud the deeper issue. How can a life-and-death struggle ever be thought of as leisurely? By recognizing that wars are fought for meaning, and not for life. We struggle against the foe to achieve our own place in the world, not merely to save our lives. Most conquerors would gladly let the enemy live, if they were willing to live as slaves. In this sense, then, the warrior is more akin to the poet than to the farmer. Poet and warrior seek to enhance our leisure; the farmer provides us with necessities. It is for this reason that Plato puts the poet and the warrior together as members of the new class of citizen that comes into being when the state passes from the naturally good and peaceful pig-state to the ideal and fevered war-state.

2. In games we learn of victory and defeat. That which determines the coherence of a game is winning and losing. We play to win. Although we may enjoy playing a game even if we lose, it cannot be said that one plays to lose, without making the logic of games unintelligible. In addition to the pleasure we may receive from merely playing a game, there is a further pleasure taken in defeating one's opponent. Exactly why we should take so much delight in defeating another is less certain and affords much richness if it is but properly plumbed. For the moment, however, it is enough merely to mark it as true, though somewhat problematic. To take delight in winning, however, should not be so overly dominant a notion that one fails to appreciate the playing itself. This too is paradoxical. If I play to win but enjoy winning to the absolute exclusion of enjoying a game, it is thought I have "forgotten that it is merely a game." The loser who plays well and accepts defeat graciously is admired perhaps even more than the winner who struggles so intensely to win he forgets to take pleasure in the play. In some almost perverted sense, then, we seem to take delight in our playing because of winning, yet at the same time we reject the notion that winning is all-important. In this, war is decidedly *not* like a game, for warriors can never allow the idea of defeat to enter their minds. Some warriors obviously *do* take pleasure in playing the game of war, and perhaps the greatest warriors always do; but such delights are not taken as justifications for war.

On the other hand, the player who plays well enough but has no driving force to achieve victory is often thought of as not entering into the spirit of the game. We feel cheated in winning against those who do not themselves care to win, or if we lose against such dispirited adversaries, the endeavor seems an entire waste of time. Thus, winning is a curiously ephemeral value in games, at times inspiring the entire endeavor with excitement, at others distracting from our enjoyment in the playing itself. Exactly how to measure these shifting values is itself an accomplishment of the highest gaming. Nevertheless, winning is a curious, though fertile, notion, and it must be examined.

To win means to conquer someone else, to show oneself superior to another in a certain area, to assert oneself as better, at least in the narrow confines determined by the game. This may be explained as simple arrogance or as a kind of flattering of one's ego. However, many of our greatest winners, in both games and war, are not otherwise arrogant at all, nor are victors necessarily egotistical. But many arrogant and egotistical people do indeed suffer from the loser's syndrome. One reason victory is so important is that it is a way of making oneself *matter*. For some reason it matters if I am better than anyone else at doing something that in any other context would be totally without value. It is, of course, completely unhelpful to say that one receives certain psychological benefits from winning, because like all psychological explanations, it merely paints the green wall green. The point is not that I can give a psychological account of how I feel when I win (feeling *good* if I win and feeling *bad* if I lose); the point is, Why does winning make me feel good? It is silly to say that winning makes me feel good *because* it makes me feel good, which is what a psychological account of winning often amounts to. Of course I feel good when I win, and in that sense, I try to win in order to feel good. That is obvious. But it does not help one jot in revealing why winning should make me feel good and losing make me feel bad.

Imagine, if you will, a game in which the goal is losing. The mind does not accept the suggestion. If there were a race in which the goal was to come in last across the finish line, there would be no race. The runners would simply stand at the starting line and wait. Therefore, to try to win is essential for the game to be played. Perhaps, then, the delight we take in winning comes from the realization of our having made the playing possible. But again, we do not play merely to play, but to win. Why?

There may be pleasure taken in achieving something by dint of our own effort, simple satisfaction derived from labor, as when we sense considerable delight in looking back over the row we have hoed or the car we have washed. This, however, cannot be the exclusive meaning to winning, for one of our greatest delights comes from winning games in which our efforts play no part at all. Consider a child's board game in which tokens advance by a roll of the dice. A child may take huge delight in counting his token across the finish line before the others, but the child knows perfectly well that he had no *art* in throwing the dice. Luck alone determines the victor in such games. Yet, we can take delight in them. Adult games of chance seem to provide a similar, and indeed almost inordinate, delight. Gambling is often enjoyed precisely because the winner does not deserve his victory; it is as if being *favored* by the gods of chance were more desirable than *earning* a victory by cleverness and strength. So, if we take delight in winning a game of chance, like poker or a child's board game, then we cannot account for the delight by an appeal to the satisfaction we take in a job well done. Again, the essence of winning eludes us if we reduce it to this account.

A far more serious and revealing dimension of this problem can be developed by raising the counternotion. Why not consider the delights of losing. We have shown above that it makes no sense to *try* to lose if this attitude is shared by all the players. But what about trying to win, losing, and finding great delight in accepting defeat? This may not be normal, but it is not unintelligible. There is surely a kind of pleasure in submitting to another's will or triumph. In certain sexual events some people seem to derive prodigious pleasure and satisfaction from being taken or used. The fact that many may label such acts as abnormal or even perverse does not keep them from being a source of pleasure. Many who are initiated into such rites assure all who would listen that such pleasures are far greater than the unspeakably common ones of merely mutual sharing. Why do we not, then, take equal or even greater delight in losing? From this observation it is obvious that some *do indeed* take pleasure in defeat, and as a consequence of this reflection, it is no longer possible to argue that the reason for winning is the pleasure taken in winning, since it is possible to enjoy defeat as well.

A further consideration of the puzzle of winning should show that the simpleminded acceptance of the value of victory is questionable. Let us imagine two people playing checkers, a game of considerable subtlety and skill, in many ways more demanding than chess. Suppose the first, a brilliant and artful player, tries valiantly to win. His opponent, however, is just a little more brilliant than he. As the game progresses, although the first player tries desperately to stop his opponent, the opponent simply outmaneuvers him. As the inevitable result ensues, surely it is possible for the first player to rejoice in the victory of the greater brilliance. It is not impossible to imagine someone actually taking greater delight in his opponent's victory simply because the opponent *ought* to win. In this sense we have a totally nonperverse delight taken in one's own defeat. And since the first player may have experienced this excellence for the first time, it may even be that the defeated player actually enjoys being defeated more than the winner enjoys his victory. By these reflections we can see that the *meaning* of victory simply cannot be accounted for by the delight, the pleasure, or even the self-importance of the winner. How, then, can we isolate the significance of winning?

It is possible, of course, to argue that winning is a *primitive* notion, not reducible to any other. Just as Moore argues for the nonreducibility of notions like "yellow" or "good," so perhaps the triumph of the victor is something that is understood directly, without mediation by other concepts. If we *do* not understand the priority of winning over losing, we simply *can*not understand it by an appeal to any other more fundamental notions. But if winning is indeed a primitive or fundamental notion that cannot be explained by simpler notions, it should at least be possible to locate the range of meaning that favors winning over losing. It cannot be that it gives psychological pleasure, for that account merely tells us what happens because of winning; it does not explain why winning itself is seen as a boon. Nor can it be the sense of getting what we have deserved, because winning is often the result of luck and we treasure such victories as highly as those we have earned. But it *does* seem to have some significance for our existential understanding. We count more as victors than as losers; to win matters, and therefore *our* winning matters as a manifestation of our own importance. The delight we take in winning is grounded in the value we place on being who we are. Winning cannot be valued merely because of the pleasure it brings, but it can be judged as superior to losing, because of the fundamental realization that being itself is a joy. In this sense, winning *is* a fundamental notion that cannot be explained by other values. The mere fact that winning is *accompanied* by feelings of self-importance or arrogant pleasure no more implies that these feelings are why winning is important than the sense of satisfaction I receive in doing good implies that I did the good merely in order to have those feelings.

If, however, one wins in order to achieve importance over others, it must be seen as a morally dubious achievement. Surely this is nothing else than mere selfishness wantonly indulged. What value can be found in this empty vaunting of my own ego at the expense of others? But the argument does not show that winning must always be selfish, indulgent, or egotistical. It shows merely that the self *matters,* that games focus on the primordial disjunction between success and failure, and that success at just *being* can be celebrated. The distinction between success and failure may well be one of the most primordial notions we can have. Plato and other Greek thinkers have pointed out, for example, that one can *fail* at being a human being. In book 1 of *The Republic* Socrates points out that to harm a man is to make him less of a man and that it is never just to do that. To become less of a man is to fail at being a man. To succeed at being a man is to approach the full realization of what it means to be a man. Thus, the idea of success and failure is absolutely fundamental to thought itself. Winning is the celebration of success. To win, even at a simple game, is to affirm the irreducible significance of success. That I can rejoice when others win in no way lessens the significance of this truth; it is still the case that winning matters by focusing on success; and that just means reaching the full realization of one's self and meaning.

In order to focus on the existential meaning of winning, I have emphasized the nonpurposive character of games. I asked, What value is there in winning a useless and unimportant game? In this way it was possible to isolate the notion of success and failure as a fundamental way in which we think. However, in my reflection on war, it is no longer possible to designate the victories as unimportant and unpurposive. Indeed, few things in the world are more purposive or more important than war. Specific wars are often seen as defending the very notion of civilization itself, as Churchill said of the Second World War. In this sense, then, wars are supremely ungamelike. Certainly it seems odd to characterize as a game anything in which men freely give their lives. Nevertheless, the existential significance of winning can be found not only in games but in war as well. However, since war is *serious* in a way that mere games are not, a special examination must be made of winning in war as opposed to winning in games.

As World War I ground mercilessly toward its fourth year, the German government was faced with a profound dilemma. Many in Germany wanted peace; both the will and the economic capability of continuing the war were eroding. Otherwise bellicose statesmen on both sides of the battle were growing more and more aghast and appalled at the massive and senseless slaughter. Yet how could Germany quit the war? Would not the victors exact huge and even cruel punishment against them? Would France, England, and the United States agree simply to stop fighting? This they could not imagine. And in this, they were quite right. Not even Woodrow Wilson would have expected the Allies to agree to a *status quo ante.* And why? Having fought so dearly and so expensively for four years, the victors would expect some homage paid to their sacrifice. To the victor belong the spoils. And although many argue that the treaty of Versailles as well as the dreadful armistice at Compiègnie were unfair, it is nevertheless understandable that the victors, especially France, should feel the need to *punish* the losers as well as to make them stop fighting. So the Germans, fearing the unjust peace, were forced to continue a war they simply could not win.

An enemy is not necessarily *forgotten* merely because the specific threat no longer exists. Sometimes countries are fought in order to stop them from doing something; other times they are not only fought, they are also *beaten.* Through violence, what preexisted the war must be eradicated. The enemy must be beaten, as in punishment (for the sake of justice), or, sadly, beaten and *taken,* as in rape. Having fought a war, it is not enough to end the war; one must conquer. France not only wanted to regain Alsace and Lorraine, to disarm the German army, to drive the kaiser from his throne, and to demand payments, it wanted to *punish* Germany. And punish Germany it did. The German Empire no longer existed; huge tracts of land that had been a part of Germany before 1914 were now not German. Severe and awesome restrictions were placed on the German army and even more on the navy. But it was necessary to punish not only the *government* of Germany but also the people of Germany. Huge, crushing indemnities were imposed, indemnities that the people, not the government, of Germany were required to pay. A *kind* of government unfamiliar to them was forced on them. Thus, the punishment was not only against the government or military personalities who had perpetrated the war, but against the Germans as such. To be a German was to be guilty. The fact that the severity of this peace was a partial cause of the subsequent rise of a new Germany, under Hitler, does not prove that the Allies ought not to have punished the losers; indeed, some use the rise of Naziism as proof that the victors were too lenient. What is significant here is that the odium was placed on *being* German. And this reveals to us what it means to be defeated in a war. To lose is to forfeit our existential meaning.

Twenty-five years later, when Germany conquered Poland, the point was driven home with even greater savagery. To be a Pole became a contemptuous joke; Poles were seen as *Untermenschen,* fit only for slaves to serve the glorious Reich. To lose in a war is to lose a certain way of existing. The Nazis, in their racism, merely gave this truth a particularly noxious scientific basis, but the peculiar emphasis on existential notions was really not new. To be a Pole, for the conquering Germans, was not to have *done* wrong but to *be* inferior. Thus, defeat in a war threatens the very existential ownness that collects and protects our unique values.

People seem to prefer a cruel regime that is their own to a benevolent rule by foreigners. In the same way that one might say, "Good or bad, this man is my brother," one also says, "Good or bad, this government is *ours.*" This is because what is at stake in a country is the citizens' own, so the government that represents them should also be their own. To be defeated is to lose this sense of being true to one's ownness.

Is this sense of ownness, which seems to matter so very much in wars between nations, carried over to the meaning of victory in games? Even if the essence of a game is the nonpurposive character of the contest, can one understand the meaning of winning in terms of this existential value? I have suggested that there is a similarity between how we understand the meaning of winning in both wars and games, but I leave unanswered the question which is more fundamental. What *is* fundamental, however, is the notion that in winning, the self is celebrated. If the combatants are individuals, the celebration is of a single self, an I; if the winners are a team, the celebration is of the self as shared, the we.

Victory is essentially a celebration. When a child delights in counting his token first across the finish line, the winning is not really the *cause* of his joy, it is merely the occasion, or opportunity, for it to be released. In this sense the joy of the child manifests itself in winning a game because winning focuses on the existence (or worth of existence) of the child. It is a child's nature to be joyful. He is still full of wonder and delight at the universe, and at peace with himself. Hence, in winning he celebrates his own nature. When adults play games, especially games of chance, the delight taken imitates the child's, precisely because the game is not the result of labor but of bestowal. Clausewitz, for example, points out that war is like a game in that there is always an element of the unpredictable, an aspect of chance. If the gods of chance favor us, we feel privileged and honored by this smile of fortune. It might be thought, however, that wars are not won by chance and that the child's delight in celebrating who he is in no way corresponds to the warrior's concern for victory. But I have tried to show that warriors do indeed fight for the meaning of their existence and that victory is a celebration of that meaning. The warrior achieves his victory by hard labor, but the *meaning* of his victory is *not* that of wages earned by labor but that of celebration of who he is. Thus, to the extent that winning and losing play an essential role in our understanding of war, war must be seen as a game, because what is celebrated in victory is the joy we take in our ownness and because wars are fought on behalf of what is our own.

This takes us back to the first point, that war is leisure. Or rather, since that sounds counterintuitive at first hearing, war is *about* our leisured existence. This is something most of us would not deny. What else do we fight for except our culture, our traditions, our religions? If leisure is taken broadly enough to include all values that follow from these seminal beliefs, then the observation that we fight for leisure is noncontroversial. But the argument proceeds from this noncontroversial point to a more demanding claim: not only is the goal or purpose of our fighting to be understood as leisure, but the fighting itself is to be seen as a form of leisure. Two characteristics give warring this unlikely quality. The first is that wars, like games, delight the mind. The second is that war, like games, is made intelligible by victory. Victory should not be seen as a *means* only, but as an end. That is, we struggle to achieve victory not only because it allows us to do something else, like keeping our traditions intact or expanding them, but also because being victorious is one of the essential ways in which the self reveals its own meaning. Whatever victory means—and I have suggested that its meaning is multifarious and perhaps not reducible to other values—it is a fundamental way we gauge our success and failure. Victory cannot be accounted for by the satisfaction we take in basic wants and needs being fulfilled. Victory carries the kind of significance we find in leisure, that is, something we do beyond taking care of our bodily needs. The proof of this can be seen by simply reflecting on the paradox of war discussed earlier; we sacrifice our surety about our bodily satisfaction for the sake of values that are not purposive. However, in order for this argument to make sense, we must now discuss the more fundamental notion: What, then, is leisure? And for this we should now turn to the philosopher selected to support this existential mark.

In the *Nichomachean Ethics*, Aristotle discusses his theory that of all the *types* of lives one can lead, the life that best satisfies the description of happiness is the contemplative life. The Greek word for leisure is *skolē*, from which we get our English word "school." It should be noted that the opposite of *skolē*, the word containing the negative alpha, *askolē*, is the Greek word for "work." Thus, *work* is a negative concept, meaning "nonleisure." For the Greeks, man's proper realm is leisure. Work is that which distracts us from our proper place in the world. Aristotle even goes so far as to say that the purpose of work is to achieve nonwork, only in the Greek the negative is on the former term.

The argument Aristotle provides is powerful in its simplicity. In the three kinds of life he considers, the life of pleasure, the life of honor, and the life of thought, only the last is self-sufficient. The life of pleasure depends on circumstance, luck, and other people. Since pleasure seems to be intensified by its absence and lessened by repetition, the sated man is an anomaly because, as sated, he has no desires; but since the pleasure consists in the satisfying of desires, we can have no pleasure if we have no desires; and if we have desires, that means we are lacking what we want. The life of honor is superior to the life of pleasure, but it too depends on things beyond our control. Honor exists only when it is bestowed by others. It can be denied without justification or warrant. The life of honor may be won by those who do not deserve it and denied those who do. But the life of thought is sustained by the thinker himself. It needs no external referent or focus outside itself. The life of the mind—and consequently the life of leisure—is self-sufficient and endless. The form of this argument is similar to Aristotle's argument in book Λ of the *Metaphysics,* where God is defined as thought thinking thought. The idea of a God is of a perfect and unending being. If such a being were to exist, its nature would have to be completely self-sufficient, that is, perfect. The only perfect thing could be thought thinking thought. In this sense, then, the life of mind, or the life of leisure, is godlike: it needs no referent outside itself to justify it.

This argument is perhaps one of the most well-known of Aristotle's many contributions to thought, and it runs as an undercurrent through most of his thinking. In many ways it is the Greek version of Schopenhauer's persuasion that the only good thing is a thing without any purpose or utility. This idea has independent worth, which need not depend on the arguments of Aristotle or Schopenhauer: what is ultimate in our understanding of things that matter is that which needs no other justification for its existence. The ancient Greek thinker, however, is more direct in his analysis, for he does not speak of values or importance but simply of being. Here there is no fact-value distinction, no disjunction between what is and what ought to be. It is a glorious combination of truth, fact, reality, and worth: that which is most real is what is most precious. In our understanding of this ultimate reality, the supreme realization comes when the focus is placed on its self-autonomy. Just as God is that which needs no other being in order to explain it, so the life of contemplation is a life that needs no other to justify it. The idea of *work* is something that necessarily depends on something other than itself. I do not work for the sake of work, I work for the sake of completing the labor or for the wage or for the satisfaction of a job well done. (Marx, I believe, contradicts this, finding in work a kind of *summum bonum* that is independent. And Saint Benedict's maxim *laborare est orare* seems to contradict it as well.) For the Greeks, however, especially Aristotle, the proper realm of humankind, that by which man can be distinguished from the other animals, is his mind. The mind can either serve man's interests as a calculative tool, or it serves itself. It is only when the mind serves itself that man's truest nature can be realized. This is what is meant by the famous Aristotelian definition: man is the rational animal.

In leisure, the pleasures of the mind are celebrated. Thus, leisure, not work, becomes the proper metaphor for self-understanding. This teaching is so antithetical to our contemporary consciousness that it needs to be developed. Two influences that disassociate the modern mind from the Greek notion of leisure are the Protestant work ethic and Marxist ideology. Both of these perspectives on human nature see labor as the natural activity for the species. In the Protestant work ethic, especially in the American tradition, salvation is achieved through hard work. The Genesis story tells us that Adam and Eve were expelled from the Garden of Eden and as part of their punishment were required to "earn their bread by the sweat of their brow." Idleness is seen as the devil's workshop; sloth is seen as one of the seven deadly sins. So deeply ingrained is this teaching of the intrinsic value of work that Milton in his epic masterpiece could not even allow Adam and Eve to relax in paradise itself; they were required to *work*, pruning the overly abundant fruit. It is hard to imagine Socrates making sense of this sanctification of work. For him, the life of reason, of discussion, of wonder, would provide a far greater Eden, and far happier days. But for the Protestant Christian, work activates the body as well as the mind. Man, for the Protestant Christian, is naturally lazy and wickedly idle, and man's nature must hence be overcome. For him, only the divine can bring about salvation, so the enterprise of man is to overcome what is natural. For the Greeks, however, man's nature is not sinful but rational, and hence leisure provides not idleness but play, in which the mind's own essence, rationality, is celebrated.

More recently, the atheistic ideology of Marx has also celebrated the laborer, even to the point of identifying the activity of the mind as mental work. Part of the reason for this emphasis on work comes, of course, from Marx's analysis of alienation. In capitalism the worker is alienated from his labor because the benefits of his toil do not revert back to him but are usurped by the owner. The property owner does not work, at least not directly with the primary resources. His idleness is not seen as good, and certainly not seen as leisure. It is, rather, something achieved by the enslavement of the worker. Thus, for a true Marxist, even modest recreation is taken with a sense of guilt. Indeed, emphasis is put on play as a form of re-creation, that is, a building up of health and energy to be used in work. Play is thus seen as a means for even better labor, completely opposite to Aristotle's notion that labor should be seen merely as a preparation for play. Under the influence of Marxism, art and philosophy are not done for the sake of pure beauty or pure truth; rather both are made to serve the workers' state. The nonpurposive is excised; leisure is seen as a form of decadence. Whatever games are allowed are justified solely in terms of their effects, such as health, propaganda, and training.

Both Marxism and the work ethic have, as a consequence of this emphasis, an undeniable grimness about their cultures. Officially sanctioned Soviet art, before the fall of the Soviet Union, was almost comically drab; the early American Puritans frowned on any and all celebration. Even Christmas was not feted in colonial America; the idea of a holy day (or holiday, as it came to be known) was deprecated as popish and smacking of that self-indulgent wickedness represented by the Catholic church. These two traditions, therefore, have considerable influence on our contemporary consciousness still, even if one is neither Marxist nor Protestant. It is difficult for the modern thinker to disassociate himself from the conviction that a man must *do* something with his life. It is a rare teacher who is willing to spend much time on refining one's sense of simple elegance. Whereas the contemporary will urge us, "Don't just sit there; *do* something!" the Greek man of leisure urges us, "Don't just do something; sit there!"

I have exaggerated this difference to make a point. However, it is essential if the true meaning of leisure is to be understood. Perhaps in our deepest and stillest moments, we all recognize that our worth is not limited by the good deeds we perform but by who we are. And it is this dimension of our worth, that precious realization of our importance just because we *are,* that is the ground of war. It is not merely that we fight *for* our leisure; the warrior himself is a man of leisure. The decisive element in war is victory, and victory is an existential notion. War is therefore a game in the most profound sense: an activity made sense of by winning. The meaning of winning is not exhausted by bringing the fighting to an end with the capacity to exert our will over the enemy; it has its own significance. It is only when the phenomenon of winning is fully understood that war itself will be made clear. It is perhaps better to define war as a desperate game than to define games as a form of nonserious war, for the idea of *winning* can be isolated in games easier than in war. The point is, games illuminate war; wars do not illuminate games.

I do not wish this discussion to imply that the gamelike quality of war in any way justifies war. The moral restraints against wanton and unnecessary wars are still valid, and no one should ever engage in a reckless war merely to satisfy these existential needs. This inquiry seeks to understand the phenomenon of war, not to prescribe behavior. It is of critical importance, however, to isolate the elements that make up war, and this discussion of games is crucial in pinpointing the uniquely existential meaning of war. Many people thoughtlessly condemn all war as a game. This indictment is shallow on two levels. It overlooks the seriousness of games, and it overlooks the seriousness of the kind of things that wars are fought for. Wars are indeed desperate games. It does not follow from this, however, that wars should not be fought at all.

WAR AS HORRIFIC

It is probably easier to show that war is horrific than to show any other mark that can be assigned to war. The evidence is overwhelming. From the grotesque oils of Goya to the clinical exactitude of the photographs in *Life* magazine, artists have not ceased to represent war in terms of awesome horror. For the sake of truth, of course, such representations are proper and fitting. Sometimes one has the feeling, however, that such depictions of war are presented as persuasions, as if, somehow, we did not know how horrible war is and had but to see these pictures of ghastly suffering to persuade us not to support the military needs of a country. This is an unfortunate policy, not because it may persuade people to adopt a pacifistic view, but because it distracts from the true meaning of war's horrors. For thousands of years we have been presented with war as dreadful, ugly, and pitiless, and we have continued to fight. In Euripides' tragedy *The Trojan Women,* war is revealed in the most merciless and shocking manner, and I know of no artwork in all of human culture to equal it in its power to demonstrate the horror of human belligerence. But that work is over two thousand years old, and has been read by countless warriors over the centuries. The cruelty of war is not a secret. No amount of lurid pornography will ever deter us from war, for the simple reason that we already know it is horrible.

This present inquiry into war as horrific is hence not to be understood as a part of antiwar propaganda. Rather, it is an essential part of our understanding of war. If we are to understand war, we must also understand what it means to be horrified; whatever it is about us that provokes horror must be revealed if war is to make sense. And the point must here be pressed: the proper word is *horrific*. There are many possible negative terms one might be tempted to assign to war. It is bad; it is wicked; it is cruel, savage, evil, terrible, senseless, mad, crazy, insane, meaningless, sinful, ugly, obscene; it is inhumane. Some of these terms should be applied to war; some should not. Probably all can be applied to some aspects of war. But even words of censure have specific meanings, and it does no good wantonly to heap every imaginable indictment on the head of Mars, as if by sheer weight the concept would be eclipsed. The term "horrific" is chosen carefully and precisely; it is not intended to collapse the several meanings of this negative list into one "superword" that connotes the worst of all possible meanings. Horror is not merely another among many negative reactions one has to war, it is the specific and special reaction to war.

The etymology of the term "horrific" suggests that it and its variants come from "hair," so that "horrific" is really "hairific" in the older usage meaning "bristling." What is horrific makes our hair stand on end. The term also, like its sister term "terrific," suggests *trembling*. The horrific makes us tremble and shake. These original usages have a kind of primeval appropriateness about them, and they can serve as a starting point for our analysis. The horrific, even in contemporary usage, suggests that the effect on us is sufficiently intense as to induce physical reaction of a fairly violent sort. Far more than the merely unpleasant or disagreeable, the horrific makes us shudder, tremble, and react in a revulsion of rejection. At the same time, there is something awesome about what is horrific. The enormity of the reaction stuns the mind, so that in spite of ourselves we are fascinated by the very thing that repulses us. The words "terrible" and "terror" have been so used in this way that in one variant, "terrific," the meaning has actually taken on positive significance. To say war is horrific, then, is to spot our reaction as a fascinated and awestruck revulsion. Although akin to "terror," the word "horror" emphasizes the notion of awe coupled with repulsion, whereas "terror" implies a greater sense of fear and dread. At the end of his masterpiece, *Heart of Darkness,* Joseph Conrad has the character Kurtz repeat over and over the words "The horror! The horror!" This has a remarkable impact on the reader; one feels that no other word would do as well. Kurtz was not merely terrified or afraid, he was struck with the fascination of his own revulsion. What Conrad reveals in his artistry is what is meant here by the word *horrific*. It fittingly describes our reaction to war.

Very often words of this sort are abused by the feeling of frustration we have in our attempts to censure something. Surely the urge to curse and swear is one of the more precious resources of poetry, for when we feel the sense of outrage at what is unacceptable, there is a remarkable impulse to *speak*. However, wonderful as it may be as a stimulant for oratory, this sense of splendid frustration often comes over those who are not friendly to language itself, and an abuse takes place. Very often those who are outraged find themselves reaching for deeper and deeper thrusts. They are dissatisfied with the censure in saying something is merely "bad"; they want to censure it with even more flaying terminology, so they go "beyond" the simple indictment of a thing's badness and resort to more satisfying verbal indulgence. They call it wicked or crazy or insane. Now, one can appreciate the need for ultimate censure, but this does not license inappropriate usage. There really is no more profound censure than to say it is bad. If one were to be even more precise, one might say morally bad, and that is the ultimate censure. That is as bad as you can get. To call war insane, or crazy, is merely to put it in the category of the unintelligible. But there are many "good" things that are unintelligible, such as love, genius, divinity, and hope. What is worse, if war is insane, there can be no moral indictment, and usually the speaker would not be so liberal. To say something is evil suggests not only a moral censure but a metaphysical impropriety or twist. To say something is wicked implies not only that the act is immoral but that the person performing the act has a defect of character. (A good person may do a bad thing in violation of his character; a wicked person does a bad thing *because* of his character.) However, "bad" also has a somewhat more modest meaning, as when we speak of a bad cold (the illness is severe) or a bad call (the umpire was wrong) or a bad day (nothing went well). In these usages, "bad" has no moral censure; it is the same as "unpleasant" or "lacking."

In this last sense, war is certainly bad. Very few people want war or enjoy it, and its consequences are highly unpleasant. To say that war is morally bad cannot be universalized, though surely some wars are morally bad and others are not. To say that war is evil is to assert a metaphysical violation; this is surely unjustified. Because war is the result of deliberate action by rational beings who must be held responsible for their actions and censured if the war is immoral, war is not crazy, insane, or absurd. Therefore, we need a meaningful and precise negative term that properly describes our censure of war, and this term is "horrific." War is also "terrific" in its original meaning, but the contemporary usage makes this term inappropriate. Furthermore, although war is terrific, it is more than what this word entails; the combination of awe and revulsion is sufficiently important to make the term "horrific" preferable.

There is one other term that might be used to signify the basic rejection that is felt in our contemplation of war, and that is "tragic." Tragedy is, of course, an art form, but the term is often used in a metaphoric way to refer to actual events. The essence of tragedy is that what is great is brought down by the very elements that provide greatness. It is the very majesty of King Lear that brings about his sorrowful end. In wars, the very greatness of nations is a part of their collapse. In the classical dramas we identify as tragic, there is a curious but wonderful conjunction of two opposing sentiments: we feel deeply moved by the lofty spirit of greatness inspired by the power of the central character, and we thrill to his overreaching will—what the Greeks called hubris—but at the same time we experience enormous grief at the noble character's fall. It is the interplay of these two opposing sentiments that is the stuff of tragedy. Such elements surely are present in our contemplation of war. Like tragedy, war is both great and sad. One could even make a revealing comparison between the hubris and sophrosyne of a tragedy on the one hand, and the moral and the existential elements of the paradox of war, on the other, for our instincts to peace are like sophrosyne, knowing one's place in the world, and our pride in what is our own, which inspires the existential meaning of war, is very much like hubris. Few, I think, would quarrel with the suggestion that war is tragic.

However, tragedy is essentially an art form. Art may indeed be a mirror to life, but the reality of war surpasses the image. In seeking to find the proper word of censure, both "terror" and "tragic" can indeed be applied to war, but neither term does full justice to what is felt. The sense of revulsion coupled with awesome fascination is only partially represented by the terms "tragic" and "terrible." For these reasons I suggest that "horrific" is indeed the proper term. Of course, none of these three terms in any way implies moral wrongness. But all three do contain the notion of regret. Perhaps, then, a final word should be investigated: "sadness." War is sad. We weep at the prodigious loss and the painful waste that is the result of war, and only the most hardened and insensitive shed no tears. But sadness does not of itself represent the totality of our sentiment. It does not go far enough to denote the extent of our grief, nor does it allow for the sense of awe and wonder that accompanies our loss. So we return to the original suggestion. There is something decidedly negative about war, something that causes us to shake our heads in grief, anger, and sadness. Given the spectacular character of the carnage, I think the single most revealing term for this peculiar censure we direct at war is "horror."

What, however, does horror tell us about ourselves? If we accept horror's original meaning, what is it about ourselves that makes our hair stand on end and our bodies tremble? One immediate realization is that horror is neither a purely mental nor a purely physical reaction. The mind is appalled and the body trembles. There is, in the experience of horror, a kind of disbelief even as it is accepted as true. A kind of numbness or paralysis overcomes us precisely because our minds find it difficult to accept that which all our positive instincts reject. It is this tension between our various faculties that renders horror its unique meaning. In addition to our acceptance of the *fact,* however, there is also a fascination for what is horrific. What is it about horror that so fascinates? If we might take a more innocent example to isolate this feature, we might consider horror as it is understood in the world of entertainment. Young people particularly seem to enjoy viewing the genre of films known as horror pictures, in which grotesque monsters prey on the innocent. One aspect of horror films, of course, is simply that fear, especially when presented with aesthetic distance, can be enjoyable. There is a delightful kind of thrill that can be enjoyed quite innocently, and it is, I think, a partial reason for the popularity of such films that they *completely* captivate us during the period of our "suspended disbelief." In his analysis of the sublime, Edmund Burke argues that one of the most compelling aspects of *terror* is that it is total; it permits of no reserve of sentiment; all of our attention is riveted in terror; there is no room left for any other feeling. This sense of total and complete absorption can, in the case of horror films, actually be enjoyed because, in spite of the absorption, the mind knows there is no real threat.

Normally, when we are afraid, we act. But terror is so immense that instead of reacting as we usually do in the case of a threat, we are immobilized. The whole point of terrorization is to remove all capacity for action from the enemy. However, if, in addition to this paralysis induced by terror, we also find ourselves fascinated by what also repulses us, we have not only terror but horror. Both fascination and repulsion are essentially aesthetic notions; that is, they are descriptions of how we feel when we witness something horrific. To be fascinated is to want to continue seeing; to be repulsed is to want to cease seeing; in horror, then, we want both to continue and to cease our sensation. The mind wants to turn away, but it cannot. This thrall is dreadful, for the threat not only induces fear, it also permeates our con-

THE ELEMENTS OF WAR — III

sciousness with helplessness. The need to act struggles with our inability to act, and this causes us to tremble and to bristle—hence horror. Being helpless is always frustrating and painful, so horror is essentially a negative sensation. Yet the totality of its involvement and the inevitable fascination for the grotesque cannot be denied.

When we speak of the horrors of war, then, we do not merely mean that such grotesque situations should be avoided. We also mean they stun the mind. And we mean that such images captivate us by their enormity and outrage. With the invention of the photograph, a mute and dreadful testament, it is possible to reproduce these horrors. We see photographs of mutilated hands, feet without toes, legs without feet, trunks without legs, faces without their proper parts; we see the mutilated corpses of children, or children pathetically orphaned, kneeling by the corpses of their mothers; we see noble cathedrals devastated by bombs, artworks that were the glory of a culture obscenely destroyed; we see the putrefied bodies of innocent animals and the wanton waste of whole fields of life-sustaining crops. We see a baby carriage broken in the mud, a child's toy or bicycle twisted in the gutter, or a sacred relic tossed thoughtlessly in the sewer. As we see these things, memorialized in photos, we are aghast. We would be aghast at them even if they were the results of a natural disaster, which they could have been. A violent earthquake or a volcanic eruption can produce similar pictures. Indeed, many of the photographic remembrances of war are indistinguishable from similar remembrances of natural disasters. What makes these pictures truly *horrific* is not their merely ghastly manifestation but the realization that such results stem from our own natures. We are horrified by these pictures because they are the result of warlikeness within ourselves. Either we think that such events can be prevented or that such events are inevitable, given our nature. It is hard to determine which suggestion is more dreadful. If such things can be prevented, why are they not prevented? This question sears our conscience. Or, if we assume an inevitability to war, then such pictures horrify us because they are the result of our nature. In either case, there is a self-loathing that oppresses the mind. Even though we ourselves may have been completely innocent of the war, we ask, Is this what *we* have done? In part, the horror of war is that it is *our* horror. We are stunned not only by the outrage but by the realization that we ourselves can or did perform such acts. This realization makes us tremble; it disgusts us and makes us turn away; but it also fascinates us. Thus, it too is horrific. The horrors of war are horrific because they are our own. We horrify ourselves.

It is essential to realize that we in no way ease the horrors of war by telling ourselves it was morally imperative to fight. Horror has its own kind of censure; it does not need the further indictment of moral wrongness. It may be absolutely justifiable to fire on an invading army to protect our own soil, but the savagery that this violence produces on the young bodies of the enemy is still horrible, and the impact of that horror on our own minds cannot be assuaged by the moral justification. Nor should it. But this horror within ourselves must be understood.

In addition to the notion of horror *of* war, there is also the problem of horror (or terror) *in* war. It has long been recognized that one of the more important aspects of a campaign is the effect of terror on a population. It is precisely because the enemy, as human, may be stunned into paralysis by the shock of such savagery visited upon his own that we might be led to use terror as an added weapon in our arsenal. Clausewitz notes the high importance of being able to demoralize the enemy, and all leaders, from Alexander to Schwarzkopf, have been aware of it as an element in their strategy. In both world wars, the Germans included *Schrecklichkeit* as part of their technique to conquer Europe. And there can be no doubt that on occasion these tactics have proven effective. Surely one of the reasons German *Blitzkriege* were effective in both Poland and France in 1939 and 1940 was that the awesome ruthlessness of these attacks produced a sense of utter helplessness on the part of the invaded peoples. Why offer resistance if it can have no effect? There is a kind of wisdom in knowing when to capitulate before a superior force, and the more titanic the horror, the easier it is to persuade the enemy to surrender.

Yet we also know from history that *Schrecklichkeit* often backfires. The brutality of the Germans against Belgium in 1914 helped stir world opinion against the invaders, and even the Belgian army itself under its stalwart king found resources of courage to resist. Göring in 1941 thought he could terrify England into submission simply by bombing its cities; the American command in Vietnam thought they could subdue the Vietcong through the intimidation of napalm. But England did not buckle under Göring, nor did the Vietcong collapse under Westmoreland's bombs. The horrors of Hiroshima and Nagasaki, however, did convince the Japanese to sign an unconditional surrender. The tactics of terror therefore sometimes backfire and sometimes are successful.

It is rewarding, then, to look more closely at the differences. When we think of those who resist successfully the tactics of terror, there is a high admiration for the courage manifested by both the people and their leaders. King Albert of Belgium in 1914 and Winston Churchill in England's resistance in 1941 are seen as special kinds of heroes whose special kind of courage penetrates the darkness of fear. In contrast, however, King Leopold of Belgium, who yielded perhaps too quickly in 1940, does not stand the test of history as well. By examining these virtues, we may learn about the vice. From those who prove masters of horror, we may spot the limits of horror. If the *use* of horror in warfare is to intimidate and hence disarm the opponent, and if the resistance to the tactics of horror is recognized as a virtue of a specially radiant kind, then we should recognize something about the nature of horror itself. In addition to making us want to turn our heads away even as it fascinates, the experience of horror also threatens to undermine our integrity and honor. The sheer ugliness of horror lessens our grip on ourselves. The experience of horror, then, has two phases. In one, our sensitivity toward what is human is offended, and we are aghast at this violation of the sacredness of humanity. We consider this to be a virtue, for they who are *not* horrified at mutilated bodies we accuse of gross insensitivity. But then, the horrific seems to go further and makes us not only despair of our humanity but abandon it, in cowardice. If the sheer enormity of the experience renders us incapable of reaction, we then submit to the wickedness of it and yield our autonomy to another. Horror, then, is both positive and negative, both virtue and vice. The interpretation hangs on the notion of courage. As we shall see in the next section, courage is a uniquely existential virtue, for it focuses on the worth of who we are. And this reveals the true dread of horror: that our *meaning* will be eclipsed. Let us examine the two phases of horror in this light.

When we claim that war is horrific, what we mean, in part, is that violence is done to our humanity. We see torn and twisted bodies, and we think, "War has no respect, no reverence, for what is human." We then begin to feel an even deeper dread: this kind of savagery is in *me*. War occurs because of something in our nature. A sense of self-loathing overcomes us, and we tremble. This is the first phase. And though it is highly unpleasant, we consider it a mark of our sensitivity to human suffering. The second phase, however, is less noble. Overcome by this trembling in our souls, we find ourselves incapable of action. The enemy has wrought this destruction, but we have no will to resist, and by our weakness we capitulate. It is more than mere fear; the horror itself becomes horrible. To overcome this dread, we need great courage, or leadership that relies on courage. The essence of horror reveals itself as the loss of humanity; the essence of courage is that it regains humanity. By the horror of war, we mean the trembling brought about by the realization of our own inhumanity. This inhumanity is either perceived in the dreadful agonies of others or dreaded in the loss of our own capacity to act. The horror of war, then, is not only the gruesome pictures of savagery (for they could be brought about by nonwar events) but the role that we ourselves play either in bringing about the savagery to others or by being paralyzed into a special kind of cowardice.

Why does horror have this peculiar quality? To answer this, we turn now to the philosopher chosen to illuminate this mark, Edmund Burke. In his *Enquiry into the Sublime and the Beautiful,* Burke's analysis of the sublime is quite different from that found in Kant, which was used to support the first mark of war, vastness. Most critics agree that Kant's analysis is superior in many ways to Burke's, but the Englishman's contribution is not without significance. In section 7 he writes, "Whatever is fitted in any sort to excite the ideas of pain, and danger, that is to say, whatever is in any sort terrible, or is conversant about terrible objects or operates in a manner analogous to terror, is a source of the *sublime;* that is, it is productive of the strongest emotion which the mind is capable of feeling." A little later, in the same section, he insists that if the terror is too pressing, there is no room for delight, but "at certain distances, and with certain modifications," the terror may be enjoyed. Burke puts much emphasis on the fact that terror is the greatest emotion one can experience. It is this that gives it the character of the sublime, namely, that there is no greater possible emotion. He explains this in a further section: "The passion caused by the great and sublime in nature when those causes operate most powerfully is Astonishment; and astonishment is that state of the soul in which all its motions are suspended, with some degree of horror. In this case the mind is so filled with its object, that it cannot contain any other." The all-encompassing character of this emotion gives it the unique quality. It is precisely because the effect is so pervasive that it is astonishing, and this astonishment is a kind of horror. Unlike Kant, Burke does not make an appeal to the faculties that are violated or appealed to in this experience, but his observations are no less insightful. What is horrific astonishes us by its ability completely to dominate our consciousness. The recognition that we can be so totally riveted by anything has its own thrall. Indeed, it thrills us by its dominance. It is this very special sense of taking delight in being dominated by an experience that deserves our interest in this context. Above, in my consideration of war as a game, mention was made of those who delight in being taken or defeated. This is similar to the account Burke gives us of our experience of horror. Even though we do not accept this with our ordinary understanding, there is a kind of unhealthy, dangerous, and fascinating seduction with what is all-powerful. It is the strangeness or newness of this sensation that so attracts us.

Horror will never be understood if it is seen merely as that which repulses us. Not only are the horrors of war manifest in the grotesque suffering of its victims, but the peculiar attraction of *danger* must be added to it. Burke insists that the confrontation of danger enlivens the spirit as no other emotion can. His account for this is less ingenious, for he claims that the reason for it is the high value we place on life. This is to explain the spectacular by means of the ordinary. Nevertheless, few would deny that dangers do enliven life, paradoxical as that may be.

Horror, of course, is not the same as danger. If our analysis is correct, the horrific, like the terrifying, benumbs us, whereas danger enlivens us. In spite of this, the threat provoked by danger *is* a part of the horrific and must be included in the account. Clausewitz has a remarkable passage in his book *On War* in which he describes the experience of danger. We must bear in mind that Clausewitz had actually experienced battle in his youth and had been under fire, so he knew whereof he spoke. The passage in question is quite brief, only four paragraphs long, but it is tremendously revealing. It is entitled "On Danger in War." He accompanies an imaginary youth into his first battle, and though he shifts his pronouns, the account has the touch of direct experience.

> Let us accompany a novice on the battlefield. As we approach, the rumble of guns grows louder and alternates with the whir of cannonballs, which begin to attract his attention. Shots begin to strike close around us. . . . Here cannonballs and bursting shells are frequent, and life begins to seem more serious than the young man had imagined. Suddenly someone you know is wounded . . . you yourself are not as steady and collected as you were. . . . the air is filled with hissing bullets that sound like a sharp crack if they pass close to one's head. For a final shock, the sight of men being killed and mutilated moves our pounding hearts to awe and pity.
>
> The novice cannot pass through these layers of increasing intensity of danger without sensing that here ideas are governed by other factors, that the light of reason is refracted in a manner quite different from that which is normal in academic speculation. (Chapter 4, Howard and Pavet translation)

Ideas, says Clausewitz, are governed by other factors. He makes it clear that this experience is not all negative; there is a thrill in it. Yet he also insists that through training and genius and, above all, courage, the experience must be partially overcome. He considers danger to be one of the "frictions" of war that keep actual battles from being thought of in terms of the pure or ideal form of war, in the Platonic sense of *eidos*. It is this "other factor" that makes Clausewitz's description of the novice's first encounter similar to the analyses of both Kant and Burke. This experience is beyond our normal sensibility. It may still be "reason," but it is "refracted" through a new prism. Because it is so unusual, however, it can, in paralyzing the spirit, be destructive.

To recapitulate: horror is a negative emotion; it paralyzes us into inaction, partly because it is a rare experience and partly because it threatens our life. However, in war what particularly enthralls is the realization that such violence stems from our own natures. We are both attracted to it and repulsed by it, and our own autonomy is threatened by the enormity of the shock. In confrontation with this huge experience, we need resources that are equal to it, and this leads us to an appreciation of courage. Thus, we are led to the final existential mark.

WAR AS HEROIC

When medals are given for uncommon valor, a remarkable phrase is used. The award, such as the Congressional Medal of Honor, is bestowed with the explanation that the recipient has acted "above and beyond the call of duty." This phrase reveals a great deal about how we think of the heroic. The award is not given to one who does his duty exceptionally well or over long periods of time. The point is, the heroic is not even within the range of our understanding of duty. Duty means "doing what one ought to do." We admire those who do their duty, but no matter how grim or spectacular, it is what is expected. To go beyond duty is to enter into an entirely nonmoral range of discourse. The language of obligation and ought is simply inadequate to reveal what we mean when we reflect on the nature of the heroic. What is so remarkable about this is that such transcendence is packaged in quite ordinary language; it is directly and openly declared in this astonishing phrase that is as common and available as normal speech. Every schoolboy is familiar with it; even the most unremarkable and nonphilosophical citizen knows what it means. A cautious and modest man who may tremble with unease at a Nietzschean title like *Beyond Good and*

Evil nevertheless blithely accepts the invocation of valor that it is above and beyond the call of duty. Stolid and unimaginative people who would, if asked, probably deny that there could ever be any value *beyond* the moral and the good nevertheless do not blanch when they hear the heroic described in this way.

Perhaps, of course, it is due to inattention or even miscomprehension; it may be that common usage has deadened the sharp edge of meaning to this phrase, but I see no reason to be so grudging to normal understanding. The average person may be only half-aware of what he says, but that does not render his language unintelligible. When pressed, few, I think, would misinterpret this remarkable phrase as some adulation of dutiful performance. It means what it says, and we are confronted with a profound understanding of what is heroic: that which cannot be understood solely in terms of what ought to be done. It is also one of the few remaining bastions of elitism. The heroic is not common. Unlike the Kantian notion of the morally good, the heroic cannot be universalized. It is perhaps for this reason that in a cynical and egalitarian age the virtue of heroism is not easily accepted. Indeed, the heroic is often greeted with contempt and disdain by those who fear excellence or who caustically dismiss greatness as a nondemocratic notion. The very fact that the heroic is understood in transmoral terms puts it out of reach for those who insist that all good things must be equally shared or meanly denied. It is they who warn us against hero-worship, without realizing that to see a hero merely as an ordinary man is to forfeit the notion of the heroic altogether.

There are, of course, heroes outside of war, but the notion of the heroic is profoundly bound up with the notion of the warrior so much so that most nonwar uses of the term "heroic" are almost metaphors. It may seem, however, that it is possible to have a war in which there are no heroes. One can certainly imagine a grim exchange of violence in which no man stands out as spectacular. All do their duty, and no one stars as heroic. In fact, there may have been historical wars without heroes, so that to define the heroic as a necessary condition for a war might be denied by this scientific observation, but I do not think this necessarily forfeits the heroic as an essential mark of war. The heroic is needed to *understand* war, not to identify it. To argue that an understanding of the heroic is necessary to an understanding of war does not mean that every war must have had heroes any more than to say that an understanding of maternal love is necessary to an understanding of motherhood means that all mothers must love their children. I am, however, suggesting that the two terms, "war" and "hero," are interdependent in this existential sense: to understand one the other must be assumed.

For any war that lasts more than a few months, governments indeed make a special effort to find a hero. Just as in the case of the effect of horror, the heroic plays a role in that elusive notion of morale. Why this should be so cannot be answered by an appeal to cheap emotionalism or propaganda. The wise war leader knows that for a people to support a war they must be able to idealize through their suffering. The heroic is a source of meaning, not of psychological manipulation. For this reason, astute leaders recognize that for a war-torn people to endure their losses they need a hero to spot as a model; they need to be reminded who they are, not tricked into idle deception. Thus, the hero functions as an ideal in the Platonic sense; although we ourselves are not heroes, we look to those who are to understand ourselves.

To say that war is heroic, then, does not mean that every act of war can be so described. Nor does it mean that every warrior is a hero, for these descriptions would violate the uniqueness that is essential for our understanding of the heroic. It does not even mean that every war has heroes. What it does mean is that we understand war in terms of the heroic. It is possible, of course, to isolate the meaning of the heroic by asking what a hero is.

A hero is understood in terms both of what he has done and of who he is, that is, his actions and his character. We call an act heroic when it entails great danger, when the result either advances the cause considerably or saves lives, when prodigious courage is manifested in the act, and when the act itself is seen as splendid or remarkable. All four of these conditions should be present, normally, if the act is to be called heroic. Thus, not all courageous acts are heroic, but all heroic acts are courageous. In addition to these conditions for a heroic act, we also have conditions for understanding a heroic character. In the original Greek meaning of the word, a hero is not an ordinary man but often a half-man, half-god: a demigod. Or, if he cannot find any divinity in his parentage, he is specially favored by one of the many gods on Olympus. A hero is the subject of near veneration in such epics as *The Iliad* and *The Odyssey*. Therefore, in seeking to understand a hero, the classical mind inevitably thought in terms of a being who is either sired or favored by the gods, hence of someone who is not judged or assessed in ordinary terms. He is also the stuff of epics, which means that *who* he is becomes a source of tales and stories to instruct the young. The hero is a paradigm or model; he is less understood than used as a means of understanding.

Thus, both as an action and as a person, the heroic represents something outstanding, a source of illumination, an ideal. There are two notions, then, that we must examine before we can properly appreciate the heroic: ideality and courage. Instinctively, the modern democrat shies away from an ideal; it smacks of aristocracy and privilege. We do not like to think there is anyone better than ourselves, and since we despise arrogance, we do not even like to think there are many less than ourselves. This deep antagonism to the ideal frustrates any natural instinct to appreciate ideality. Courage, on the other hand, can be recognized and appreciated by the egalitarian; however, even this virtue needs special analysis in order to bring out its essence. Since it is usually wiser to begin with what is not alien, I shall initiate this inquiry by a consideration of courage and then shall turn to Plato for an understanding of ideality.

Courage

Plato identifies courage as the virtue of the warrior class, which corresponds to the spirit in the individual. Thus, it is, for Plato, a spiritual virtue; that is, we understand it as part of our spirit, not our reason. But courage is also a peculiarly existential virtue. It can be understood as the celebration of our own existence.

Most people, I believe, would agree that courage is distinct from either justice or knowledge. That is, merely because I *know* what I ought to do, it does not follow I will be able to do it. Furthermore, to imagine a state in which the good are rewarded and the bad punished (justice) does not inform me of that spiritual resource by which men carry out dangerous but necessary tasks. Furthermore, when we think of courage, we also think of some wonderful but mysterious resource within our spiritual being that somehow puts us on a plane of special meaning. It is a virtue we seem not only to admire but actually to love. The acts of courage that thrill us most are perhaps those which are least expected, coming from people whom one does not normally identify as brave. It occurs in many places outside of warfare, and indeed some of the more private and intimate forms of courage reveal a great deal more about the human species than the more spectacular performances on the battlefield. Indeed, most will make the distinction between sheer animal bravery (which can be admired in the same way natural strength or beauty is admired: as a gift) and courage. Few virtues are judged as manifesting the true character of someone as is courage. When a person would almost rather suffer death itself than have to perform a truly difficult task and yet performs the task anyway, we often realize just who this person is. On the other hand, genuine cowardice often evokes not anger or even outrage but contempt. These remarks suggest that courage tells us about who we really are, that courage is a virtue that we cherish as a guardian of our fundamental meaning. I am *eclipsed* by cowardice, but courage radiates from my character.

Let us consider the state of a man's mind and heart just at the onset of a difficult, unpleasant, and even dangerous task. Let us assume that he has already figured out that this act should be done, so there is no question of what is right. Let us also assume that there are no extraneous forces that would somehow distract him from his duty. Now, what does he ask himself? He does not ask, Is this what I ought to do? for he has already decided that. He does not ask whether his knowledge is impaired or adequate; he assumes that the facts are known and the judgment decided. He does not pray for more intelligence; indeed he may wish that he were less intelligent, since he would, if he could, avoid this confrontation. What he desperately hopes is simply that he has the wherewithal to carry it out. At the moment of his commitment what he fears is that he will not be capable of doing his duty; he fears he will be lacking in some primordial, all-important sense of who he is. Courage is the virtue that demands of ourselves sufficient strength to be true to our own being. I ask, Do I have the stuff? What I dread is not some purely physical failure but the unendurable prospect of having to live with myself, knowing that I am inadequate as a human being. In many ways, courage is the most private of all virtues, for it requires of us the will to accept ourselves as we are. When confronted by the need for courage, we are concerned not with what is right or what is moral or what will bring us pleasure or happiness, but quite simply whether we are *sufficient.* If the man is religious, he may pray, "Oh, Lord, give me strength," which is really a rather revealing request, for one is either strong or is not. Who can "give" strength? We do not pray merely for *success*—for both the craven and the virtuous do that—but also for the strength to confront our fears nobly.

Among all the virtues, courage alone is unpleasant. No one wants to have to be courageous, for being courageous presupposes a threat that challenges us severely. We all would like a world in which justice reigned; we enjoy being pious or wise or self-satisfied. We may admire courage in others, but we would all prefer never to have *to be* courageous, for if one enjoyed being courageous one would be involved in a contradiction. Socrates argues in the dialogue *Laches,* which is about courage, that the man who enters a battle fearfully and uncertain of the outcome has more courage than one who enters the battle assured and certain of victory. This, it seems, is an almost universally approved judgment: unless there is fear, there can be no courage. If the ordeal were easy or enjoyable, there would be no courage necessary to undertake it. For this reason, courage should be seen as a uniquely *existential* virtue, for what is at stake is the worth of one's own personal integrity. It may be painful, perhaps even fatal, but I will endure this agony because of who I am; my existence matters, and I will not defile it with shame or cowardice. Such reflections draw on remarkable resources, and the mind can only wonder at them.

Another aspect of courage is whether it can be taught or learned or developed. Suppose one knows that one must soon confront a demanding and unpleasant situation. How does one prepare for courage? There may be countless psychological tricks we use to prepare ourselves for such events, but perhaps the most effective is the simple one appealed to above: we remind ourselves that what is at stake is our own sense of self-worth. If I am about to confront a dreadful situation, the conflict is usually between two quite distinct fears: the fear of the threat itself and the counterfear that I shall not have the courage to confront it honorably. Without the second fear all courage becomes mere prudence; I should simply get out of the way of the first threat. To sustain one's own courage, then, requires an appeal to one's sense of one's own worth. Cowardice is simply not worthy of me.

Suppose, however, some simply admit that they just do not think that their integrity is that important, that they would rather be safe and danger-free than threatened. Suppose some say they simply are not worthy and prefer to avoid all unpleasantness regardless of the loss of self-esteem. There are such people. We may sympathize with their plight, or we may seek to instill in them some sense of self-worth; but as long as this nihilistic attitude persists, we cannot help thinking of them as somehow lacking. There is no logical formula one can use to prove to such persons that they matter sufficiently to be courageous, but we *do* know that *unless* they have a sense of self-worth they cannot be courageous.

Remarkably, cowardice itself often seems to produce a kind of courage. Caesar says in Shakespeare's play that the coward dies a thousand deaths; the brave man dies but once. However, if that is true, the coward must come back to life 999 times, and one wonders if there is not more power in that restoration than in one heroic sacrifice. The human person provides a wealth of fascinating struggles between cowardice and courage, and the various kinds of courage are not always the most obvious. It may take a deeper kind of courage to be a coward in some ways. The point is, even the most complex psychological confusion about a person's will does not darken our understanding of the basic insight: courage depends on a realization of one's self-worth, and our repulsion at the coward hangs on this same realization of the emptiness of one who has abandoned it. Courage is an existential virtue; indeed it may be the paradigm of self-confrontation.

In Richard Wagner's opera, *Siegfried,* the young hero confesses to his wily guardian, the dwarf Mime, that he has never known fear. Mime attempts to explain to the young Siegfried what fear must really be like. He describes the tingling sensation, the thrill running through the veins, the quickening of the pulse, and the charge of vital dread. But the naturally brave and lively Siegfried does not comprehend what Mime is talking about. However, he senses its importance and expresses the wish that he knew what fear really was. (A hero wants to know what fear is?) Even when the bold young man fights the dragon, Fafner, he does not experience fear. It is not until he witnesses the radiant beauty of Brünnhilde that he suddenly breaks out into the familiar tremor of mortal dread. The myth suggests that only in love, indeed, love of the beautiful, can true fear be realized, and thence only can true courage be realized. The brave Siegfried becomes the courageous Siegfried, and only in this realization does he become a hero. Of course, only in this peculiar state of loving-fearfulness does he become vulnerable, and as vulnerable he becomes tragic. There is a great deal to learn from the mythical consciousness, and Wagner's opera succeeds in showing us the true connection between these profound self-revealing virtues: only through fear can one love; only through love-induced fear can one become vulnerable; only as vulnerable does it matter if we succeed or no; only as confronting our fearsome vulnerability do we realize who we are — and that is what it means to be heroic.

Courage is properly the virtue of the warrior not only because bravery is needed for warriors but also because the warrior is defending the worth of our existence, which is what courage appeals to. The celebration of this self-worth is called glory, and perhaps no single word in the English language has been more grossly misunderstood and abused. Glory is not the same as fame, or adulation. Today the term is used almost exclusively in a contemptuous sense. The true notion of glory contains the notion of deep respect and joy for what is splendid, and the defense and celebration of what is one's own is truly glorious.

The essence of courage lies in our unwillingness to forfeit our own worth. When one is confronted with a threatening situation, what matters is that one does not lose respect for oneself. Accordingly, when we find it necessary to inspire another to do what is courageous, we instinctively find it better to appeal to his own self-esteem: "Remember who you are. This is difficult, to be sure, but you are not the kind of person who could live with himself knowing you did not have the stuff." In Shakespeare's *Richard II,* the self-doubting king finds resolve only when he reminds himself who he is:

Aumerle: Comfort, my liege. Remember who you are.
King: I had forgot myself. Am I not king? Awake, thou coward majesty! thou sleepest.

Later on in this same play, when the king capitulates and surrenders his crown to "that vile politician, Bolingbroke," we feel frustrated at his action. We know that Richard *has* been heroic, and so his presented cowardice troubles us deeply. We cannot but feel that Richard's tragedy is one in which he has forgotten who he is. Shakespeare as a tragic genius is willing to help us up to a point. (Is it, for example, that Richard's is the tragedy of *language?* That he *talks himself into* his own ruin?) But the poet is unwilling to explain too much, for the whole point is that Richard is *not* true to himself. To explain Richard's failure by pointing out psychological weaknesses would not explain but explain away. As king, Richard acted in an unkingly way; hence our sense of tragedy is heightened by his inauthenticity. For the same reason, Heidegger has spotted resoluteness as the essence of authenticity.

In trying to grasp as fully as we can the nature of courage, we must also examine the nature of cowardice. If the above paragraph is anywhere near the truth, we then recognize cowardice as a kind of inauthenticity, a weakness of the self. Indeed, we often think of cowardice as *the* vice in which the self is denied. We are offended by all vices, of course; but our reaction to cowardice is more sadness and revulsion than anger or outrage. In extreme cases of cowardice, we may even feel the vice is *obscene,* that is, that from which we turn our faces. It is painful to watch. Sins committed out of passion, anger, lust, greed, or even ignorance can be forgiven; but cowardice is difficult to forgive just because it is so intimate. We can forgive cowardice, of course, because we all recognize that the same weakness is within us. This is why Satan is a problem. We are told by both theologian and poet that Satan's crime was pride; he reached beyond himself and challenged God. But this splendid personage remains something of a hero for us, especially as he is presented in *Paradise Lost* or in Marlowe's *Tragedy of Doctor Faustus.* Perhaps a profounder theology would present his rebellion as a kind of cowardice. For all his evil ways, his protest that he would rather reign in hell than serve in heaven sounds a deep chord within all of us. It is a rich suggestion to characterize Satan's fault as similar to Richard's: he had forgotten who he was. Richard's forgetting himself was cowardice; why not see Satan in a similar way?

These ruminations are not meant to distract from the profound question at hand. Both courage and cowardice are essential to our understanding. They are the polarities of the most profound truth worthy of our contemplation: our own self-acceptance. To be a coward is not to care who we are. To be courageous is to care who we are. Thus, courage is, in essence, the virtue *about* our existence as meaningful. This is what is meant by characterizing it as an *existential* virtue. However, the mark under discussion is not courage but heroism. In addition to being courageous, a true hero must be an ideal.

Ideality

Men do idealize. It is part of our nature as knowing and reasoning beings. And this must be emphasized: ideality is a form of *cognition*. We idealize in order to understand. It is not an idle form of adulation or worship; it is something that is as necessary to the mind as conceptualization or abstraction. It is a function of our consciousness to be able to take a notion and intensify it or amplify it to its highest degree of perfection. If I comprehend the idea of swiftness, it is possible for me to idealize this notion so that I can imagine the swiftest being. Few would doubt this faculty, though whether its function lies in the imagination or elsewhere is perhaps moot. However, though few would deny that we can idealize, fewer still would argue that idealization provides a kind of *learning*. Yet, a moment's reflection will show that paradoxical as it may seem, we do learn from our capacity to idealize. It is a paradox because in idealizing we learn about ourselves by the projection of excellence beyond ourselves.

Suppose I wish to reflect on what it means to move. I realize that I am a spatial being and that an essential part of what and who I am consists in my taking up space. I do not question *that* I am a spatial being, nor am I concerned at the moment with how I come to know about my extension in space. I simply want to reflect on what being in space *means*. One way in which I can further or deepen my understanding is to attend a ballet and watch a great dancer. He moves better than I; indeed, he may be the

THE ELEMENTS OF WAR—III

greatest dancer, in which case he moves better than anyone else. Now, by comparing the inelegant movements of my own body with the dazzling perfection of the dancer's, I can see that *moving* is something at which I can either succeed or fail. From this difference, and with the help of the dancer, I can see that the possibilities of motion present themselves to me as meaningful. The dancer, for example, stretches his hand out in supplication; I can see that this gesture reveals what it means to have such emotion and need. But the paradox is that I learn about what it means *for me* to move by watching someone move better than I. How do I make sense of this? We say the dancer *idealizes* human motion, so that even though I cannot move as elegantly as he, what is illuminated by his excellence is not only his moving but my moving as well. This is how ideality works. The ideal functions as a source of illumination for the various modes or ways of existing.

The hero is therefore not merely a courageous person who endures danger for the sake of others, he is also a source of understanding, an ideal from which we derive meaning. This is why we often speak of a hero in terms of the spectacular. He who does the extraordinary thing, the bold one, he who ventures into the remarkable and unusual, deserves the title. It may be one's duty to be courageous, but it is above and beyond the call of duty to achieve the heroic. By definition, the hero is one who stands out, who focuses our attention simply by being different in a remarkable way. However, in his uniqueness he is not merely *odd;* by being spectacular he does not merely *differ* from the rest; rather his uniqueness serves as a source of self-understanding. War brings us to the extremity of our cares and concerns not only because of the threat of death but because the entire communal existence is questioned. The hero draws our attention to what is ecstatic; he shows us who we are precisely by surpassing who we are. There is something paradoxical in all ideality, then: by focusing on something other than myself I learn about myself.

To say that war is heroic is not merely to say that there are heroes *in* war, it is to say that war is understood heroically, that is, as a source or ideal by which we understand ourselves as revealed in courage. War, like many other notions, *is* what it is *as* we understand it. To define war properly is to focus on how we understand it, and one essential way we have of understanding is the notion of ideality. In this, the two elements of the heroic, courage and ideality, are conjoined. How, then, are we to understand the nature of ideality? In seeking to comprehend this all-important notion, we turn now to a consideration of the thinker chosen as the support of this mark, Plato. Above, we have already seen this thinker's contribution in the analysis of the holy, as it is presented in the dialogue *Euthyphro.* Now we turn to his doctrine of ideality.

In his famous discussion of *aitia* (cause) in the *Phaedo,* Socrates points out that he, unlike the Anaxagorean physicists who explain merely by listing the conditions that bring the thing in question about, prefers to explain by "pointing out how a thing is best." He contrasts the physicist's account of his being in prison (that he is there because of his bones, muscles, and sinews) with his own account, which is to show how it is best for him, as a citizen of Athens, to be there. Now, this seemingly innocent difference is in fact crucial to the understanding of Plato. For it emphasizes that one understands only when one sees things in the light of perfection.

Thus, when one seeks to understand justice, one must reason out an ideal state which does not exist but by which all actual (and hence lesser) states are illuminated. It is important to note that Plato has not denied that there may exist a useful discipline called Anaxagorean science, that maybe one can find out all the conditions that are prior to and seem to be the agency of a thing's existence; but such information, even if forthcoming, does not provide understanding. For to *understand* something is to grasp its meaning, not its actuality. Thus, the logical form of Plato's theory of explanation is not "I know that *x*" but rather "I understand what *x* means."

According to Plato, all things that are to be understood permit of success or failure. I understand running, for example, by noting the difference between those who run badly and those who run well. It is only because there is a difference between running badly and running well that I can *understand what running means.* Thus, mud, for example, of which there exists no better or worse instances, since all mud is just mud, cannot properly be said to have a Form; that is, it cannot properly be thought about or be understood. Socrates' disappointment and ultimate rejection of Anaxagoras is of supreme importance because he accuses the physicist of asking the wrong question, of "confusing conditions for causes." There is, to be sure, no principle of excellence in the determination of matters of fact; but then, precisely because of this lack of the principle of excellence, there can, merely from the awareness of matters of fact, be no understanding.

To understand in the light of excellence presupposes ideality. That is, I must be able to proceed from the qualities of a particular situation to the enlargement or engrandizement of such qualities. The supreme of such perfections of meaning are Plato's ideas, or Forms. Hence, the Forms, in their universality, are not the "least common denominators" that include all particulars that bear their name. Strictly speaking, the Forms do not "include"

any particular thing, since all actual and particular things must lack sufficient perfection to be included in the Form. They are, rather, illuminated by
the Form; they *participate* in the perfection but do not fully possess it. The
Forms operate, like the sun, not as objects of knowledge but as the source of
illumination by which other things are understood. In other words, since I
can recognize that some men are better at playing the lyre than others, such
qualitative difference can be understood only in terms of an ideal player. For
to understand, according to Plato, *means* to judge in the light of the
projected perfection. If all lyre players were equally good, one could not
make such judgments and hence could not understand lyre playing, though
one might surely know that there is such a thing. How is it possible,
however, for the mind or the soul to project from the givenness of playing
the lyre to the ideal lyre playing? How does the mind come into contact with
the Forms, or the ideas?

In the *Phaedrus* Socrates gives us an account of such projection. What is
the difference, he asks, between someone who observes a beautiful youth
without lust or passion and one who sees the same youth with lust and
passion? The difference, Socrates tells us, is that through the eros of the
latter, the passionate admirer of beauty is "lifted up" to the level of the
Forms. This is to say that eros universalizes or idealizes. Although anyone
may appreciate the beauty of the youth, only he who is overcome by the
madness of eros sees such beauty idealistically, or in universal terms.

Now, to say that eros idealizes is not without phenomenological support.
We might say that Romeo idealizes Juliet and through such idealization is
led to rhapsodic insight and articulation of the meaning of love itself. The
passion of eros forces the mind to see things idealistically, but only under
such ideality can the comprehension of the meaning of things be accomplished,
for ideals are those principles by which we understand. Only by means of
the ideal state can I understand justice, even if its actual occurrence is found
only in the pale and imitative instances of actually existing states. Ideas are
like the sun: they illuminate the things under their light; they are not
themselves looked at. Thus, we *stand under* when we under-stand; we
stand under the light of illumination of an idea wherever we understand
something.

But if eros is that which lifts us to the level of the ideal, eros is also that
which renders an account of both knowing and not knowing that ideal. In
the *Symposium* Socrates assures us that it is due to eros that we are
"between" knowledge and ignorance, between the beautiful and the ugly,
between having and not having. Eros was born, according to Diotima's

myth, of the mortal woman Poverty conspiring to be impregnated by the male god Plenty. Eros is thus the true offspring of both his parents: from his mortal mother he is finite; from his divine father, infinite. He is both possession and lack, beauty and ugliness, wisdom and ignorance. Love is that by which reasoning can be suspended between two opposites, and therefore it alone can explain how idealization is possible. Idealization is formally interesting because it allows suspension between actuality and possibility. When I understand through idealization, I am aware both of what is and what ought to be. One's relation to the truth is therefore not that of the possessor, but neither is it that of the nonpossessor; since one's relation to the truth is that of eros, one loves the truth, and hence neither fully has nor completely lacks the beloved truth.

The nature of Plato's ideality is thus understood by an appeal to the erotic. But this present discussion is concerned with ideality as a part of the heroic. Does this mean that the *heroic* is itself erotic? Certainly in a Platonic sense this can be asserted, since both the heroic and the erotic function as forms of ideality. Even outside the Platonic opus, however, the understanding often links the two notions. In an earlier discussion, I noted that one of the differences between our feelings for a police officer and a warrior is that although the former is admired, the latter is loved, because the warrior's bravery protects what is our own. Furthermore, the warrior is often thought of in terms of patriotism, the love of country. War, then, is linked with love. But surely there is no greater dichotomy than that which exists between love and war. During the Vietnam War, one of the most popular youth slogans was "Make love, not war!" suggesting a radical disjunction between the two. Perhaps, however, the Greek suggestion is a more profound one: Is not the god of war, Ares, a sibling to the god of love?

This analysis of Plato's texts has shown us why the heroic must be understood in terms of ideality. And it is because of this understanding that we can now see why war itself is heroic. It is heroic because in war the meaning of our existence is idealized, and the virtue that protects existence, courage, is embodied. The heroic, therefore, is not only a major mark of war, it is essential to our understanding of it.

This completes the analyses of the nine existential marks of war. Each of the nine marks reveals the peculiarly existential meaning to war and, when taken together, reveal an "existential description" of the term. No matter how profound and deep our existential appreciation may be, however, war cannot be considered without a moral resistance to it. Thus, it remains a paradox, in which the existential contrasts with the moral. But the concerns that make up our existential meaning are precious indeed: notions like the sacred, the historical, the sublime (both in vastness and in horror), the communal, and the heroic are not idle pleasantries or things to be rejected easily. In *describing* war in this way, there can be no doubt that in some sense we have also revealed the *justification* of it. This does not mean that the inquiry is prejudicial or circular, for in rendering an account it was necessary to show why such ideas are valued. But the inquiry into description can never of itself be an inquiry into the source of the principles.

Part Three

THE PRINCIPLE

5

The We-They Principle

This chapter is divided into three parts. The first considers the philosophical foundation of the we-they principle. The second employs this we-they distinction in establishing a ranking of the institutions that concretize the principle in what may be called the order of belonging. The third applies this principle directly to the traditional accounts of war.

THE PHILOSOPHICAL GROUNDING

We dwell in a world in which the existence of others is essential for our meaning. This is not something we have psychologically decided on, nor is it the result of sociological development. To be with others is simply a fundamental way in which we exist. We do not derive this notion from single, isolated beings who subsequently experience other isolated beings and then form a group, nor is it something that occurs only when we happen to be in the presence of others; rather it is a condition of how we exist at all, something that must be assumed if our existence is to be made meaningful. It therefore takes on the status of a principle, and since it is about the meaning of existence, it should be designated an "existential principle." Because an existential principle, like any other principle, illuminates or explains other things, it is not often itself explained, though of course it can be articulated and analyzed. Our being with others is therefore a priori; it is through this principle that we make sense of our existential reality. It is by means of this principle that we can think about who we are.

We find ourselves confronted in two ways by the presence and meaningfulness of those who are with us. Either we accept them as belonging to our own meaningfulness, or we see them as beings that are existentially other. Thus, our being-with is either of the same or the different. If the former, it is understood as "we"; if the latter, as "they." Since this distinction provides the basis for thinking of ourselves in this primordially disjunctive way, it can be used as the title: the we-they principle. This principle is an a priori existential rule that governs the way we must think about the meaning of our existence. The we is not derived from a plurality of I's, as if our original form of existence were as an isolated and denuded self, or private mind, and the notion of the we were achieved merely by additions to this primordial unit. Indeed, the we is primordial to the I: "we are" comes before "I am."

Each of the pronouns has not only an external referent (I, the author; you, the reader) but a unique existential meaning that precedes these assignments. Grammarians point out that the word "pronoun" means "taking the place of a noun," which suggests the prior status of the noun over the pronoun. Grammatically, of course, this is correct. But the grammarian's order is reversed in existential philosophy: the pronoun precedes the noun. ("I think, therefore I am" precedes "Descartes thinks, therefore Descartes exists.") Here our inquiry is not directed toward the referents of these pronouns (that is, the nouns) but their independent meaning. Rather than see the pronoun "I" as a variable for some indefinite, knowing subject, it is now possible to ask, What does it mean to be an I? It should be obvious that this question does not ask for the personal referent, but the way of thinking requisite for understanding what it means to exist in the various ways in which the term "I" is used. It surely is partially correct to characterize this modality as being the subject of a conscious act, but that is not the whole or even the major part of its meaning. When I use these pronouns in this special existential sense, I shall capitalize them and preface them with the definite article, unless this renders the sentence awkward. Thus, when I use the phrase "the We," I am using it to designate this special existential sense. With this in mind we can now inquire directly into pronominal meanings.

The I cannot just be, all by itself. It either shares with a Thou, disjoins from a They, or objectifies an It. But I and Thou reveals We. The We, more original than either Thou or I, since it makes them possible, is either affirmative (as in love), or negative, against the They (as in war). The two phenomena, love and war, are themselves not primordial, for they are made possible by the existential logic of the pronouns, which are primordial. These pronominal meanings, therefore, are almost always conceived in terms of tandem pronouns, such as I–Thou, I–It, We–They, and Thou–It. Since it is possible for the mind to think in universal terms, it also becomes possible to think in terms of the We-All or I-All, in which the consciousness interprets itself as representative of all and any consciousness.

The above paragraph perhaps deserves further elucidation. What we mean when we say that "the I cannot just be, all by itself," is that there is no such thing as a pure, denuded, abstract mind that merely cognizes. To be conscious, after all, is merely a part of being at all. As a human being, I have eyes, but these organs are meaningless without light and other objects. But neither am I just a "seeing" being. If I have a body, it is also a sexual thing, and that means either male or female. But maleness is meaningless without the female; the self becomes meaningful only in terms of the other. Even the formal logicians recognize there is no subject without an object, no true without a false. The existential thinker merely recognizes more variants of this primordial disjunction, and assigns them different modalities by means of the various pronouns, ranging from *all, I, we,* through *you, thou, us,* to *them, him, her, it* —however, always and only in tandem. There is no I without a you to love, or an it to see, or a they to confront. It is, properly speaking, improper to speak of the pronominal tandems as relations, as if one were to understand them in terms of two entities standing in some external relation to one another. They are properly existential principles because they take their meaning not from the pair of entities related, but simply from how we must think about the meaning of our existence. The we-they principle is thus not a relation between one unit (we) and another unit (they).

It must be emphasized that one cannot *derive* the notion of the We from the simpler I and Thou; it is the other way around. The reason for this order can be seen upon reflection. The I is incomplete without an opposing or sharing counterterm such as Thou or It. But I–Thou already reveals a We. The most fundamental sense of meaning is our own being in a world, which already is either ours or not ours. It is, of course, possible to individuate even further, to focus solely on one's private self; but this requires a special intensification of meaning. There simply can be no more fundamental notion than the meaningfulness of one's own existence, and since this primary realization is either positive or negative (own or not own), this distinction between what is our own and what is not our own becomes the very disjunction by which *thinking* itself is possible, that is, the distinction between the authentic and the inauthentic. Even if we were to begin with the I, that modality would immediately be judged as either affirmative (I–Thou) or negative (I against They). This is the very fundament of thinking and being. Unless I can make such a distinction, there can be no meaning at all.

And this is an important realization. What is at issue here is meaning. The peculiar form of misology that threatens here is not skepticism or relativism but *nihilism*. Existential ideas do not refer to things but to meanings. The very principle that allows one to confront this threat to reason is the difference between existing authentically and existing inauthentically, that is, between what is ours and what is not ours. Here the term does not refer to possessions but to modes of existing.

The personal pronouns, like "I" and "We," become governed existentially by the possessive pronouns, like "ours," "mine," "theirs"; and this in turn becomes governed by the adjective "own." What is authentic becomes what is our own as a way of existing. The meaning of this term is less the sense of possession than the sense of belonging to. It is a translation of the German *eigen,* from which the term *eigentlich* (authentic) is derived. To lose this sense of one's *own* is to abandon any meaningfulness, and hence to embrace nihilism. To be a nihilist is to deny that there is any way of being that is our own; for the nihilist, what is one's own has no meaning. The threat here is not that what is our own may yield to what is not, but rather that the distinction itself will simply collapse. Unless I can distinguish between what is our own and what is not, no meaningfulness is possible at all.

This is the foundation of the we-they principle. The pronouns in the title do not refer to anything; they merely reveal *how we think.* Like all principles, this existential principle does not determine *specific* judgments, any more than the principle of cause and effect determines what the cause of any given thing is. The we-they principle is simply a rule that governs the standards by which certain judgments are made. Since it is possible to isolate the existential meanings of an idea from the thinglike referent, the notions of we-ness and they-ness can be articulated philosophically. On the basis of this primary understanding, it is possible to talk about an "existential value," that is, the weight or rank given to ways of existing in opposition to other kinds of value, such as moral or psychological values. But the principle itself is not, strictly speaking, a principle of value; it is an ontological principle, for its foundation is in the very basic way in which I think about what it means to be. The ground of the we-they principle is, quite simply, the way in which we think about being. Thus, it is more fundamental than any kind of evaluating or judging.

One of the things that the authentic I can do, of course, is to concern itself with moral questions. Whether from a deontological sense of obligation or from a utilitarian projection of possible happiness, an I that considers these matters nevertheless is presupposed by them. Although authenticity and morality are distinct, a sense of who one is must precede a decision about how to act. Thus, the question of authenticity comes before the question of obligation. And since the worth of the I is generated from the prior worth of the we, it follows there can be no moral judgment that cancels out the worth of the I or the We. This is not to say that anything that benefits the we is therefore more important than what ought to be done. It is merely to say that any proper moral judgment will in fact be consistent with the integrity of the we. Thus, I would be morally prohibited from offending someone else merely for my own advantage, but no moral law would ever require me to forgo my existential integrity. This is true not only for moral questions but for any question of value whatsoever: all legitimate value claims must be consistent with the worth of the I and the We. It is only because my existence matters that I can care about such things as morality, aesthetics, or even happiness. Pleasure, of course, would still be preferable to pain, but to argue that one ought to have pleasure or even that it is good to have pleasure would simply reduce itself to a tautology: if I define pleasure as the satisfaction of my wants, then to say I want pleasure is tautological, for I am merely saying that I want what I want, which may be true but is not very illuminating.

The existential worth of existing is therefore fundamental and cannot be outranked by any other consideration. Unless I am first meaningful, I cannot be good; unless I first care about who I am, I cannot genuinely care about anything else, even my conduct. To threaten this ground of all values, the worth of my own being, then becomes the supreme assault against me. To defend it and protect it is simply without peer. It is beyond human appeal or persuasion.

If it is granted that this supreme and irreducible judgment of worth is characterized by the notion of what is one's *own*, the question now raised must be, Is the concept of what is one's own more truly realized in one's private self (the I) or in one's shared existence (the we)? Or perhaps both are equally valid. What reasons can be adduced to show the legitimacy of the we as equal in significance to, or perhaps even more fundamental than, the I? Let us briefly consider certain historical and classical arguments. Descartes argues in his *Meditations* that the *cogito* isolates the individual soul. In the *First Meditation* he claims to suspend all former judgments and knowledge in order to get at the single, irrefutable truth that resists his methodic doubt, and on this basis he discovers the truth of the realization that if I think, I am. This is surely an ingenious proof, deserving of its enviable position in history, but many have attacked it from equally ingenious positions. One point that should be made about it is this: when Descartes "suspends" all previous knowledge, we cannot and do not take him completely seriously. In the first place, he continues to inquire, to speculate, to weigh arguments — and to do this he needs language. The language of his inquiry, whether Latin or French, has a unique history; it is imbued with subtle and powerful prejudices; it functions according to certain rules of grammar and syntax. The point here is not that Latin is incapable of translation into English, but simply that Latin or any other language brings with it a whole way of speaking and thinking. Language is cultural, and to some extent that cultural persuasion manifests itself even in speculative uses such as philosophy. This is not to say the *cogito* is invalid, or even to say that Descartes's method is flawed. It is merely to point out that any use of language appeals to a cultural reality that cannot completely be overcome. To this extent the fact that Descartes wrote first in Latin and then in French reveals the we in his inquiry.

However, there is a more serious point. In his inquiry, Descartes obviously believes that his argument will be accepted by anyone who follows his procedure. In other words, the *Meditations* are not intended as private autobiography; rather they are presented as having universal validity. The *cogito* proves not only that Descartes exists but that anyone who says it exists. So that in effect he is saying that when *we* think, we are assured of *our* existence. And by these pronouns he means the entire human race: we, the human beings who can think. The uniqueness and specificity of the I that Descartes slips in so that he can aver a human soul has been severely criticized by many subsequent thinkers.

Does this suggest, then, that by "we" is meant merely the universal and abstract subject? This interpretation must be resisted. However, no less a thinker than Immanuel Kant protested against Descartes along these lines. Kant argues that Descartes's *cogito* does not prove an isolated and specific soul or thinking thing, but rather it provides us merely with what he calls 'consciousness in general', that is, the abstract unification of all the rules and principles by which we think. Thus, what is revealed in transcendental (Kantian) thought is the human mind abstractly conceived. It is not the I of Descartes but rather the All as an abstract universal. When you and I think about our minds, we isolate those elements of our particular consciousness from those which are shared by every consciousness and thus achieve 'consciousness in general'. Far more epistemically versatile than Descartes's 'soul', this 'general consciousness' has lost all specific pronominal reference: it is neither I nor we, but all. As a critique of Descartes, this argument is probably valid, but it does leave the inquiry on the level of a purely formal analysis.

For Martin Heidegger, however, this purely formal analysis can be seen as valid if it is focused solely on *consciousness*. But if our concern is broader and deeper, the area of analysis should not be consciousness but existence itself. In this case, the pronouns return with a vengeance. From the existential point of view, the self is not isolated, as with Descartes's 'soul', nor is it universal but abstract, as is Kant's 'consciousness'; rather, being-in-the-world (to use Heidegger's term) is completely charged with all kinds of shared meanings. According to Heidegger, being-with is an a priori mode of Dasein (human existence). Thus, to understand oneself, one must begin, not with either a lonely soul or an abstract consciousness, but with a being permeated with existential care, so that being-with is equal to being-oneself and, indeed, influences it.

These thinkers show by their argumentation that there are difficulties in conceiving of the self solely in terms of the I. One final visit from the history of philosophy may help to show the significance of this idea. Plato, in his *Republic*, divides the soul into three parts: appetite, spirit, and mind. It does not take much imagination to see these three parts of the soul as embodiments of the three pronouns: I, we, and all. The appetite is that which appeals to one and only one person: I am hungry, you are thirsty, and so forth. The rules of reason, as Kant proves, are applicable to all, and they constitute mind. It is the middle stage of Plato's tripartite soul that is so provocative. He calls it spirit, and it seems to meet the needs understood by the we. It is also interesting to note that, for Plato, spirit is the part of the soul that reflects the position of the warrior in the state, whose illuminating virtue is courage. What Plato means by this division is that no single part, or aspect, of the soul is sufficient. (The Greeks did not find the language of "parts" implying any strict materialism.) Thus, if the guiding virtue of spirit is courage, and if the corresponding class within the *Republic* is the warrior class, it is easy to see how Plato gives support for the argument that war is based on the existential value of ranking what is one's own above all other concerns.

We do not accept the language of souls today, so Plato's arguments may lose some of their force. This would be unfortunate. The basic insights are still sound, and can be retranslated into modern terminology. What Plato identifies as the spirit can be seen as the existential principle of we-they. The sole arbiter of authenticity is no longer the lonely, independent self, courageously confronting all comers as alien to its uniqueness. To be sure, we do recognize such notions as constituting a way of achieving authenticity, but it is not the only way. The I may indeed provide us with a way of thinking about ourselves, but so does the we. Plato has shown that courage can be seen in terms of a state as well as in terms of an individual; indeed, he claims that it is "writ larger" and easier to understand. If we add this insight to that of Heidegger's that our being in the world is deeply influenced by our being with others, we can see the roots of the we-they principle.

How, though, does the principle actually work? One appeals to a principle usually to establish or determine some kind of judgment. One may recognize some authority to the notion of belonging to a we and opposing oneself against a they, but how exactly does the principle actually establish a judgment? The actual determination is this: self-knowledge—or, perhaps better, self-understanding—is of supreme importance. All other values are secondary to it. This principle establishes the judgment that what is ultimately important is provided by the distinction between what is our own and that which is other, and the reason is that without meaning no other value is possible. Since meaning can be realized only by holding what is one's own as primary, the self-nonself principles of which the we-they principle is paramount, outrank all other principles. This does not give license to anyone seeking to establish this meaning at the cost of morality; it does show, however, that the moral law does not compel someone to abandon his own commitment to a meaningful existence, and hence this value is ultimate.

This tension between the existential and the moral needs vigorous and critical analysis, for the danger of misunderstanding here has grave consequences. In no way must this tension be seen as justifying any disregard of the moral imperatives that are absolute. At the same time, the existential ground of morality is equally compelling and deserves full appreciation.

Moral judgments, which are universal and absolute and permit of no exception, are themselves possible only because of who we are. It is thus the intrinsic worth of our existence that ultimately grounds the absolute morality that dictates what we ought to do. Even Immanuel Kant, the most stringent and authoritative moralist in the philosophical repertoire argues precisely this way. It is respect for our own natures as lawlike, Kant argues, that demands all rational beings be treated as ends and never as means only. Thus, for Kant, what we ought to do is based on the fundamental worth of who we are: rational beings. This in no way lessens the authority of morality but, rather, enhances it by giving it an existential base. Consider the prescription or imperative against murder. We assert this as universal and absolute; that is, there can be no exceptions to it. Yet Kant and other moralists insist it is not only permissible but even obligatory to kill someone who is trying to kill ourselves or others, providing such killing is the only meaningful way to stop him. Is this inconsistent? The prohibition is against murder, not killing; and if we define murder as unjustified, willful killing, to prevent such a thing by killing the would-be murderer does not violate the imperative. But it remains a huge problem that needs clarification. Why do we say that murder is wrong in the first place? Because persons so victimized are of intrinsic worth, that is, because they must be treated as ends in themselves. Why is killing the murderer not similarly prohibited? Because the would-be murderer is a threat to the principle itself: he is willing and acting contrary to the universality of law. Killing the murderer does two things: it stops the murderer from violating the moral law, which would debase himself, and it protects those who would be his victims. It is the first of these that is more significant, although it is the second that is the more emotionally appealing. The point is, the murderer must be kept from violating the very principle that makes him a worthy being: respect for his own rationality. In allowing the would-be murderer to carry out his crime, one is not treating him as an end in himself, for as an end in himself, the would-be murderer is bound to respect, and hence be held responsible for, both his will and his action. Hence, to stop the would-be murderer by killing him is to treat him as a rational being; that is, it is a moral thing to do.

The reason for killing the would-be murderer is based on the existentially prior worth of the would-be murder; who he *is* (as a rational being) comes before the reasoning that certain actions are immoral. It is not only the intrinsic worth of his would-be victims that justifies killing him, it is equally the intrinsic worth of the would-be murder, who must be treated as an end in himself—as a morally responsible being—and not merely as a means. This is to say that, formally speaking, the existential ground of all moral judgments must be presupposed if the moral judgments are to make sense. This can be articulated by saying that who we are ranks above what we do. Yet, "who we are" also provides the ground for making absolute, universal, lawlike moral principles. The soldier, defending his homeland, kills (though does not murder) the enemy soldier, because as enemy, the alien threatens the very ground of all morality, that who we are matters. Yet killing another human being continues, rightly, to disturb us simply because we respect the moral law that ascribes to every rational being the intrinsic worth of being as an end in itself. The particular alien soldier may himself be innocent of any crime, but as alien he cannot be allowed to usurp our integrity as rational beings. Indeed it is morally *wrong* to allow or abet the enemy's destroying what is ours. Thus, to speak of the "existential outranking the moral" simply means the former is more fundamental than the latter; it does *not* mean that any private self-interest can provide loopholes in the universality of the moral law. The proper law simply could never forfeit our existential worth.

It must be remembered that the primordial and fundamental status of our existential worth is not a justification for private interests, because our very commitment to law itself places the we above the I. It is only because we revere the universality of the moral law that we must first hold as absolutely precious the sanctity of what it means to be who we are. This does not mean that the individual outranks the community, so that a private, personal interest, even as lofty as the concern for one's own life, in any way outranks our duty to protect our institutional meaning. The noble ranking of "who we are" establishes the basis of meaning, not the mere continuance of life. If this were not the case, sacrifice would not be noble, it would be improper; daring would not be admirable but forbidden; and "life lived well" would always have to yield to "life lived long." This would be the end of philosophy as well as the end of the hegemony of reason itself.

Thus, strictly and formally, there can *be* no genuine conflict between existential and moral principles. Rather, both the absolute moral judgment, which alone gives imperatives directing action, and the existential understanding that grounds moral judgment and hence cannot conflict with it presuppose the ultimate worth of how we exist because of who we are. Yet both do present certain instincts and sensitivities that can and often do conflict. Respect for the lives and decency of others, which must follow from our moral consciousness, may conflict with the feelings we have for who we are, and the principles about who we are themselves ground all moral judgment. We would not be human were such conflicts *in sentiment* not to occur, nor would we be worthy of our calling as members of the species were such conflicts not the cause of the deepest anguish and frustration. In no instance is this anguish deeper than in war, but it is also the case that nothing other than war can so profoundly ennoble us by the stark yet radiant realization of this truth. For who we are matters, in part, only because truth matters, and war reveals this more brilliantly than any other mode of existence.

To sum up briefly: the we-they principle is *existential.* This means it tells us about the meaning of our existence; it illumines who and what we are, not what we ought to do. It is a priori. This means it must be thought prior to any actual commitment or belonging. It is a *ranking* principle. This means that it tells us how to rank our values: specifically, to rank the worth of the meaning of our existence, though not the length of it, above the worth of any other judgment whatsoever. It is *fundamental.* This means that the principle is not derived from any other principle, so that the existential analysis is presupposed by all other analyses. The we-they principle is, then, ontologically first.

THE ORDER OF BELONGING

The we-they principle is an a priori rule concerning the existential meaning of how human beings belong to each other. But people belong in various ways and with varying hierarchies, and so the question inevitably arises, Is there any *rational order* to how we think of these institutions? Or are we left with a purely arbitrary phenomenon completely devoid of principle, with some people identifying with one group or organization, while others find greater meaning in quite other institutions? At first glance it seems that the identification with an institution is completely subjective and that the ranking of any order is purely a matter of opinion. For it is obvious that people do indeed differ in their evaluations as to which groups are more important to them. Some identify with their families, others with their country, still others with their religion or political party. There seems to be no way to determine which institution deserves our highest allegiance, given the vast differences among people's personal interests.

Nevertheless, it is possible to determine a hierarchy that is nonsubjective and nonarbitrary, based on the analysis of what these various institutions mean. It is not suggested by this ranking what *ought* to be done in every case, although there is often a correspondence between one's moral obligation and one's loyalty to a group. Nor is it suggested that this ranking corresponds to what is the case. In the present analysis, the ranking is purely an existential one; that is, the hierarchy is determined on the basis of meaning. The institution that provides the greater source of meaningfulness is ranked above the institutions that provide less. There are countless possible groups or institutions with which we identify ourselves and find a sense of belonging, a source of understanding who we are, from family and local community to nation, race, religion, and even humanity itself. Not all institutions are the grounds of war, of course; one does not go to war for the sake of a chess club or a drinking fraternity. But among those groups that have historically provoked the fierce loyalty sufficient to cause men to fight for it, there are some that are more noble than others. In this argument, then, we are seeking to rank the ways of belonging in terms of historical institutions that provide us with the existential understanding of the we-self.

When we think about who we are and seek to identify those groups or institutions that give us meaning, there seem to be two different kinds of identifications: those with which we were born and cannot change and those which seem to be the result of choice or selection. Although I was born an American, it is not impossible for me to expatriate; although my native tongue is English, I can decide to learn another language and forgo ever speaking my mother tongue again. I can choose political parties at will and change my allegiance to them. But I cannot change the color of my skin or the gender of my birth—at least without spectacular surgery. And although it is possible to reject my culture and my heritage for another, it is far more difficult and rare to do this than it is to change one's political allegiance. Thus, there is, at least prima facie, a distinction between those groups that are chosen or selected, and those that are inherited or innate. This distinction itself is, of course, somewhat relative; it is impossible for me to alter my racial characteristics, extremely difficult though not impossible to change my culture, fairly easy to change my beliefs, and perhaps too easy to change my political inclinations. Nevertheless, a rough kind of distinction can be made between what might be called the *inherited* belonging and the opted, or *political*, belonging. In the first group can be included such institutions as one's family, one's national or racial identity, and one's religious community; in the second group are included such units as one's political party, one's government, and one's state. One's country seems to straddle both divisions. As listed, these groups constitute a simple but natural hierarchy in the following manner:

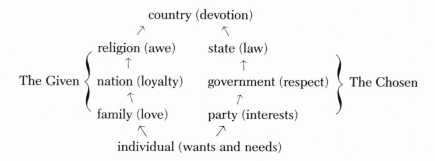

This order is purely existential; it is not meant to imply a moral hierarchy. As presented, the ranking suggests that the higher institutions usually, though not inevitably, demand greater allegiance than the lower ones, especially in the political series in the right column. On the whole, the entire series in the left-hand column outranks that in the right-hand column. Furthermore, according to this diagram, a government outranks a party, and a state outranks a government. In the right-hand column (the political order) there is a natural development of allegiance, whereas in the left-hand column the development is not meant to be inevitable. The hierarchy represented here is often repudiated by individuals or institutions for various reasons, of course, but there is, I think, a certain coherence to this structure of allegiance that helps explain, though it cannot prescribe, how human beings rank their allegiance to institutions to which they belong. Each of these seven institutions has been defended and expanded by war; adherence to them is often a cause of war; for each of them men are willing on occasion to sacrifice their lives. What each means, and how they develop from each other, then, is an important question.

The task of the present section is to inquire into what it means to be in each of these categories. What does it mean to belong to a party, a government, or a state? What does it mean to belong to a family, a nation, or a religion? To what extent do both the inherited and the political categories overlap and conjoin the institution of a country? And why? One purpose for the examination of such an existential hierarchy is to spot and identify what it means to deviate from it. For example, when someone allows his political interest to outrank his national or even state interests, how do we think about such things? For the sake of the natural development of the argument, I shall begin by considering the political institutions, starting from the bottom and working up.

Party.   I identify "party" with political interests. Whenever a man seeks to *do* something, whenever he seeks to bring about *change* so as to establish an order to the community that satisfies his interests, he finds he can best accomplish his ends by joining up with those who share similar ideas. Insofar as these interests are met with resistance, that is, when others have differing or conflicting interests, there is a natural tendency among human beings to associate with others for the sake of persuasion. In modern times, this association is with the political party.

There have been political organizations similar to the modern party from the very beginning of human history. In ancient Greece one can read of the democrats, for example, plotting the overthrow of the Thirty and prosecuting Socrates for his allegiance to those who believed in a return to aristocratic rule. There have always been factions, cliques, cabals, and alliances in every court or government known to humankind. But modern political parties apparently began with the Whigs and Tories following the Restoration of the Stuart monarchy after the Commonwealth in England. With the rise of Parliament as an autonomous power and with it the rise of acceptable divergence of political opinion, it was possible for there to be disagreement without the fear or threat of treason. During the reign of the Tudors, anyone organizing political influences to bring down the government would have been branded a traitor; after the Restoration it soon became quite acceptable for one political party to seek to throw out the ruling party; and this was not only seen as not treasonous, it was perceived as a healthy and natural political phenomenon. Since then, the notion of a political party has come to mean an acceptable way of organizing support for one's political preference for how one should rule the country. Parties, then, have come to mean organizations founded on certain moral or practical principles that seek legally to take control of the institution that actually controls the nation, the government. Even parties committed to violent takeover, like the Nazi party in Germany in the 1930s or the Marxist parties in other times and places, are nevertheless seen primarily as legitimate organizations that want to run the government according to their lights. Even the Marxists and Nazis wanted to come to power by legitimate means if they could. Their commitment to violence was only in the last resort, if legal means could not bring them the government.

How we think about parties, therefore, is revealing in terms of the hierarchy of our belonging. Commitment to a party is usually seen as secondary to the nation or even government. There are some parties, of course, dedicated to changing the constitutional structure of government, but even they see the party as distinct from the government. Usually, parties seek to win control of a government whose constitutional character is seen as more sacred than the principles that dominate the political party's own ideology. Thus, a Whig may hate a Tory, and a Republican may hate a Democrat, but the Whig would love England and the Republican would love America even when governed by their foes.

At the outbreak of World War I, for example, the French Socialists, although they had ardently supported antiwar policies and strongly resisted the government, found that when France was in danger they could not resist the government's request for their services in the war against Germany. Some of these patriots had, as politicians, supported the notion of a world government and, as Socialists, were deeply opposed to the conservatives. Although they saw their support as for the country and not the government per se, they realized they could not serve the one without serving the other. This strikes us as revealing but understandable. Inevitably, we find the reluctant support of partisans more sacrificial and appealing than that of the enthusiasts, for it reveals the high significance of one's commitment. Political disputes about policy could not deter their love of France.

We think quite otherwise about those who reverse the order. When an Austrian Nazi works against the overthrow of the republic, or when a Polish Communist sacrifices the autonomy of Poland on the basis of an international party, the feeling is less of admiration than of wonder. We do not doubt the sincerity of the political beliefs, nor do we base our judgment solely on the rightness or wrongness of these policies; we simply feel that a man who has sacrificed his country for the sake of a party has misplaced his affections. We feel this way because of the inherent hierarchy of what might be called the order of belonging. To be a Democrat or a Republican is to be an American with a particular view about how the country should be governed, and although the political passions may run high, the one is seen as being in service of the other. The Democrat thinks his party should govern America just because America matters. Thus, a party member who sacrifices the country for the sake of the party has confused the order of his allegiance. It is to confuse ends with means. It is to confuse the servant with the master.

But there is a further reason for this ranking. Although the founders of a party may have lofty notions of their political organization and men may join for the noblest of reasons, the parties are seen as the working place for the daily, often gritty, and sometimes dirty business of political affairs. It is considered proper to slug out the petty and contentious disputes of political power on the party level, so that by the time it comes before the structures of the nation the bitterness can be left on the lower level. This is true even of a particular man. He may rise to power in the back rooms and cloakrooms of petty politics, but when he reaches national office, he must at least assume a dignity beyond that of his partisan origins. Even when this dignity is only *assumed,* the difference is important. We just think about party in a different way than we think about the government or nation.

To some extent, the idea of a one-party government collapses the distinction, and this is usually to be regretted. But even in one-party systems like the former Soviet Union or Nazi Germany, the official distinction between party and government is maintained. Again, the reason is that the way we think about the two institutions is so fundamentally different that it is beneficial to retain the distinction even if only formally. One's allegiance is almost always greater toward the higher end of the list.

Government. In the modern world, parties exist in order to control the government. But the government can fall without the state falling. In parliamentary democracies, one speaks of the government falling when the ruling party has lost its support from the people. This does not mean that the nation or even the state has collapsed. Those who actually control the machinery of power are the government. A party, or a coalition of parties, may control the government, and the government controls the state. The term "government" has two meanings that are often used indiscriminately, though the two meanings should be kept distinct. The first refers to those in power, as when we speak of "the present government" (in America this sense is often designated "administration": we do not speak, as the British do, of the fall of the Bush government but of the Bush administration). The second meaning to the term refers to the structure or constitutional framework that determines the manner in which a people may be ruled. In this sense, when we speak of the government of the United States, we do not mean the administration in the White House but the constitutional system of power and rights that persists through the lives of various administrations. Nevertheless, the government is never identified with the state. For one thing, the term "government" obviously refers to those who govern, whereas the state seems to include those governed as well.

Since, in most modern states, those who possess power in the various governments are identified in terms of their party membership, it might be thought that the allegiance to party is the basis of one's allegiance to the government, but this is not true. Men who do not share the beliefs or policies of a party in power nevertheless may respect and honor the government just because it has been entrusted with the rule and defense of the state and nation. In part, of course, this respect may simply be grounded in prudence, knowing that if one resists the rule of the party in power one will be targeted by the greater authority of law. But the honor we bestow on ruling governments even when they are of the opposition party is not merely based on fear, it is also grounded on a reverence for legitimacy. A man may be furious in outrage with the policies of the ruling government but may have sufficient respect for the notion of law that he will honor the statutes, even if with reluctance. And this, it seems, is the most important point distinguishing party from government: the one has interests; the other, law. Although there may be parties that support deeply moral convictions and the laws in existence may frustrate these ideas, the laws demand respect independent of their moral ground. This is not to say that no matter how wicked or unjust it is, a law must be obeyed, for that is an exaggerated position. But it is to say that, once passed, a bill that has been resisted now becomes law, and as law demands a respect not deserved by mere interests, even if those interests are worthy and noble.

If parties seek to control the government, it is the role of the government to control the state. Because the government has the authority of law behind it, the nature of our allegiance to it is different. Although we may greatly prefer the policies of our party that is not in power, we respect the law passed by the party in possession of the government just because of our own lawlikeness. We belong to a party because of what we approve; we belong to a government because of respect.

State. The system of laws that binds us together as ruled and ruler is known as the state. The state is essentially a legal institution, and whatever respect it has, or even affection, is due to our understanding of the necessity of law. I may eschew political parties and may be indifferent to government, but the state is both my protector and the source of possible punishment. To reject the idea of a state is to prefer a purely natural or animal existence. If the party represents my interests and the government represents power, then the state represents law. I have allegiance to the state just because I respect the need, authority, and beauty of a world of law. To be sure, there is a coldness, an almost unfeeling and inhuman quality, to our understanding of a state, for it is all rules and regulations, not warm and emotional people. But it is just because this rigorous and formal structure can be appealed to as a fair and even tribunal that it has a kind of allegiance that neither the party nor the government can evoke. The state not only represents the power and authority of law, but it also embodies the rights and protections of the citizens, even against the ruling powers. It is the state that protects me from wanton police, unconstitutional policies, and from criminals that share my homeland. I may have affection for the state, and high admiration, or may be distrustful of it, or even fearful. But unless it is deeply corrupt and evil to the core, it demands my respect. However, the state as such does not represent me as a member of a people with a history and tradition; this is reserved for the nation. Like the government, the state may fail; but the nation remains.

The Family. The natural progress from the party, through the government, to the state should focus now on the nation; but before we turn to that ranking institution, it is necessary first to consider the family, and this for two reasons. In the first place, a nation is often seen as the family writ large; and in the second, without families there would be no nation. The family is, simply, the most original and basic of all natural institutions, stemming from the phenomena of mating and birth and the seemingly natural affections that develop from such unions. But our understanding of the family cannot be grounded solely or even essentially in such biological genealogy; human history and literature go far beyond the native significance of procreation and offspring.

Few characters in all literature emerge with quite the same significance as the young, heroic girl who dies for her brother and whose name provides the title of ·Sophocles' noblest work, *Antigone.* Not only is this drama a masterpiece of incalculable skill and beauty, the heroine herself stands as both a portal and citadel of our understanding of the heroic and noble: a portal, for her role is so early among the created fictions of the artist; a citadel because few, if any, works of literary genius can equal this creation. Yet, she confounds simplistic analysis and ready categorization. Who is this girl? Why does Sophocles go to such magnificent lengths to present her to us as he does? Why is she, in many ways, a better representative of the tragic hero than even her hapless father?

It may perhaps be more insightful if we attempt to answer these questions by asking another one, more obliquely. Who is Polynieces? The answer is obvious: he is Antigone's brother. In saying this, we suggest that she is far more readily identifiable than he: everyone knows who Antigone is; she gives reference to her brother; her brother is known only because of her. Perhaps this is even true of her uncle. One can imagine such a question in a high school identification exam: Who is Creon? Why, Antigone's uncle, of course. The answer is scored correct. Yet, in a deeper sense, if we return to our original question and ask, Who is Antigone? the answer is that she is Polyniece's sister. She is *also* Creon's niece, as well as his loyal subject, but it is being Polynieces' sister that really matters. And if we want to know what it *means* to be a sister, there is no story in all of human literature that better expresses it. For Antigone, torn between two loyal ties, that to her brother and that to her king and uncle, sacrifices herself in a way that confounds all nonspiritual understanding. There is nothing more fundamental than our understanding of her when, faced with death and the stigma of national disloyalty, she cannot forget who she is, her brother's sister. She does not choose this gruesome anguish; she accepts it. She seeks no glory, as did her father, though she will not share whatever meaning there is with her sister, Ismene, who, we must admit, is less of a sister. But, in showing us, through her courage, what it means to be a sister, Antigone has uncovered much more. For we accept Antigone's loyalty and her affection as being *true.* Most of us might feel that we might fail if so tested, reasons might be given that she ought to have acted otherwise, some may see her merely as a victim of outdated kingly power, but she nevertheless *reveals* as few characters in fiction ever have. Hegel claims that the love of a sister for a brother is the purest of all human loves, but I doubt if he would have known that had it not been for *Antigone.* What her character does is to reveal the ultimate claim on our loyalties: first the family and then the nation. For she does honor them both, but her courage establishes the hierarchy. Creon realizes afterward that his own rule as king depends precisely on the kind of loyalty that Antigone manifests; there can be no state, no kingdom, no nation unless there is first that love of what is our own, that sharing of blood and flesh that is a family. Men have gone to war to defend their families, but without families there would have been no spirit of war at all.

It should be noted that Antigone does not choose her loyalty to her brother *rather* than her loyalty to Creon as king, for to be loyal to the one is to be loyal to the other. Her choice simply reveals the hierarchy: to be loyal to a nation is merely an extension of familial piety. We cannot be true to ourselves unless we are true to those who are of our own; disloyalty to what is one's own is disloyalty to oneself. The tragedy reveals this. Antigone shows us what it means to *belong* at all. Hers is the passion of all inherited belonging, and from this familial origin develops the larger family, the nation.

Nation. As World War I ground to a dreary and bitter end, Woodrow Wilson became the champion of an ever more popular notion, that only Frenchmen should be allowed to govern France; Germans, Germany; and Poles, Poland. This was known as the principle of self-determination. The idea was that no ethnic, racial, or national group should govern over people not of that group. Wilson, of course, was not the first person to have held such a view, but since he represented the leader among the victorious powers, and since the United States at that time enjoyed remarkably high prestige among nations for its moral vision, the idea was often identified as Wilsonian. And what could make more sense? Surely this doctrine represents one of the most enlightened policies to come out of the early twentieth century. On the basis of this doctrine, vast plans were laid for the redistribution of thousands of people. Turkish farmers who had lived all their lives on Greek soil were to be transferred to Turkey to replace Greek farmers whose families had lived on Turkish soil for generations. The inconvenience, perhaps even personal tragedy, of a few farmers could not be measured against the more universal good: Greek should rule Greek; Turk, Turk.

It occurred to almost no one at the time that this doctrine was in fact an extension of a rather profound racism and that in less than twenty years Adolf Hitler would use the principle to establish his claim for the Sudetenland of Czechoslovakia. Suppose I argue that America should be ruled by Americans. What would this mean? That our president must be a native Indian? That only white, Anglo-Saxons should be president? That anyone with an American citizenship should be able to rule? But the Greek farmer in Turkey had Turkish citizenship; the German living in the Sudetenland had Czech citizenship. What is a nation, anyway?

The term "nation" originally was used to designate a racial or at least cultural identity. When Shylock complains in *The Merchant of Venice* that his enemy hates "his Nation," he means the Jewish race. Today, in the United States when we speak of the Navajo nation, we do not mean a politically autonomous state, we mean the people who are racially identified as the Navajo people. The etymology of the term strongly emphasizes this meaning; its root is the Latin *natus,* birth. One's nationality refers to one's racial or ethnic origins. In America we speak of our country being made of various nationalities: English, German, Irish, Jewish, African. But, of course, these terms are puzzling. Who is a German? Someone who comes from Germany? But a Jew could come from Germany. And where does a Jew come from? Until 1949 it would have been absurd to say that a Jew came from Israel. And Africa is a continent, not a nation. There is as much difference between the Northeast African Egyptians and the Zulus as there is between a Scot and an Italian. What, then, did Wilson mean when he suggested that nations should be governed by their own nationality?

Whatever it means, nationality is surely an important notion; why else should Wilson argue that only on its basis should future governments be founded? If it is admittedly a somewhat ephemeral notion, it is nonetheless a profound one, for in its absence all rule is merely conquest. Should an Austrian government rule in Italy, that is imperialism; but if Italian Fascists control the government of Rome, that is legitimate rule. As counterintuitive as this may seem at first, surely there is something to it. Frenchmen should rule France. Why? When the Austrians ruled Italy, there was an Austrian *state,* but there was also an Italian *nation.* What this means is that although the Italians recognized and even respected the rulers from Austria, they did not see them as belonging to what was their own. A nation, therefore, is an ethnic, racial, and cultural unit that establishes *ownness* in a way that no mere political structure can. But racial and ethnic characteristics are inherited, they follow from the same genetic roots as one's language and one's facial characteristics. The modern notion of nation, however, is not restricted solely to such genetic factors. In America, especially, there seems to be a profound realization that Japanese Americans, African Americans, and Asian Americans are just as profoundly a part of the nation as are European Americans. However, as remarkable as this may be, it is unusual, though not completely unique. In Europe, it is easy to spot a German as German, an Italian as Italian, a Frenchman as French. Indians who live in England consider themselves British, and Algerians living in France consider themselves French, but these accommodations do not detract from the basic image we have of the peoples who constitute the nation-states of Europe.

Because of the dreadful cruelty in Nazi Germany, it is difficult for the modern thinker to have much respect for racism, but it cannot be denied that racial and ethnic differences do make up an essential part of what we mean by a nation. In the seventeenth and eighteenth centuries there developed the notion of the nation-state, which, reaching its peak in the nineteenth century, seemed to combine both the political and the ethnic resources of a people. The hyphen is important, for it both conjoins and disjoins: it recognizes the political unity of a powerful state and at the same time accepts the notion of a racial and ethnic peculiarity. A nation-state was seen as a natural combination of the two aspects of human needs for living together: the rulers shared a common heritage with those who were ruled.

Is it possible to support one's nation and not one's state? Of course, as was certainly the case of the Italian patriots who hated their own government and state, the ruling Austrians. Which is higher? Again, it is obvious from this example that the nation has a higher claim to our ownness than the merely political state. But there can be no doubt that the incipient racial and ethnic determination of nations also contains an abuse. Perhaps in this sense, it is improper to define the United States as a nation-state.

In 1861, of course, the difference between state and nation became critical. A Virginian, prior to the outbreak of the war, may have said he loved his state, Virginia, and his nation, the United States; but after the secession he shifted his love of the nation to the Confederacy. But "state" does not merely mean the individual states; there is also the state of the United States, as when we talk of the secretary of state. The language seems remarkably reversed here, for the average Southerner surely thought more highly of his individual state, such as Virginia, than he did of his nation, either the United States or the Confederacy. Indeed, by calling the new nation a confederacy, the Southerner emphasized the autonomy of the state, which is also why Lincoln continually talked of the Union. But no Southerner ever thought of his particular state as a *nation,* though that emphasis put on such things as race, ethnicity, and language would make one think that Virginia ought really to be a nation. The nineteenth-century Italian loved his nation but hated his state, the nineteenth-century Southerner hated his nation but loved his state. To which, then, belongs the greater appeal to loyalty and devotion? Perhaps, indeed, we need a different term altogether.

Religion. The placement of this institution in the present scheme is complicated by attitudinal shifts toward what religious belief means. In contemporary, Western society one's religion is a matter of personal choice and is often arbitrary and idle. One changes religions as easily as hairstyles, and no one seems to mind too terribly much what one believes. In this sense, the term "religion" properly belongs in the right-hand column of my scheme: it is merely an extension of one's political party. In other times and places, however, one's religion is far more fundamental and native to one's existence. There were partially theocratic eras in history, and there are partially theocratic states today, for example, Israel, Iran, and Nepal. But even in the officially nontheistic democratic and socialistic states of the present age in which religion, when permitted, is a purely private matter with no governmental or even cultural support, it often functions as an institution of traditionalist sentiment and memory. People go to church not only because of a theological belief but because of the pressure of social and familial values. Even a nonpracticing Christian, for example, feels a strong sense of nostalgia around Christmas and may be loath to rear his children deprived of such ceremonial advantage. In this sense, religion is not an opted ideology, accepted on rational principles, but an inherited disposition for communal worship. It seems important then to distinguish the private experience of religious feeling and the necessarily more public sense of religious community. As a *causus belli,* of course, religion must be seen as a communal, perhaps even inherited, institution. Nevertheless, these two different senses of religion are not completely separated. What one privately believes often is the result of cultural education, and it might be argued that the nature of religious experience per se is that of a *given* rather than an *achieved* wisdom.

There are, then, two questions that should be addressed in this context: (1) What is the existential nature of the religious experience? And (2) what is it about such existential awareness that demands communal participation? The first question may be posed in the vernacular by asking simply, if somewhat crudely, "What is it like being a believer?" The second question can be asked, "Why do people build cathedrals?" Perhaps if we understand these two questions we can ask the third, "Why do people go to war over religious disputes?"

At first glance, religious belief seems to be an acceptance of a metaphysical order that ultimately supports everything that happens but is often in contradiction with our ordinary understanding of these events. Because the believer often seems to espouse truths that are in blatant defiance of our own eyes, religious belief is sometimes considered irrational or fanatical. Certainly it seems the prerogative of the believer to disdain ordinary reasons for the interpretation of one's purpose and goal in life, whatever these may be. Thus, religion seems the antithesis of rationality. On the other hand, the poverty of light that natural science and pure logic throw on the deep questions of life and meaning cannot be denied. There is a sterility and emptiness in the purely scientific vision of human affairs, and the complete nonbeliever may seem sufficiently lacking in spiritual understanding to make a cautious thinker hesitate to opt simply for the picture of a purely naturalistic human being.

It is, I think, improper and distracting to view religion as a metaphysical picture of the world, as if it were an ideology. In the first place, most believers are simply not metaphysicians and have little inclination to be so; in the second place, such a picture misses the most essential characteristic of religious understanding, which is existential gratitude. In order to isolate this notion and bring it to the forefront of consciousness, a variation on Descartes's *Second Meditation* may be helpful.

According to Descartes, I think, therefore I am; but I need not be, so I am contingent. But at this point in the argument we can deviate from Descartes a bit. Being contingent means I need not be, so my actual existence presents me with a question. Why do I exist rather than not? I may not know any specific purpose or reason for my existence, but I do know that my existence is not demanded by reason or logical necessity. Hence my existence is gratuitous. It is precisely because I *need not be* that, reflecting on this, I am grateful. (*Not* "I *feel* grateful" but simply "I *am* grateful.") Gratitude is not merely a feeling that may or may not occur; it is an essential characteristic of my existential meaning. To be is to be given existence, since otherwise I would be a necessary being. Existential gratitude is the awareness that my existence is not necessary and that therefore it must be given. But what is given in this special sense is bestowed, and that just means that I *matter*. Bestowals are granted because of the worth of the one to whom something is bestowed. To say that there is no reason for my existence is to say that the meaning of existence cannot be thought about, and that is to limit the uses of reason to the mere determination of unimportant questions, which itself is an attitude of misology.

Self-reflection entails the concept of gratitude and reverence toward the ineffable mystery of being, and this is nothing else than spirituality, which, when concretized, becomes religion. The ordinary person may express his own spirituality and religiosity by asserting something as vague as the "belief that there is something more to the world than nature, something more to myself than body, and something more to existence than what is temporal and transient," but this formulation adopts the metaphysical language of entities, establishing a claim as to the kinds of things that exist. They may indeed be *believed*, but the ground of such belief is not the entities themselves but an awareness of the meaning of existence. To be aware of the *meaningfulness* of my contingency is to be thankful that I exist at all. To concretize this thankfulness, to give it an object, may be the demand of a certain prejudice to our experience, but in any event it leads to the establishment of theological entities: God, a created world, and some form of communication between the finite and the infinite, which is usually some form of historically grounded incident, establishing a system of doctrines and rituals — in short, a religion.

To be is to be grateful. This, in short, is the religious reality. Thus, to be irreligious or atheistic is to be thankless, to consider one's existing a mere fortuity of events; it is to be fortunate rather than grateful. It is from this primordial modality of gratitude that all other existential ways of being religious stem, such as being fearful, worshipful, forgiven, guilty, punitive, immortal, and prayerful.

But even if this analysis is correct, why does religion offer one a sense of *belonging?* Why is it not the case that one is simply grateful for being an individual, rather than grateful for being a member of a privileged few, a chosen race, or a baptized congregation? Part of the reason for this is the obvious one that I am not only grateful *that* I exist but *how* I exist. Thus, I am not only grateful to be at all but also grateful to be a son of these parents, a child of this nation, a citizen of this state. But that is not the only reason. The gratitude for existence that is religious is also worshipful, which means that to be grateful seeks a way of manifesting its gratitude in rites, rituals, and traditions. These rites are revered as *inherited* for the same reason that existence itself is seen as bestowed, seen as a gift: because they are *given.* To revere one's origins as sacred is to honor one's religious tradition, and both of these stem from an honoring of one's bestowed existence. This is a part of what it means to be a contingent being.

What, then, is the nature of this belonging? What is the kind of institution that is ranked and revered? Individual religions, which are nothing but structures giving institutional concretization to the primordial existentiality, can be grotesque and unfair, morally dubious and racist, bewildering and culturally retardant. Though they need not be, of course. But, if they are believed, they are a formidable source of commitment and loyalty. Usually these religious institutions are not in opposition to one's national and ethnic heritage. Thus, to fight for America or England or Germany is to fight for Christian lands as Christian soldiers; to fight for Iran is to fight for salvation and Islam, to defend Israel is to defend Judaism. It is a happy fortune when one can conjoin one's nation with one's religion. Occasionally, however, there is opposition, as a Jew must confront in Germany or as any theist whatsoever must confront a Communist atheism. In this case, however, the believer usually hopes to conjoin his two heritages: he hopes his countrymen will convert to the true faith or at least will tolerate it. But in any event, since the postterrestrial lives of the believers and the believers' children may be at stake, the loyalty a religion demands from a believer is fierce and uncompromising.

This ground of existential gratitude distinguishes religion from metaphysical ideologies like Marxism and fascism. Too often ideologies and religions are compared as equally compelling to the mind and spirit of humankind. There is no doubt that ideologies do indeed attract many people, particularly those which appeal to some kind of inevitability. Any system attracts by appealing to powers and forces beyond one's personal influence; in this sense they are similar to religion. God and the revolution both go on even if you and I fail in our efforts or even die. And both religion and revolutionary ideology often win from zealots a truly remarkable loyalty that is often as frightening as it is inspiring. But a religion is much more than a mere system of beliefs; it is founded on a profound sense of gratitude, and unlike ideological systems, it promotes mystery, wonder, and awe. The very persuasion of an ideological system is its scientific basis, the notion of explainability and coherence. But religion rejoices in the ineffable, the unexplained, the exotic. As gracious, religion is above and beyond; as secular, the ideological system is finite, workable, and ultimately civil, if not civilized. Thus, as a focus of human allegiance and belonging, which is what we are concerned with here, the ideological system is best when it is political and chosen. The distinction is critical: in the system, we choose it; in religion, we are chosen.

Nevertheless, in the history of human allegiance, religion, as great as it is as a source of identification, remains second to the idea of one's country. In spite of the divine element in religion, one's association with one's country usually, though not always, has a more immediate appeal.

Country. More than any of the other terms, this one suggests a *place.* And yet, the purely geographical characteristic of one's country seems an unlikely source for such depth of commitment. If a political party represents one's interests, a government one's power, a state one's respect for law, a nation one's sense of belonging to a people, why should a mere *place* rank higher than the other four? Surely *where* one lives is not as important as *how* one lives; surely the accidents of place cannot determine the worth of man as much as his commitment and virtue. Indeed, of all the natural predicates assigned to the human person, where he is seems the least significant.

Yet, it cannot be denied that should one ask a young warrior why he fights, his answer would almost always be, not for a party or a government or a state or even a nation, but simply his country. Does he fight for a place? It is not just any place, of course; it is his *home.* And because the term "country" refers to one's home, it makes it the most sacred of all institutions. Home is not only place in the sense of geographical location; rather it is place in the sense of where one belongs. Home is the source of value, the origin of language, the hearth from which all the household gods spring, the location necessary to be oneself. In Italian, the term is *patria,* my country as a father. The land is my father, as in German *Vaterland.* My country is the land of my fathers, the place and hence the origin of my familial existence, of the looks I inherit, the accent in my voice, the lap from which I drink the milk of culture, judgment, and care. This is the stuff of patriotism, it is the love of what is my own. It ranks higher than state or nation because as a place it locates and gives identity; as place it is actual and sensible, not abstract or formal; as a place it can be both beautiful and familiar. One's homeland can be loved, not merely respected or admired. Thus, it is "my country" for which I die and not my nation or state or government or party.

What is so remarkable about this order of belonging is that the hierarchy is completely opposite to that of the moral rank. Surely what is important to me as a moral agent comprises my concerns for actions and policies. Surely the least important thing governing my conduct is where I come from. If I am concerned about the welfare of my fellow citizens, and if I strongly believe in certain policies that I feel will bring about these benefits, there is no institution that will put me in direct control of these activities more quickly than a political party. If I feel deeply about the poor, I may want to join a socialist party; if I care about the freedom guaranteed by the constitution that governs my lawmakers, I may want to join a conservative party. A party is an institution of change and action, a country is merely something to love. Or consider the difference between a state and a nation. Morally, the state outranks the nation, for states are legal structures, built and founded for the sake of justice and domestic success. A nation, on the other hand, is an inheritance, something akin to one's race, an institution over which I have little or no control. I can vote and persuade others to change the structure of a state if I feel there is injustice in it, but nothing I can do can alter the peculiar character of the blond Teutons or the dark-skinned Italians or the propensity of the Scottish to red hair or the innate love of pleasure in the French. I was not asked to be born an American, so why does it matter? I am asked to belong to a party, and since I am free to join or not, the party is ethically more important than the nation, the state more important than the country. Or so the moralist must see it. But the existential philosopher must turn these priorities around.

The political and cultural orders of belonging are not completely separate, of course. A party may favor a religion; a nation cannot be separated from its art. And of course, there are conflicts, some of them awesome and wonderful. One's family ties can conflict with one's political beliefs; a commitment to the law may upset a religious duty; loyalty to one institution may clash with an equally powerful loyalty to another. This discussion is not meant to provide any moral lessons about how to resolve these enormous problems. But the ranking of the political order is especially meant to show the importance of how we think about such senses of belonging. When two brothers faced each other on opposing sides of a battle during the Civil War, the dreadful conflict between loyalties was existentially huge: Which matters more? The family or the country? There *is* a hierarchy, but it is not a moral one. It can help us understand who we are, but it cannot help us decide what we ought to do.

It cannot be denied that this order has, as presented, a seemingly arbitrary stopping place. Why stop at a country? Surely there is an even higher and nobler institution that outranks our country, and that is the human race as such. To no more lofty group, family, nation, or culture can I belong than the family of man, the species humankind, this wonderful global village whose mutual sharings of differing tongues and customs provides the richest resource of identification and belonging possible. And does not the recognition of the even greater family of nations outclass all provincial concerns that are petty by comparison? If I must belong, why not to the race of humankind? Why this country, that government, these political parties? Is it possible to identify one's we-self with the greatest we of all, namely, all of us?

Surely there is significance to the idea of "we, the world"; and if the notion of country must outrank a mere government, cannot the notion of the world outrank any given country? And if this is true, does not all the uniqueness of this language, that tradition, and "our" culture collapse? Why must I defend the uniqueness of my country, when the higher allegiance is to mankind as such? Must identity to a particular we always be so provincial and narrow?

There is, of course, an identity with the species and with the planet. Any one who has any education or culture at all knows of the great contributions that each nation and people give to the whole. I can thrill to the poetry of a Shakespeare and a Goethe, the music of a Bach, a Verdi, and a Bizet, the novels of a Dostoyevsky and a Mann, the philosophers of Greece, Germany, and America. And in recognizing a monumental gratitude to all these nations, do I not despise the narrowness of nationalism, the partisan bigotry of impoverished chauvinism? There are times when I rejoice not at being merely an American but also a human. But rather than forfeit the legitimacy of the order of belonging, my joy in being human actually enhances it. For, quite simply, I am human because I am American; Shakespeare is a world-class genius because he wrote in English and shared an English culture. We do and should identify with the world, but only as members of other institutional orders. Just as Antigone is a great figure in Greek culture because she was first Polynieces' sister, so too Beethoven is a world musician because his was a German soul with a German spirit. If, by this protest, one asks, Can I "identify" with a world without these "lesser" units? the answer is no. With whom are you identifying? Other humans, to be sure, but they are Japanese humans, African humans, and Spanish humans. There are no humans that do not speak a native tongue, that do not have particular sex and skin color and tradition. We belong to this earth, and in some senses, surely the moral ones, our belonging to the world outranks our petty concern. But our existential meaning is no less real because of this. I may indeed have a profound affection for the world, my home, but I still identify with what is my own within the world. Why is this the case?

In the development of the hierarchy of belonging, it may at first seem that the ranking is determined by quantity. Just as there are more people in a state than in a government, and more people in a nation than in a family, so it might be thought that the world's population being greater than my country, the former should outrank the latter. But the hierarchy is qualitative, not quantitative. A worldwide political party may have more members than I have countrymen but I still rank the homeland above the party. Furthermore, as was seen in the analysis of the concept of the we-they distinction, the we must always be understood in terms of opposition to a they. The world as such cannot be the foundation of our belonging for there would be none that were excluded and, hence, genuinely none included.

Yet in spite of this, there can be no doubt that we do have affection for the human race, and not a mere abstract awareness of our class inclusion in the concept. When I read of African sufferers or Chinese victims or see the lonely anguish of Indonesian orphans, I am not merely abstractly aware of my duty to them, but unless I am remarkably insensitive, I also sense a profound identification with their misery. Their suffering becomes a part of me; I sense the strong pull of what might be called the brotherhood of man. In such cases I am indifferent to their racial and cultural differences. (Although I may wonder, Why don't we do something about them? and not even reflect that I have already used terms like "we" and "them" to announce my distress.) But the sentiment I manifest toward them is just different from that I feel toward those with whom I share cultural similarities. Toward them it is essentially a profound moral feeling, which, as Kant points out, is what it means to have universality. This is just to say that I owe all human beings the full respect of the moral law just because they are human, but what I owe to those who are my own, however that is understood, is other than the universal moral law. To argue that I "belong" to the world in the same way that I belong to a nation or a people is to confuse the moral with the existential understanding.

Each of the seven institutions in this order of belonging has been the source of wars. The Montagues and the Capulets fought because of their families; the Reds and the Whites in the Russian Civil Wars, because of their political beliefs; countless times religious wars were fought on the plains of Europe. Governments clashed in the American Civil War; nations, in the Boer war; states, in the various wars of independence. But most often, wars are fought between *countries,* although this strict philosophical distinction is usually not followed in political discourse where we speak of "nations" and not countries at war. This must be understood as a mere verbal difference, however. Political language does not always distinguish between the "country" and the "nation" as I have above. Thus, when historians and politicians speak of "nations at war," we should translate this as "countries at war" if we are to adhere to the strict existential meanings in our sketch of the order of belonging.

This sketch is now complete. It is now fitting to consider just why it is that we go to war and what institutions provide us with the opportunity. It is the conviction of this analysis, of course, that the reason any war is carried out is the triumph of the *we* over the *they;* in order to see how this is the case, we must revisit the classical and traditional accounts of war.

TRADITIONAL ACCOUNTS OF WAR

Patriotism. From our reading of early history we find that war is usually carried out between two opposing countries or nations. Athenians fight against Spartans, Greeks against Persians, Romans against the Carthaginians, France against Germany, America against Japan. Even wars that do not seem immediately to fit this notion, such as civil wars, are readily reinterpreted along these nationalistic lines: the South thought of itself as an independent nation in seeking to secede from the Union. In wars of independence, the point is to establish a new nation. So patriotism, the love of one's country or nation, seems to be the most obvious cause of modern war.

In the preceding section we analyzed the order of belonging and discovered some powerful reasons patriotism, as the militant affection for one's homeland, sponsors warfare. One's homeland is the source of so many values, including tradition, language, history, and ethnic identity, that it is quite easy to see why, when these values are threatened, one would take up arms to defend them. But it is not only these inherited and precious values that cause one to fight for one country and against another.

Sometimes nations fight for a particular moral cause, as when the Allies joined together to defeat the Axis powers in 1940. Hitler was simply so morally repugnant that he had to be stopped, and the existence of armed nations alone provided the enemies of National Socialism the opportunity to stop the moral contagion. In that case, a nation became a vessel for the overriding morality; we fought against the Nazis because they were bad, and for the Allies because they were, in this case, representing the good. This is a pleasant fortuity when the existential value and the moral value coincide, but the fact that it does not always do so does not stop us from appreciating the nation as a power that can accomplish good things. Such examples, however, should not distract the reader from the central principle that men fight for meaning rather than for justice. This provides one reason to appeal to patriotism as a reason for war: because people believe their nation can achieve what is good.

Nations therefore provide us with such precious ideas as our culture, our values, and our history. Sometimes they even provide us with the means for achieving justice. It is therefore easy to see why some people fight to defend their country. It does not follow from this that if we were to remove patriotism from the hearts of men, all wars would cease; far less does it follow that the idea of patriotism should be removed. Is it, then, the major cause for war? What must be realized is that patriotism is merely a concrete form of the universal principle of we-they. The Armenian poet Stephen Orbelian over seven hundred years ago wrote, "I love my country because it is mine." This simple but profound remark reveals much of what has been discussed in this chapter. The point is, patriotism as such is insufficient to explain the remarkable energy, value, and life that men expend on behalf of their country. It is not the noun alone that counts; it is the adjective: not their *country* but *their* country. A country or a nation is perhaps the most important concretization of the we-they principle, and the notion of the love for one's country cannot be reduced to simplistic and naïve views about the value of place and tradition. To be sure, place and tradition are important, but they themselves take their significance from the more primordial notion of we-they.

Religion. Second only to patriotism is the view that religious beliefs and the differences that exist between these beliefs are the genuine causes of war. There are some wars that are self-consciously identified as religious wars, such as the Crusades or Philip II's Catholic wars against emerging European Protestantism. In addition, there are countless nationalistic wars with religious overtones, such as that launched when Catholic Spain invaded Protestant England. Even today the spectacle of religious wars haunts the mind with the maniacal violence of Iraq and Yugoslavia, as well as the grim, constant horror of Northern Ireland. Usually this characterization is met with considerable sadness, as if battling over differences of religion were somehow unworthy of the human species. To the modern, atheistic mind, to fight for religion seems a kind of madness.

Religion, of course, for those who believe, may be even more important than one's country. The believer, after all, is convinced that his own salvation depends on his creed; if his children are not allowed to practice their religion, they will be damned. Such beliefs obviously, if sincere, are powerful motivating forces, and there is little argument one can bring against an ardent believer to persuade him to lay down his arms merely for the sake of a happier or longer life here on earth if the promise of a future paradise sustains him. Again, however, as in the case of patriotism, the existential underpinning lies in the reality of the we-they distinction. We the believers, they the infidel. Religion is a profound and sustaining force in the lives of those who believe, and of course, depending on what they believe, it may be absolutely necessary for them to defend with their lives what is holy and sacred. Scientific or secular atheism may disdain this total commitment, but it has no primary appeal to the hearts of men. Nor is greater illumination achieved by appealing to ignorance, as if all believers were hugely naïve and grossly unenlightened and all atheists were simply wiser than lesser men. It is, of course, a characteristic of our species to believe that our own preferences are superior, that our own view of the world is clearer than that of others. In seeking to understand the phenomenon of war, however, it is essential to see that such deeply rooted beliefs can provide a whole people with remarkable devotion to a cause and that once this cause is seen as "theirs," the commitment to it may exceed all possible energies necessary to stop it. Given that none of us is infinitely wise, the differences between religions cannot be swept away by indifference. In our contemporary, American consciousness religions are often thought of as quaint pleasantries like the color of one's hair or eyes. But religions are not so ineffectual or trivial. Coexistence of religions may be accomplished on a temporary level, but if the essence of one religion conflicts with that of another, appeals to tolerance will not ease the struggle. Some religions forbid a man to have more than one wife; others urge polygamy. These are irreconcilable notions, and if both of these religions also require that the state be governed by its religious precepts, then a peaceful accommodation is just impossible. The zeal of the patriot is eclipsed by the more fiery support of a true believer, for he has God on his side. And if, in the struggle of the we over the they, God belongs to the we, the contest can only be violent.

Ideology. The modern indifference to religion has, however, been replaced with another form of commitment to belief that is not less treacherous and violent, though, as we have seen, the believers in an inevitable world ideology differ from religious believers in two important ways: (1) the notion of postterrestrial happiness and (2) the triumph of gratitude as a mode of existence. If religion was the motivating factor in past wars, the more recent experience of two great iron armies clanging and crashing into each other on Europe's eastern front in the struggle for the ascendancy of atheistic ideology is no less dreadful than the most virulent of religious wars. Atheistic Naziism struggled with atheistic communism on the broad and bloody plains of eastern Europe with a savagery rarely matched in previous conflicts. We should, however, think of ideology as a separate category from religion, for the former has no doctrine of postterrestrial existence and the latter appeals to an authority beyond human criticism. In fact, however, both provide similar kinds of foundation for the notion of the we over the they. In both religion and ideology, the we is identified with a metaphysical order that far outstrips the petty concerns with daily life. One finds oneself absorbed in the wider and more important dimensions of the worldview offered by either religion or ideology, and this belief provides the ground for all meaning whatsoever. Essential to both ideology and religion is the notion of sacrifice, in which an individual who otherwise would be lost in the flood of futility offered to the unbeliever is redeemed by participation in the greater reality. At first glance one might be led to believe that religions and ideologies militate against the existential we by their deprecation of the individual and their emphasis on communal subservience to the distant and the unattainable goal, but this is not true. Few who have not experienced it can attest to the tremendous satisfaction that comes from identifying with a world movement, however ephemeral, and from celebrating their absorption into the existential we of these metaphysical orders. Indeed, such an experience is all the more heady and exciting because the we is identified with a world inevitability, a kind of necessity that intimidates the mere contingencies of everyday life. In this sense, the we is what must be, whereas the they is what must be overcome. For this reason, one's identification with an ideology like communism, fascism, or Naziism in the time of war is formidable and resistant to mere appeals to humanity.

Thus, ideology provides, as does religion, a concrete institution equal to that of the nation as a cause of wars but lacking the great historical tradition of patriotic wars. However, history seems to suggest that although ideologies may supplant religions in some way, the lure of the nation often cancels out an ideological host. During the early (pre-Bonaparte) days of the French revolutionary army, the urgency of the troops that led to such immediate and high success was due, in part, to the soldiers' belief that they were spreading republican ideals. However, what began as revolutionary expanse quickly became identified not with the principles of the Revolution but the hegemony of France. When the early armies of the newly found Soviet Union began their attacks on their neighbors, the expectation was that the workers of the world would abandon their allegiance to their respective countries and join with the Bolsheviks. This, of course, did not happen, and indeed the Red Army became the Russian army. For some reason, armies gathered to defend and widen a religion or ideology usually become national armies. Philip II's armies were originally seen as warriors for the Catholic religion in Europe, but they, too, soon became simply armies of Spanish conquest. Thus, even though there have been genuine religious and ideological wars, many adopt the guise of nationalistic wars in spite of themselves. It may well be the case that this is due, in part, to the nature of military organization and tradition. After all, Hitler did not invade democracy or Christianity; he invaded Poland and France. The Allies may well have thought they were defending such noble beliefs, but in fact they fought as Englishmen, Americans, and Frenchmen. Within civil wars, of course, the role of religion or ideology may play a larger role than in wars between states, but the instinct for nationhood is very strong. The fact that ideological wars usually turn into national disputes cannot be avoided in our quest to understand the true nature of the we-they principle as it reveals itself in war.

Social Causes. The modern mind seems to have some difficulty accepting the appeals of vast metaphysical systems and prefers to give causal accounts more in keeping with the scientific spirit of the age. For this reason some theorists in recent times have appealed to causes that are within the realm of sociological explanation or even psychological determination. Thus, two fairly modern accounts of war are economic and political.

Many people seem to think there is something inherently wrong with the unequal distribution of wealth. These egalitarians are quick to point out that what has been designated the nationalistic, the religious, and the ideological causes of war are in effect really grounded in economics. The poor, achieving nothing but desperation for their labors, seek to find redress and, when the system fails, turn to violence. By this account, the truly profound reason for Germany's invasion of France in World War I was the fact that Germany needed economic expansion and recognition; the South was led to secede from the Union for economic reasons; the Vietnam War was fought for the oil and mineral wealth of the area. There is a certain bent of mind that insists on seeing every political and social upheaval as grounded in the greed of the rich and the desperation of the poor. There may, of course, be some contributing factor of this kind in many wars. It is even possible to admit that one could feel a sense of identification with the social economic groups: *we*, the poor, against *them*, the rich. There can be no doubt that sometimes the economic conditions lead people to identify with more conventional institutions of war; an impoverished and starving multitude may well identify with a religion or an ideology that seeks to give meaning to their struggle and perhaps even arm them against a common enemy. However, economic rebellion is usually a matter within a state, not a matter between states. And of course, herein lies a problem with description. In the present turmoil in Northern Ireland, we have poor, Catholic Irish fighting against wealthy, Protestant Englishmen. Are they fighting because they are poor or Irish or Catholic? If among the poor are some Marxist social revolutionaries, which is the guiding principle of explanation? It seems clear that if one is speaking of *war* and not merely of social unrest or even internal revolutions, one must focus on those institutions that are grounded in a profound sense of identification with what is our own (the we). It is much easier to understand the identification with "we, the Irish," rather than "we, the poor." Poverty has nothing in its meaning to provide unity; its concern is almost exclusively relief. I do not *want* to be poor, hence it is difficult for me to feel much unity with other poor people, except for ordinary sympathy. But I may *want* to be American and hence can find much greater sense of unity with fellow Americans. I may join up with the fellow impoverished, but the union is purely utilitarian and fleeting; it would last only as long as the mutual poverty lasted. The hope would be, however, that being American would outlast the struggle; hence there is more reason to identify with my country than with my economic class. It is more significant to feel "we Americans" than "we, the poor."

Another contemporary explanation is to be found in the phenomenon of political leadership. War, some say, is caused by a particularly gifted political leader being able to mesmerize an entire nation into a blind obedience to his will. This view seems to take a phenomenon like Hitler or Amin as paradigmatic of all causes of war. There is no doubt that such men do indeed cause unusual havoc and violence, but to account for war, even the wars these men provoke, as due solely to their power to lead and the public's capacity to be duped is to misunderstand the event. No one denies that people can be beguiled, that nations can often be misled into enterprises far beyond their ability to achieve, that men often reach for goals that are not wise, prudent, or good. No one denies that the impulse for self-preservation and the existential value of one's own worth, valid and important as they are in themselves, can go astray. Yielding to the demagoguery of men like Hitler, Amin, Hussein, and Napoleon often leads otherwise noble peoples into senseless military adventurism. But these events do not happen in existential vacuums. One must ask, What is appealed to by such men? How do the Hitlers and Husseins of the world work their poison on us? There must be something about us other than mere ignorance or even stupidity that makes us follow them.

A primitive may believe that the rains are caused by the angry gods and wonder what fault he has committed when a storm rages. Such erroneous belief does not invalidate the principle of cause and effect, however. We say merely that the principle, though still valid, has been misapplied or misused. So, when an evil but gifted political leader inspires a nation to a disastrous war, the fault is not with the we-they principle as such but with its use. The political accounts of war are important, obviously, but they are not sufficiently profound to provide us with an understanding of ourselves, so necessary if war is to be thinkable.

What I have tried to suggest in these remarks is simply that the traditional accounts of war all presuppose the more fundamental and existential principle of thinking about our meaningfulness in terms of we against them, the we-they principle. Whether it be the classical theories of nationalism and religion or the more contemporary views of ideology, economics, and politics, in order to make sense of war we must recognize that the sustaining institution must provide an adequate vehicle for the appreciation and articulation of the we-they principle. In this sense, the nation or the country remains the most impressive and, in the last analysis, the paradigm of all the others. There are excellent reasons one should love one's country, even if the conduct of that country is not always the most enviable. It may be logically possible to imagine a person living a meaningful life without a country, but it is not existentially possible to do so.

Up to this point the main task has been simply to isolate the we-they principle and show its function in the phenomenon of war. It is necessary now, however, to bring this principle briefly into contact with other human concerns to show its relevance and the nature of its application. An unwary reader may think that this principle provides an all-encompassing license, that all wars and all warlike activities are mysteriously justified by an appeal to this existential principle. Since existential meaning must come before ethical consideration, it may seem that this validates all war and all conduct within wars. This is not so. Nevertheless, it is perhaps advisable to consider in detail how our thinking includes the principle in terms of our normal evaluations.

Recent history has provided us with an uncommonly rare opportunity to examine this question. The Second World War was fought with unusual savagery and over remarkably clear moral issues. But even the stark moral clarity of that war does not eclipse the deep agony of thought when confronting the values involved. There were assuredly many German soldiers who were decent, moral, honest, and upright human beings, unafraid of self-examination and willing to hold themselves responsible for what they did. Normally it is no great intellectual matter to justify the conduct of men on both sides of a conflict. Every man has an obligation to defend his country, and although there may have been an immoral act by some leader at the beginning of a conflict, individual soldiers are not thought of as immoral as they carry out their sanguinary duties on either side of the line. However, in the case of Hitlerian Germany, the nature of the assault was so morally dubious that one wonders how to think about what it meant to be a German soldier. Yet few, I think, would argue that all German soldiers were morally wrong in fighting for their country. What does this mean? Let us imagine a morally good man who is a German soldier in 1940. It seems to me most people would not hesitate to make the following judgments about him:

1. We would not judge his fighting in the army as immoral.
2. We *might* expect him to resist through legal means the Nazi government, though to expect him to participate in an actual overthrow would assume extraordinary moral courage and great wisdom.
3. However, we would never expect him to plot against his own fellow combatants. Indeed, were he to inform his enemy (the Allies) of his

own troop movements, we would think of him as a traitor to his own country.

4. We would hold him responsible for any war crimes, violation of international law, and "crimes against humanity."

I consider these four judgments to represent a fairly common attitude; they are presented here not as gospel, but merely as the kind of judgments that are often made. If we assume they are correct, what must be presupposed in order for them to be true? In the case of (1), we find an interesting isolation of values. On the one hand, Nazi Germany can be seen as the embodiment of evil, and its overthrow at that time must have been the supreme social good. Yet we do not judge the German soldier as immoral. Why? Because we distinguish between the evaluation of the regime and the private obligation; we consider one's duty to one's country *regardless of the essential position* of that country to be unassailable. This all-important distinction does not depend on a naïveté on the part of the soldier and a paternalistic superiority on the part of the government. In other words, the *reason* we make this distinction is not that governments are more intelligent or even more responsible or that soldiers or citizens are simply not in a position to know the facts. Even if the soldier in question were a brilliant moralist at a university, the distinction would still be made. We hold the obligation to defend one's country to be independent of the ethical concerns of that country's policy. Does this mean that regardless of how wicked a regime is, a citizen or soldier must defend it? If this means to defend one's country as one's own, the answer is yes. If it means to defend a specific regime, the answer is no. The soldier in question would of course be in a position to resist the regime before the outbreak of war; indeed, even after the war began he could still work for the overthrow of the government. However, since in the time of war it is difficult to upset a government in power without damaging the country itself, the assessment varies considerably. But the principle is simple: as long as the integrity of the country itself is not threatened, there is no moral restraint on seeking to overthrow a dubious government. The generals who tried to assassinate Hitler in 1944 did so not because they were inspired by transnational morality but because they believed Hitler was destroying *Germany.*

This brings us to a consideration of (2). It is considered a rather extraordinary act to confront one's own government and at the same time hold dear the sacredness of one's own country. Thus, although we might hope that the citizens of a country would on their own overthrow a bad ruler, we reserve the title of extraordinarily brave for someone actually willing to carry this out during the time of war. This means another distinction: we do not hold a man morally responsible for not overthrowing a Hitler during the time of war, simply because that demands extraordinary virtues and one cannot universalize the extraordinary. But we certainly do hope and wish that such people act accordingly. However, even under the most terrible of regimes (and Hitler's certainly qualifies), it is never expected that one will turn against his *country,* only his government.

The analysis of the principles assumed to make (3) valid provides an even deeper truth. For a soldier to plot against his own government during a time of war might be acceptable if the regime was evil enough; but for a soldier to plot against his own regiment would simply be treachery, and the man would be thought of as a traitor. Even though the regiment may well be fighting to establish a regime that is ethically dubious, it is morally required for an individual not to violate his own loyalty. In this sense, loyalty to what is one's own is independent of the ethical evaluation of the institution to which one is loyal. Only in one way can sense be made of this judgment, only if the existential worth provided by the we-they principle is not eclipsed by the ethical censure against the regime.

But how is this kind of thinking *possible?* Surely there is much to be said for the counterargument that no one should ever support institutions or men who are bringing about morally dubious rules. Why do we insist that even Nazi Germans should have the right of loyalty to what is their own? The answer to this is the key to the entire analysis: because one must assert one's own meaningfulness before one can be held morally responsible at all. *Who* I am is more important than what I do. The reason we believe that individual soldiers should not be censured for their loyalty to Germany is quite simple: loyalty to what is theirs has worth independent of the good or bad they might do as members of that society. Ordinarily, one seeks justice *within* a state, but one seeks meaning *by means* of a state. This accounts for the difference between how we feel about a police officer (working within the state) and how we feel about a soldier (working on behalf of one's own state and against the threat of an alien state).

These are the prima facie presuppositions that must be made in order to account for the first three judgments we make about the soldier who defends a morally dubious state. The philosophical underpinnings of these prima facie judgments must await further development in the next chapters. However, one final judgment must now be considered before we proceed. In the Second World War, which we are using as an example, there were some members of both the German and Japanese military governments who were later found guilty of war crimes and crimes against humanity. What is the nature of this judgment? How is it possible to assert (4) after having argued for (3)?

When a *soldier* commits war crimes, what we mean is simply this: that certain violent acts against peoples were carried out that had no military necessity about them or that served in no way to establish the integrity of one's own country. This, then, is not inconsistent with (3) or even with the principle of we-they. The judgment is made that the man guilty of war crimes was using his position within the military establishment in order to carry out acts that either were for his own private gratification or were sponsored by an allegiance that had nothing to do with one's loyalty or devotion to one's country and the integrity of one's existential worth. There really is no great moral problem here; it is the same kind of judgment we would make against any soldier in any army who violated the rules of warfare. The only problem might be when the state that should have carried out the censure, that is, the offender's own state, either no longer exists or has ceased to function as an arbiter of justice. There is, of course, the tricky legal question: By what right does one state, using its own legal apparatus, prosecute a citizen of another state? This, however, though fascinating, is essentially a moral or even legal question and in no way directly affects the tension between existential worth and the moral law. What is important here is merely to show that the argument supporting the fundamental character of existential worth does not collapse when questions of this sort are raised.

However, war crimes are not the same as crimes against humanity. By this latter term is meant acts or deeds perpetrated on behalf of a morally dubious policy or government. The anti-Semitic laws of the Third Reich are often thought of as constituting crimes against humanity. This notion is admittedly a troublesome one regardless of which way it is thought of. In the first place, we are reluctant to allow any independent sovereign state complete and total license, as if there were no tribunal save those established within a state; on the other hand, we are similarly distressed at the idea that one state can tell another what to do. If one were to argue that the concept of crimes against humanity means that there are moral restrictions to which any state ought minimally to adhere, there would surely be few objections. This is merely to understand what we think a state ought to be. But to argue that the notion contradicts the hierarchy of the we-they over the ethical principles is to misunderstand. The crimes against humanity are crimes against humanity within states. The we-they principle does not state that any and every act on behalf of one's integrity is permitted; it merely states that no moral decision or ethical judgment can contradict the primary right for meaning. Nor does the notion of crimes against humanity in any way argue for a world state or even a world tribunal. It simply shows us that one of the ways in which we think is to recognize that moral restraints are not only imposed on individuals within states but also on the governments themselves. The primacy of the right to meaningfulness (the we-they principle) is in no way undermined by this realization.

Even so, the ideas of both war crimes and crimes against humanity have very deep and troublesome roots. The thorny question *Quid jure?* haunts all who would raise these uneasy moral interrogations.

I have raised four points about how most people seem to think with regard to the German soldier; I have done so in order to isolate the significance of the we-they principle as an underlying rule that establishes a fundamental value beyond which no local or provincial concern may make an appeal. There is something deeply puzzling about these judgments, and something remarkably exciting about them as well. It is perhaps one of the most remarkable kinds of evaluations that we make; just because I am fighting against an enemy, I do not need to deny him his own personal integrity. Even though I may hate the Nazi regime, I do not therefore deny to the individual German soldier his right to fight for his country. I submit that no sense can be made of this judgment without some kind of existential hierarchy, in which a man's right to fight for and establish his own meaning cannot be forfeit merely by the fact that his nation is morally in the wrong.

However, this discussion of the German soldier during World War II has raised another question that perhaps should be treated here. When we speak of a German soldier, we do not necessarily mean a Nazi soldier. When we think of the term "Nazi," we also mean someone who is a fervent racist, committed to the superiority of the Aryan race and to the subhumanity of other races, particularly the Jewish race. Racism has often been an unfortunate cancer on the body politic, and the American official attitude toward blacks before the Emancipation Proclamation and the Thirteenth Amendment was no less unsavory than the official attitude of Hitler's Reich. But the Nazis were so spectacular in their execution of this policy that Hitler goes down in history as one of the archfiends of all time, and his wickedness is often equated with his racism. Thus, for those who have come after 1945, the chief social evil, second only to the fear of a nuclear holocaust, is racist bigotry. In all liberal conscience, the remnants of this scourge must be eradicated before we can rest without guilt. But herein lies the itch. Is not racism merely another form of the we over the they? And does not the monumental ugliness of racism reflect back on the we-they principle in a negative way? If the we-they principle supports racism, then by a kind of moral *modus tollens* do we not forfeit all respect for the principle as well? This question deserves serious reflection.

Racism. Today racism is officially presented as simple bigotry. The schools, television, films, and popular novels constantly depict their criminals and villains as racial bigots; on the other hand, teams that share many racial players, heroes who have racially different friends, and lovers with racially different mates are celebrated as enlightened and morally superior. As forms of moral instruction, such rhetoric is probably helpful in establishing a deep Western commitment to overthrow the tendencies of the past that resulted in such inhumane horrors as the Jewish Holocaust and the black slave trade. America, at least, is officially committed to a nonracist state, and most Americans are rightfully proud of the interracial success of the postwar spiritual ethos. We have grown used to blacks, Hispanics, Jews, and American Indians leading our sports teams to victory, being elected to the top posts of government, becoming independent millionaires, and winning the hearts of the young in the entertainment fields. No one denies that there are still many individual racial bigots and large pockets of resentment, but the official and ever-widening support is far more tolerant. The public ethos judges these remaining prejudicial racists as simply un-American. The sad shock of the Los Angeles riots in 1992 offended us all just because both victims and perpetrators were our own fellow citizens.

But to view all racial judgment as merely bigotry is nevertheless misleading and for the philosopher is seriously distracting. Not all forms of racial pride or ethnic awareness are wicked, nor are they necessarily forms of bigotry. There is no reason to reject all forms of racial consciousness. It is philosophically imperative to try to straighten out how we think about this elusive notion.

It is important first to recognize that the notion is indeed elusive. Why do we ever think of a racist action as immoral? We may think we have a perfectly clear idea of this, but reflection often shows the clarity to be illusory. Consider the following imaginary situation. Suppose one reads an account in the newspaper of a young man who was beaten by three youths in the street so savagely he was hospitalized. Few would deny that this is a dreadful and immoral act. Suppose, however, the next edition of the papers informs us that the police are entertaining three *reasons* for the assault: (1) that the assault was gang-related, (2) that the victim was a rapist who had just defiled the sister of the three brothers who had beaten him up in revenge, and (3) that the victim was a Jew beaten up by neo-Nazis. Is our response the same in all three cases? To be sure, in all three cases the crime is condemned as unwarranted and immoral. But the further judgments one makes are radically different. If the crime was gang-related, this may well have been just another battle in the long war between street gangs. Had the victim been accompanied by four of his gang, the three perpetrators may have been the victims, and this simply alters the way we think. We do not condone the beating, but we understand the causes. In the second case, some may even go so far as to condone the act. If the victim of the beating had indeed raped the sister of the three brothers who attacked him, some might think that justice was done. Even those who would not think so, the majority probably, would nevertheless consider the attack as mitigated and, if not justified, at least excused. Our sympathy for the victim is much less than in the first case, and we would expect the punishment of the offenders to be less than in the first case. But when we turn to the third case, where the victim is a Jew and the perpetrators are neo-Nazis, the feeling is quite different altogether. Here we feel not only that an assault has been committed but also that *another kind* of offense, an offense against a way of thinking, has been committed. We feel that the offenders deserve far more punishment than those who were the perpetrators in the first and second cases. But *why* do we feel this?

If Nazi thugs beat up a Jewish boy, we condemn the action. Why? Because the Jewish boy was innocent? But we would condemn *any* group who beat up *any* innocent victim. Is our reaction that one ought not to beat up any innocent victim? If that is the response, then there is nothing racial about our condemnation at all. Suppose, however, someone objects that racism is to be condemned because it is the *cause* of actions that are immoral. But we would do this in nonracial cases as well. Love could be the cause of one person beating up another. Do we condemn love? Anger, jealousy, greed, revenge, frustration, punishment, warning, and so forth are all candidates for the *cause* of a wrongdoing. But we do not universally indict all such causes. Racism seems to be a special kind of thing, a special kind of cause.

Why do we condemn racism? If the answer is, because racism leads to immoral acts like beatings and murder, then we have misjudged the situation, for it is the immorality of such things as beatings and murder that deserve the censure; we do not have to add that they were caused by racism. Suppose a man was a racist but did nothing improper because of it. Would we consider him evil?

One reason why, in the three cases suggested above, the mind reacts more vehemently in the racial case is that it brings back memories of two great social evils, slavery and the Holocaust. The story of a Jewish boy being beaten by Nazi thugs immediately reminds us of Germany in the thirties and forties, and the natural repulsion against those dismal times may simply add a certain amount of depression to our ordinary moral judgment that innocent people do not deserve to be beaten up. But if *this* is what we mean by our rejection of racism, then it is little more than nostalgia and hardly worth our consideration.

The point must be emphasized. If, in the three speculative accounts of why the boy was beaten, the moral judgment is the same, then racism is indicted merely as a possible cause of immoral acts and should thus be ranked along with other psychologically disturbing conditions as jealousy, envy, love, and confusion. But racism does not seem to be equated with these other possible candidates of motivation to crime.

The social reformer may glibly assume that if racial categories were eliminated, such unfortunate occurrences as the youth being beaten might also be eliminated and that hence race *ought* to be unimportant. But the Jewish boy who is the victim of a beating or the black who is the victim of discrimination does not feel that race is unimportant; indeed, they feel their own race *is* important. The peculiar syllogism is that such social evils are caused by racial differences, and hence racial distinctions should be eliminated. But surely the opposite is the case. The victims do not want their race to be unimportant, they want their race to matter. Racial awareness is not the same as racial bigotry. There is a tendency to eliminate those things that matter *just because they matter,* which is pernicious. If racial distinctions cause difficulty, pretend they do not exist. If religion causes strife, insist religions do not matter. If gender difference causes stress, de-emphasize the contrast of the sexes. If diversities in wealth seem unequal, redistribute it so that all are economically common. The inference is that if nothing matters, no one will care; and peace, or at least bovine equanimity, will be the reward. Such nihilistic cures vex the soul more than the ills they were meant to alleviate. It turns Plato's reasoning in *The Republic* on its head: Glaucon protests that in the so-called pig-state there are no luxuries, and so we introduce the warrior class and the noble virtues; but now we see luxury as the cause of war, and by eradicating it we get rid of the warriors. There is surely both nonsense and danger in trying to solve social problems by achieved indifference. Paradoxically, it is only when racial differences are revered as important, perhaps even solemnly important, that bigotry can be overcome.

And this, I think, is surely why we feel that the third reason for the beating is so repugnant. Not because race is unimportant and the thugs mistakenly thought it was important, but, quite to the contrary, because race *is* important and the thugs have trivialized it by making it the object of their contempt.

The three possible reasons for the beating of the youth therefore manifest an important dimension of our thinking. If the reason is that of race, what is added to our dismay is that something very important has been abused. Not only is a man's life threatened, so is the way in which his life is lived. Racism, therefore, reveals itself as antithetical to racial significance. We consider it an evil not merely because it can be the cause for other morally dubious acts but also because it is, in itself, an abuse of an essential way in which we think about ourselves; hence, it is an offense against meaning. To put this in the context of our present vocabulary, the beating of the youth in itself is a moral wrong, but the racism that inspires it is an *existential* error. A thief who steals another's property may be furious if someone steals from him; he does not comprehend that for him to steal from another is to debase the entire notion of property; so too the vulgar racist who assaults another because of his race is undermining the very notion of his own racial nature. Whenever I abuse another, I undermine the reason that supports the abuse: if it is because of race, I am curiously inconsistent. Racial awareness, and indeed racial importance, must be distinguished from racism, not because racism leads to morally dubious conduct, for that leaves racism as morally neutral, but because racism is the opposite of racial awareness and importance.

The notion of one's own racial nature is an essential part of who one is. It is part of our culture, heritage, and tradition, even and especially in a country like America deeply committed now to achieving racial equality before the law. Good Americans *want* their country to be multiracial; they do not want their country to be raceless or racially nihilistic. What, then, does it mean to be racial (as opposed to racist)?

The Judeo-Christian and Western traditions have for the past several centuries focused ever more penetratingly on those notions that reveal the meaning of existence. Ever since Kant showed that moral obligations stem from the nature of rationality itself, thinkers have sought to show that what constitutes the importance of human beings is more than the mere rectitude of their acts. Kant himself recognized the autonomy of the aesthetic principle, for example, showing that it was not enough merely to be moral in order to be worthwhile. He argued that in addition to the moral law there are also other principles, not utilitarian or useful, that the mind uses in order to complete its understanding of itself. In the nineteenth century, many thinkers followed this transcendental approach and sought out ways of identifying characteristics that were essential for the struggle against nihilism. Nietzsche, for example, exulted in any concept that would allow him to go beyond the purely moral perspective (beyond good and evil). But in his search for what later came to be known as existential notions, he would often appeal to terms like "race" to give his thought a concrete basis. He argues, for example, that the origins of the moral judgments themselves must be seen in notion of a class or race of superior beings. In other words, I uphold a reverence for the moral law only because of who I am, as a member of the elite or superior group. In his *Toward a Genealogy of Morals,* for example, Nietzsche argues quite clearly that the origin or source of promise keeping lies in the elitist notion that such acts as promise breaking are beneath those of the noble class. Thus, it is not that keeping promises makes me worthy; it is rather the other way around: I am first a worthy person, therefore I keep promises. The impact and profundity of this analysis simply cannot be overstressed. The moral law is founded on the existential worth: who I am determines what I ought to do. Although this insight goes far beyond Kant, it is nevertheless prepared by Kant, and it is of capital importance in our understanding not only of Nietzsche himself but of the entire development of the existential consciousness. That race should be used as one of these existential notions is almost inevitable.

In Wagner's great operatic and dramatic masterpiece, *The Ring of the Niebelungs,* one understands the titanic struggle not between equal types but between the lowly dwarfs, the stupid giants, the foolish but wonderful gods, and finally the emerging new race, that of the loving but tragically flawed human beings. "Which race rules beneath the earth?" the Wanderer, Wotan, asks Mime, who responds correctly, "The dwarfs." Which race rules above the earth? The gods. Which race rules on earth? The power-hungry giants. Only the sacrificial loving of a once divine Brünnhilde can resolve the epic struggle among forces characterized not by the goodness of acts but by the racial destinies of the different types. Dwarfs may do good or bad things, but they are still only dwarfs; the gods may do good or bad things, but they remain gods. For Wagner, the dwarfs are simply incapable of love because of their greed for power; the gods can love, but because of their terrible oaths and commitment to what has been promised, they too cannot find in their love any redemption. Only the free beings, sired in divinity but mortally wrenched from their paternity by the very oaths of Fricka can forgive and find redemption. This appeal to the "races" is, in Wagner's art, simply sublime. For Wagner the man, however, the cheap and petty racism of his life must be thrust aside with psychological violence if we are to appreciate his genius. The idea that race is a determinant of the worth of a man thus becomes a noble thought, but like all great ideas, it can be twisted into an ugly and destructive idea by those incapable of sustaining the loftiness of the original insight. Wagner the artist seems to have depleted Wagner the man; that is unfortunate for him but wonderful for us.

This discussion, I think, does much to help us understand that grim phenomenon of the noble German nation yielding to the petty tyranny of a racist like Adolf Hitler. It is supremely ironic and historically poignant that the second half of Hitler's *Mein Kampf* was published in the same year as Heidegger's *Being and Time*, 1927. The Germans, after the Versailles treaty, were treated as simply bad; to be German was to be bad. The Weimar Republic was not a German state, it was a Franco-American-English creation imposed from without, depriving the German people of what was their own. The German people found reasons for supporting the guttersnipe Hitler simply because he offered them something more important than being nice, namely, being themselves. That this was a tragic and perhaps even fatal error in no way lessens its explanative power. Deprive a people of their existential worth and you either destroy them or, if they are resourceful enough, they will destroy you. This is not the place to go into detail about how one must understand the tragic support Germans gave to Hitler, but surely it cannot be explained away by silly psychological descriptions of the Teutonic peoples as overly militaristic lovers of parades, beguiled by pomposity in their leaders.

Racism, if it is to be understood properly, must be seen as a deviant form of something immensely important and profoundly worthwhile. Race (as opposed to racism) is an essential way in which we understand ourselves and hence is an existential characteristic that is fundamental to the constitution of the we-they principle. In seeking to overcome racism, one must not inadvertently overcome the importance and legitimacy of racial awareness and the validity of the we-they principle. What makes racism deviant is not that it results in morally improper acts, but rather that it undermines its own racial significance by abusing the racial pride of another. Thus, rather than provide an argument against the validity of the we-they principle, race supports this all-important principle in the understanding of our own meaning. We should strive, not to become *color-blind,* as if it really were better *not to* see, but color-*appreciative,* rejoicing that we *can* see.

Part Four

THE MEANING

6

The Essence of War

With the help of the nine existential marks, it is possible to describe the phenomenon of war. There are, of course, further predicates that could be applied to war; for any interesting phenomenon, they are almost endless, though some are surely more important than others. It is now our task, however, to seek to *define* rather than merely to describe; and to do this properly, one must identify the 'essence'. Descriptions help us to identify and recognize a concept, but essentialist definitions are meant to help us understand how we *think* about the term. The predicates used to describe can be questionable, of course, and different thinkers may not agree about which predicates should be included; but the question about their appropriateness is simply one of adequacy and aptness. It can be resolved by reference to facts or by disputation of history. But to define, by identifying a particular 'essence', is something that can be argued about in the most serious way. For the choice of an 'essence' reveals the most fundamental way in which we think about a term.

You and I may, for example, agree completely about the description of the term "dance." We may share exactly the same judgments about which phenomena should be called dance and which not. There would be no disagreement about the use of term; at no time would you identify one event as dancing and I disagree. Yet, even though there would be no quarrel about our use of the term, it would not follow that we agree about its essence. You may think that the essence of dance is motion, whereas I may think it rhythm. This dispute would not be resolved by appealing to the phenomenon, since that is assumed. But it is a serious dispute nonetheless, for the difference reveals a fundamental distinction in the way we *think*. By expressing these two definitions of dance, we recognize that we think very differently about what dancing *means*. Although a certain degree of tolerance is required for decent behavior, the dispute is not an arbitrary one; we do not think that the matter is entirely subjective, for I would maintain that those who spot the essence of dance as motion rather than rhythm are missing something important in the appreciation of dance. To be sure, such a dispute may well reveal more about those who maintain the claim, but this does not involve a lack of objectivity to the enterprise. Of course, the list of meaningful candidates to identify the essence of dance is quite limited, and the dispute about the definition would not wantonly open up to absurdist suggestions; the essence of dance could not be color, for example.

The fact that certain phenomena can be approached from differing notions of what their essence is means that any serious attempt to come to grips with a term must weigh and evaluate these various definitions. It is for this reason that the description of war by means of the nine marks is necessary before the present inquiry. We must know how to identify a thing before we can question how to think about what it means.

There are ready suggestions about the essence of war. War, some say, is nothing but power. Others say that war is the result of the inequities of certain economic systems. If these suggestions are taken seriously, they mean that to understand war one must first understand power or economic injustice. But further, if the term "essence" is used correctly, it also means that all of the marks of war must be thought in terms of the essence. This might be possible with the term "power," but not really with the second suggestion. For if men fight wars because of economic injustice, then the essence would be envy or greed or righteousness. To argue, for example, that all (or most) wars are *caused* by greed or a sense of outraged justice is not to say that these notions constitute their essence. In fact, the causes of war, particularly in the political sense, are very often quite distracting from

our understanding of the true essence. How a war begins does not determine the quality or character of the event itself. There are many wars that
have developed far beyond their origins; a simple border dispute may grow
into a desperate struggle to maintain integrity.

In order for a particular candidate to be taken seriously as the essence of
war, it must serve as a source of illumination to all of war's marks and faces.
Power is certainly a better candidate than greed simply because greed does
not further our understanding of such important qualities of war as bravery,
sacrifice, and outrage, for example. Again, the preparation provided by the
existential analyses of the nine marks is here beneficial; we know what it is
we are trying to define. The test of the definition, then, is whether the
essence identified succeeds in illuminating the description. It is important to
realize why we dispute *the* essence. There may be several important
candidates, all of which reveal the meaning of war's many facets, but we do
not find ourselves merely listing a series of essences as we can and have
done in the case of the descriptive marks. For we are after the isolation of a
single principle or idea that is the most important in our understanding of
the event. This is why there can be serious and beneficial *quarrels* over the
single essence of the term.

Nevertheless, it is helpful to consider several suggestions. Although
it is my philosophical persuasion that the fourth suggestion in this list is
probably the most telling and hence *is* the essence, the breadth and profundity of this issue demands that a serious consideration be given to the most
attractive notions. In the following evaluations I have called the various
attempts to identify the essence *suggestions*. I do this because, unlike the
marks of description, they cannot merely be added up. Strictly speaking,
only one of these four should properly be identified as the essence of war.
Nevertheless, I am going to violate this strictness, and having exposed my
preference for the fourth one, I shall make no further argument for its
superiority.

HATRED

Given the prodigious cruelty perpetrated by the sons of Ares, it is not
surprising that many thinkers and religious teachers have taught that the
essence of war is hate. In early 1939, the poet Auden, grieving at the
shadows cast by the looming threat of war, wrote:

In the nightmare of the dark
All the dogs of Europe bark,
And the living nations wait,
Each sequestered in its hate.

And surely Auden was right; there was little else on the horizon at that time
than the steaming cauldron of almost spectacular hatred, which later that
same year broke out into open conflict. When we visit a war zone, we can
see it in the eyes of the men who would be warriors; a blazing fire of near
fanaticism, a passionate frenzy of malice for the enemy. Even when the war
is just, the cause right, the effort noble, those who carry out the dread
business are haters. The officers, the sergeants, the leaders of men look for it
in their troops; they look for those who hate, and reward them as good
soldiers when it is manifest. A recruit is told he must learn to hate. Otherwise pleasant and friendly youngsters learn it quickly. Surely it takes some
special kind of passion to join in a wave assault against entrenched posts,
and hatred is among the few emotions strong enough to make danger a
trifle. Even if, in the last analysis, one would want to deny that hate is the
essence of war, it nevertheless belongs close to the deeper spirit of Mars.

It would in fact be untruthful and hence unphilosophical to deny that
hatred is an important part of war, even if it is not the essence of it. Perhaps,
indeed, in some sense hatred is the essence. And since most decent and
humane thinking seems to indict hatred and opt instead for love, it is crucial
to understand this suggestion fully. For the point is not merely an incidental
one: we do not merely say that among many, if not most, soldiers there is in
fact a personal hatred for the enemy. This we could lament as a mere
misfortune. Rather we are implying by this suggestion that the passion of
hatred is necessary for war, that unless men hated, they would not go to war.
The suggestion also means that if we are to understand war, we must first
understand what it means to hate. What, then, is the meaning of hate? Of
course, we *know* what it means. It is one of the original words in the
language; it has a primary status, like "eat," "see," and "yellow"; it is
nonderivative. Yet, to know what it is does not mean we know how to think
about it, and that is what we need to do in the present context.

Since the term itself is original in our language, perhaps the best approach
is an oblique one. Children use the term readily, and were their grandparents not around to correct them, they would announce to all that they hate
spinach and having to go to bed and the spoiled kid next door. When their
emotions are unguarded, they even say they hate their parents. It is interest-

ing what adults say when this happens. We say that the children do not really mean what they say, that they do not really *hate* their siblings or classical music or taking medicine. Yet this is a curious persuasion. Why do parents simply disbelieve these protestations? Is it because they do not feel the children are capable of such intense feelings as hatred? Surely a child, who lives much closer to his feelings than the more reflective adult, is capable of intensity. It might be wondered if the child is capable of anything else: they are totally happy or totally sad, so if they feel animosity or ill will, it is completely unalloyed. Perhaps, then, Johnny really does hate taking a bath. Furthermore, if we deny children the intensity of hating, why attribute to them the opposite emotion? If they cannot hate, can they, then, love?

Nevertheless, we resist this overly facile declension. Perhaps children are incapable of deep love, but we feel convinced that, except in rare cases, a child does not truly hate when he says he hates something. And we say this, it seems, because we reserve the term for a sustained, self-conscious, and virulent passion; the term seems to entail an unwillingness to forget and a positive commitment against forgiveness. So spectacular is this intensity that we often provide for adults the same kind of dubiety about their feeling; we tend to disbelieve many attestations of hatred. We say someone does not *really* hate those he says he does. It is as if hate, like love, were a rare phenomenon, or as if its occurrences in the world were but pale imitations of the *real* thing. However, it is perhaps unwise to say this of love or hate. Why do we think that Romeo really loved Juliet more than the ordinary man in the street loves his wife? What is the function of the adverb "really" in such judgments? Do we *really* hate? Perhaps it is ubiquitous. Perhaps we hate and love wantonly.

Is it ever possible to hate nobly? Let us imagine a young policeman investigating a cruel rape and murder of a tender young girl. As he gently covers the mutilated body of the lovely child, he experiences a sense of outrage at the injustice of the act, and as he reflects on his sentiments, he expresses a deep and abiding hatred for the perpetrator. Sustained by this white-hot anger, he dedicates himself to the task of bringing the criminal to justice. It may well be that only the intensity of his feeling brings him to the culprit. Would this not be an instance of noble hatred? Ah, but you say this is not hatred. A noble anger, perhaps; or better, a noble outrage. But not hatred. Why do we say this?

We say this, I think, because in our understanding of hatred we usually include a sense of personal diminution, a smallness of spirit, or at least an enslavement by the passion. In hatred we become smaller; our worth becomes less. Hatred is thought of as a kind of spiritual contagion, a disease of the soul. It is unhealthy. The noble outrage of the young policeman does not diminish his stature as a human being. Yet, is this too perhaps not overly facile? If one asked the policeman if he hated the criminal, would he not agree? And is such self-evaluation to be doubted merely because it makes us uncomfortable? If we insist that hatred corrodes the soundness of the spirit, then are we correct in saying the soldier hates the enemy?

Let us look more closely at the hatred of the warrior. Is it not often as noble as the outrage of the policeman who hates the perpetrator of a crime? Surely at times it is justified. A soldier sees his best friend mangled in a torturous death; he sees his homeland violated by enemy bombs, his family decimated by enemy artillery. Can he abhor the bomb and not hate the bomber? Or, if he does *not* hate the men who did this, how are we to judge his affection for what is his own? And this requires a bold confrontation with direct meaning. Let us imagine a young man who witnesses his mother raped and slain, his father emasculated, his dear wife and baby used as playthings for wanton men. Now, let us imagine him as hating and as not hating those who defiled his family. Which do we admire more? Suppose within minutes following this sacrilege he smiles at them and says he forgives them. Do we say, "What an admirable fellow; he has only love within"? Or do we ask, "If he cannot hate, can he really love?"

It is sometimes suggested that we must hate the sin and love the sinner. But is such a separation possible? Is not the sin a sin because it is done by a sinner? We also speak of forgiveness, saying we must forgive those who wrong us. This may be true. But might it not be the case that true (real?) forgiveness can occur only after hatred? If I have never hated my enemy, can I forgive him? Or, to put the insight in another way, when I forgive someone whom I hate, is not that a greater achievement? May it not be that to forgive without first hating is really only to overlook the enormity of the wrong? Why is this notion of hate so elusive?

Perhaps we can gain an insight into hate by contrasting it with its seeming opposite, love. If we take the suggestion above seriously in saying that hate diminishes, then perhaps love increases the worth of one's existence. If hatred makes one small, then love makes one big. However, again, these overly simplistic comparisons appear to conceal more than they reveal. Both love and hate surely are passions of an enormous sort; they are not trivial matters that merely distract us idly. They both captivate and dominate us, often to the point of total eclipse of every other value. In sonnet 57 Shakespeare tells us that as the lover he is in bondage to the beloved:

THE ESSENCE OF WAR

"Being your slave, what should I do but tend / Upon the hours and times of your desire?" These confessions of the poet-lover are deeply disturbing; we do not like to hear them, for they express a truth so frighteningly intimate that we recoil from recognizing them as our own. But love can indeed make us into silent, suffering helots, it can deprive us of our reason, our sense, and even our dignity. On the other hand, consider the nature of Antony's outrage over the brutal slaying of Caesar. His hatred for the assassins stirs him to prodigious acts of revenge. Through his hatred, Antony becomes master; through his love, the poet in the sonnet becomes a slave. By this analysis it seems that hatred is nobler than love. To those who, stymied by this reading, would argue that such uses of the terms are inappropriate, it must be pointed out that too many poets, the true guardians of our language, have expressed these feelings for it to be random. Bondage is indeed a part of love, though admittedly not usually in such radical form; and a sense of masterful purpose often results from hatred. We cannot escape the full significance of these truths merely by redefining the terms "love" and "hate" so as to exclude these variations. We are seeking to understand ourselves as possible haters; we are not trying to dictate definitions that would keep our prejudices intact.

If we accept the notion that sometimes hate is necessary for our integrity, as in the case of the outraged policeman, we have seen that one suggestion is to hate the sin and love the sinner. This must now be considered more deeply. Is it possible to love or hate anything except another person? Can I hate an abstract notion like "sin"? Or is it not the case that only the sinner can be hated, since only he can be loved? Are not hatred and love alike in this, that although we doubtlessly do speak of both hating and loving nonpersons such as institutions, their original meanings are derived from passions toward other human beings? And if we accept this insight as a starting point of inquiry, we must ask why it is that hate and love are properly of people and not things. Is not hate, like love, to be understood existentially? Just as the father gives a gift to the boy because of who he is, the son, so the victim hates his offender not only because of what he has done but because of who he is. Hatred, thus, goes beyond the wrongness of the act and focuses its passion on the ground or source of that action: the enemy's will, or soul.

Why, though, do we do this? Why do we reject not only the wrongness of the act but the existential worth of the perpetrator? It seems we do this for two reasons. In the first place, the passion one can have against an *act,* per se, is limited. Partly because the past is over and gone and what we reject is no longer, and because that is frustrating. But more important, the act is not only limited in duration, it is limited in its nature. We think of an act as an event that happens in time, one that is made articulate in terms of causes and conditions. Acts can be regretted, lamented, removed from our memory, and even feared. But, we cannot really hate an act.

The second reason we focus on the worth of the agent rather than on the effects of his acts is that the agent is the ground or source of the suffering caused by the act. That is, when I look upon the poor outraged child, I lament the suffering she had to endure; but when I think about the one who defiled her, I can hate, precisely because what offends me is the freely chosen malignancy and corruption of the spirit. If I ask, Why did this man rape my daughter? and I am told that he desired her and disregarded her protests to fulfill his lust, I do not find myself rejecting those biological laws that attract men to women; rather, I find myself focusing on the person who is responsible for the outrage. As a human being, the moral agent is responsible for what he has done. But this would merely support the moral judgment that the man is guilty of wrongdoing. Granted that the perpetrator has performed a wicked act, does this not merely justify my censure and establish a basis for my claim "He ought not to have done that"? This is a judgment I would make had the criminal raped any woman, not just my daughter. Does not the fact that she is *mine* matter at all? If my reaction to this outrage is nothing more than my reaction to any man raping any woman, which is what the purely moral censure implies, then the fact that she is mine adds nothing to my indictment. But surely this is nearly impossible. Or, to make the point more directly, if I responded in a purely moral way, would I not be evidencing a dreadful *lack?* And the character of this lack has especially revealing significance: what I would lack would be any realization that who she is and who I am *matters.* Because she, as my daughter, matters to me, and because I, as her loving father, matter to her, when I turn my passion against the perpetrator, it is not merely because of what he has done or merely because of its consequences but, remaining on the same level of explanation, because of who he is. Just as the existence of my daughter *as* my daughter is the source of love and need not first be approved by some good act, so the existence of my enemy as enemy is the source of my hatred. The enemy is hated only partly because of what he has done; true hate reviles not his action but his existence. Granted the crime is necessary to show me who he is, but I understand that the crime would not have occurred unless the man was who he was, my enemy. Hatred is thus the passionate focus on the negative worth of the enemy as enemy; that is, I hate him because of who he is rather than what he has done. Terrible as what he has done is, hatred shifts from that outrage to the ground of it.

Not to hate the sinner who has perpetrated this outrageous and intimate assault against who I am is to exist in such a way as to belittle the importance of who I am. Hatred therefore becomes a manifestation of existential significance. Hatred also focuses on the existential meaning of the enemy: I hate him because of who he is.

Suppose someone says that he loves justice but does not hate injustice, that he loves beauty but does not hate the ugly, that he loves his country but does not hate the enemies of his country who would destroy it if they could. Suppose someone says he loves his innocent and gentle child but does not hate the self-indulgent villain who rapes her. What does the word "love" mean in these cases? Not to hate often seems to entail a terrible belittlement of the outrage that grounds the hate. If I do not hate the rapist of my daughter, am I then unwilling to hold the sacredness of my daughter's integrity as dear to me?

In spite of these observations, the mind is reluctant to hold hatred as something laudable and essential. One reason for hating hate itself seems to be that hatred becomes a debilitating passion; it destroys our ability to function normally in the world; it can, at times, make us do things that are greatly to our disadvantage. These observations are doubtlessly true, but as I have noted above, they are also the same dangers that come from love. Perhaps, then, what we mean is that both love and hate are dangerous in extreme. Many lovers have destroyed their own lives as well as others' by their irrational passion; those who hate passionately also bring about disasters. Perhaps, then, it is not hate that causes us to do inhumane acts but excessive hate. This becomes a mere persuasion for moderation.

Another indictment often brought against hatred is that it makes forgiveness impossible. Pinched by self-eclipsing hatred, I not only cannot forgive the criminal or the enemy, I cannot even forgive myself. Hence a life of hatred is seen as profoundly debilitating and inauthentic. It is also seen as the source of many wicked actions, so it is demeaned as a morally objectionable passion. Some go so far as to indict hatred as a sin in and of itself, but this seems indefensible. If I lie out of fear or steal because of love or attempt suicide out of grief, one does not indict fear, love, or grief; one indicts merely the actions that follow from such emotions. If, because of hatred, I torture another, I am guilty of torture, not of hatred. Suppose I simply hate my enemy; I do not plan his demise or plot his torture or arrange for any misfortune to befall him. I simply hate him. Is this morally wrong? Especially if hatred is an emotion or a passion that I cannot control, one cannot indict such a state as morally wrong. In fact, to say that one *ought not* to hate may be a meaningless utterance, since passions are not voluntary. In the same way that a moralist cannot indict someone simply for loving his best friend's wife, but can if that someone actually does something about it, so can one not censure another simply for hating. I may urge someone to try to stop hating, since it is not good to endure such emotional bondage, but it does not follow that I must indict this person for doing something morally wrong.

It is obvious that hatred makes forgiveness either impossible or very difficult. Because of the divine characteristic usually assigned to genuine forgiveness, one deficiency usually seen in hatred is that it renders this quality of mercy unlikely. However, it seems to me that one can make a strong case for the counterargument. No one can truly forgive unless one forgives a hated enemy. Hatred manifests the depth of feeling toward what was outraged; I hate because what was violated was sacred to me, whether it was the life or happiness of someone I love or a personal quality of my own, such as my honor or reputation. Normally one does not hate another for some slight wrong. Thus, to forgive someone who has been hated is surely a greater achievement of spirit than to forgive one who has not been hated. If the analysis of forgiveness as given above is correct, the act of mercy focuses on the existential worth of the forgiven, and as such it is close to love. But hate also focuses on the existential worth of another. If I forgive someone I have loved before the wrong, then the forgiveness is a consequence of that love: I forgive that someone because I loved him or her. But if I forgive someone I have hated, the isolation of the existential from the moral is not a consequence of a previous state but an establishment of independent existential realization. The forgiveness of a beloved merely tells us about the eclipsing power of love; to forgive a once hated enemy tells us about the depth of character of the forgiver.

Hatred, therefore, is a passion that must be understood existentially rather than morally. By this, at least, is meant that we do not accuse a hater of moral wrongdoing just by hating. We might feel very sad about someone hating, but we cannot hold him responsible for a feeling. However, we seem to believe that it is possible for one to change from hating to nonhating or even to forgiveness, so that hatred cannot merely be a feeling. If I urge my brother to stop hating his enemy, I must assume my brother *can* do something about being or not being a hater. On the other hand, we have seen that a man who does not hate even when his own beloved is ravaged may be seen as deficient in some way. Thus, although hatred is usually seen as an unfortunate state to be in, we do not make the inference that it is better to be unable to hate at all. We say this because, in a profound sense, to be incapable of hating is to be incapable of loving, at least in a deep way. This does not mean that all lovers have indeed hated; it merely means that to be able to love deeply means to hold the existential worth of someone as precious and sacred; and with the sacred, the idea of the sacrilegious and the profane become possible.

Surely one of the more curious qualities of hatred is that it can be enjoyed. We find ourselves actually taking delight in our hate; we are reluctant to give up hating, because this would deprive us of a curious delight we take in imagining our enemy suffering fantastic torments. If we are singularly depraved by this emotion, we may become actually sadistic in our delight. Even if we do not actually do anything, the private entertainment within the mind may be sufficiently ghoulish and cruel that to indulge in such mental sadism may entail the notion of sickness. But here we must pause and ask an important question. Is the mere fact that I can take pleasure in my hatred enough to warrant the indictment that I am mentally ill? I think not. Perhaps when hatred becomes a wanton indulgence of the mind, it may distract us from our normal activity, but again this parallel also can be said of love. Love and hate are both an indulgence of the mind; love and hate can both be the source of private and internal pleasures. Nevertheless, hedonism is an important characteristic of hatred.

Lest we confuse our terms, it is essential to distinguish hatred from either cruelty or sadism. True, many who hate are also cruel and sadistic, but I can hate without being either. Hatred may cause me to be cruel and may even uncover my sadistic tendencies, but to hate, in and of itself, does not necessarily entail cruelty. This is important because often when we indict hatred we confuse the two. It may be the case that hatred is the essence of war, but it cannot be argued that cruelty is the essence. Cruelty and sadism are psychological perversions; they are used to describe the character of a man or his emotional state as the ground of an action. Cruelty and sadism are not passions as hatred is. In the same way, we would say, for example, that love is a passion but the feeling of romantic tenderness is a psychological characteristic that should not be confused with the passion of love itself.

If we disjoin our understanding of hatred from such emotional states as cruelty and sadism, we must also make an effort to distinguish hatred from moral censure. A concern for justice is not the same as revenge. One's instinct to punish the wrongdoer probably should not be identified as a kind of hatred. True justice, of course, cannot see the incarceration of a criminal merely as a means to protect the society or as an opportunity to rehabilitate the felon; it is essential for justice that the wrongdoer be punished. In its most primitive sense, justice is an evening out, an imposition of pain on one who has caused pain in another. If you strike me with a painful blow, it is considered justice for me to strike you an equally painful blow. Remarkably, however, the modern spirit seems to think that this punitive element of justice is unworthy of a civilized person or society. The power of the state is there to protect the citizenry from *further* crime or, through education, to transform the criminal into a noncriminal, but the power of the state is *not* seen as legitimate when it is used to punish the criminal merely for the sake of the punishment. This attitude, I think, in fact removes justice altogether. For if the function of the state with regard to criminals is merely to protect the citizenry from further crimes or to rehabilitate the criminal, this means that the state is indifferent to the profound sense that the wrongdoer deserves to be *punished.* A brief thought experiment will reveal this truth. Consider a man who has committed a felonious act, such as murder or rape. It is possible to imagine that such a man, having committed this act, is simply no longer a threat to society at all. It is possible that such a person is in no need of rehabilitation; he might act as a model citizen for the rest of his life. Not only is such a case imaginable, it is often the case in real life. Many of the murderers now in our prisons are completely safe, their psychologists and counselors know perfectly well that they will never use violence again. Often, murderers were driven to their crime just because their victim was the sole cause of their misery: a hated spouse, a cruel father, a suffocating personality. Nevertheless, even though such persons can be judged completely safe and totally rehabilitated, few would deny that they ought to be punished. The prisoner is in an institution not because he will learn to be a better citizen or because he is unsafe, but simply because he deserves to be there.

There are those, of course, who argue that to insist on punishment is uncivilized, that the state has no right to incarcerate merely for the sake of making someone pay for his crimes. These people argue that one's instinct to make a perpetrator pay for his wrongdoing is merely revenge or hatred. This is a disturbing persuasion, for what it amounts to is that justice, in its most primitive sense, simply is not a virtue. The state should protect us from madmen and should seek to cure the mentally ill by whatever means it can, but the state does not *punish* madmen, it punishes only criminals. To equate the restrictions we place against the dangerously insane with the restrictions against a criminal is to deny the most fundamental way in which we think about the meaning of justice: that the good should be rewarded and the bad punished. Thus, to want to punish the wicked, to want to have the wicked suffer, is not a form of hatred but a form of justice.

By these distinctions, however, we have now made our understanding of hatred somewhat more difficult. We have argued that hatred is not the same thing as cruelty or sadism; we have also said that hatred is not the same thing as a desire that the wicked be punished or even that the wicked suffer because of their crimes. What, then, is hatred? If this passion cannot be understood merely as a desire to see another suffer, since the just man desires that the wicked suffer and the sadist desires that the undeserving suffer, then hatred cannot be understood in these terms.

Some wars, of course, can also be seen as acts of justice, even when they are not purely defensive wars. Thus, a nation that seeks to punish another nation for some outrageous act insulting to the decency of mankind need not be seen as acting out of cruelty or hatred but simply as seeking justice. Some people believe, for example, that the Allies should have invaded Germany—even if Germany had not first declared war on them—because of the enormous cruelty the German nation was visiting upon the Jews. This may not be legal, and indeed it may not even be just, but it is certainly a *reason* that can be given, and it deserves our appraisal.

These reflections show that to isolate the true meaning of hatred is not an easy task. If hatred is not justice or cruelty or sadism, if it has many of the same constituents as love, if the passion of hatred must be isolated from its effects, then the task is surely one of existential isolation. That is, we must focus on what it means *to* hate, and we must recognize that such a passion has as its object the sheer existence of the hated. The hated is the enemy, and the enemy must be seen as that which is other than ourselves or, more important, that which threatens what is our own. That such a judgment is a passionate one attests to the fact that what is our own matters; indeed, it may be that what is our own is the very foundation of anything mattering at all.

The hatred that may possibly be the essence of war, however, is not the same as the hatred of one person for another. War hatred is a peculiarly communal passion, on behalf of a people and against a people. To say that hatred is the essence of war is not merely to say that some people within one society happen to hate some people within another society. Nor is it to say that all the citizens of a country hate the citizens of another. Perhaps some may argue that the hatred in the case of war is of the leaders, but this is unlikely. It is probably true that Hitler hated his enemies, since he seemed to be able to hate everyone and anyone, but this case is unusual. Did Nicholas II hate his cousin, the kaiser, at the outbreak of World War I? Or the kaiser his other cousin, King George of England? Did Lincoln hate the relatives of his wife? If hatred exists between nations, as it obviously does at times, how must we understand this?

Certainly, in the case of an invaded people, it is easy to comprehend how, let us say, the Polish people hated the invading Germans in World War II. When a Polish soldier saw the carnage and cruelty visited upon his own family and friends, it is entirely understandable that he would fight with savagery against his enemy. And perhaps it is the fear of such outrage that inspires much of what is known as the passion of war. Whether the Blues be the true enemy of the Reds or no, if the Blues fear the Reds will come and rape their women, destroy their lands, and deny them their own form of government, then it is easy to see why the Blues may hate the Reds even if the Reds have no plan to invade at all. The escalation of mutual mistrust may develop at such a pace that mere speculation and imagination may supplant true atrocities. In this case, hatred is grounded on the fear of outrage against what is one's own, and its lack of ground in reality has no appeal to the frenzied imagination. Although such distrust often does play a role in starting a war, it cannot be the sole or even most important cause. And even if it were, it would not provide us with an understanding of the nature of the communal hate that can exist between nations.

It might be thought that the parallel between people and states is sufficient to explain this phenomenon. But the parallel is more suggestive than explanative. I can easily grasp how I may hate the rapist who defiled my daughter, but how can a whole nation of many millions hate the collective whole of another group of millions? When I hate my daughter's rapist, I may take delight in imagining him undergoing torment, but surely I do not imagine everyone of the millions who populate an enemy country undergoing similar torment. To say that nation A hates nation B seems to suggest that an abstract collective unit hates another abstract collective unit, and that is just absurd. Nevertheless, nations do hate each other, and this must be understood.

When the Polish youth witnesses his own people ravaged by the German invader, he does not merely hate the specific soldiers who shot the guns that killed his parents. His hatred is turned not only against the murderer but against the German murderer. Nor is it merely a hatred of those who gave the command or even the chief of state; it is, in truth, a hatred of their being

German, something common to each and every German just because of their nationality. Although the Polish warrior may personally know good Germans whom he does not individually hate, even *their* Germanness is hated. Is this intelligible? At first glance it may seem unintelligible because it is not possible to hate a concept. But, a deeper understanding must be reached. It is indeed possible for the warrior of Poland to hate the invader because of his Germanness, just as it is possible for him to love his family and friends because of their Polishness. He himself, as Polish, is not an abstraction, nor are his family and fellow patriots abstractions, and they are Polish. That is, being Polish is an essential part of who they are, and when loved or hated, that quality is also loved or hated. It is true we only love people and not concepts. But a person's nationality is not a concept; it is a part of his being who he is. In the time of war, the Pole *is,* as Pole, an enemy to the German. The Pole does not hate the abstract concept "Germanism"; he hates Germans. To love his fellow countrymen is possible because he sees *as his own* that which makes him a co-nationalist with the others. This is not something added on to who he is; it is an integral part of who he is. To be German is to be alien to that ownness, and since love is the affirmation of what is one's own, hate is the rejection of what is alien or threatening to what is one's own. Not to hate is to exist in such a way that who one is does not matter, just as not to love is to be indifferent to who one is and what one belongs to. This point gains significance when we realize that being German is not hated during the time of peace, so that being German is inimical only when it threatens being Polish: the Polish warrior hates the German because the German is a threat to who he is. That is what hate is: to let being who one is matter by negating the being of another.

An objection might be made that hate is an emotion and not a mode of being. That is, who I am cannot be articulated merely in terms of what I feel, much less in terms of what I do. Of course, to argue that hatred is the essence of war and not merely a cause is to articulate it in terms of existential modality rather than mere emotional feelings. To be a hater is more fundamental than to feel hate. To feel the emotion without the existential foundation is a form of self-indulgence; it is to hate merely for the sake of the twisted pleasure it brings. To hate beyond the limits of self-control is surely unwise and imprudent, but it is a vice because of the excess; one can be a slave to any passion, even love. But to be a hater is a mode of being in which what is one's own is threatened by the mere existence of what is alien or other. Because of its status as a fundamental way of being, it can be considered a candidate for the essence of war, whereas any mere emotion could not be.

This "being Polish" or "being German" is, as I have said, not a mere abstraction. The culture, the language, and the tradition of Poland and the Polish people make up who a Pole is; there are very real differences between a Polish youth and a German youth. Explicate this difference either genetically or environmentally, it makes no difference to the existential judgment. The hatred of the Polish defender for the invading German entails a realization that the culture, history, and heritage of the Germans are a part of what makes them a threat to Poland. It may be seen as too much militarism, for example, or too great a tradition of law, or the incipient praise of arrogance in German education. (It is for this reason that I felt advised to use an actual historical example in this case.) The young Polish warrior, either actually experiencing the cruelty to his people or believing it is going to happen, sees the German as the threat and counter to all that is his own. To don the uniform of his country and to take up arms against the foe is to assert that being Polish matters, whereas for the enemy to be German undermines that very integrity. In this sense, war may well be essentially hatred. To be a warrior is to embrace violence against a hated enemy, understanding by hatred an intense isolation of the meaning of who the enemy is as enemy, that is, one who not only is other but also threatens what is our own.

When the drill sergeant seeks to instill hatred in the soul of the young recruit, he not only prepares the youth for frightening situations — by giving him a passion sufficiently distracting to override his fear — he also instills in the recruit a sense of what it means to be fighting for one's country as a part of what is one's own. The enemy is seen as a threat to what is one's own, and the sacredness of the homeland is thus contrasted with the profanity of the enemy. Wartime hatred of the enemy is a curious phenomenon, for the years of peace that follow often see a remarkable transformation of the passion. In some cases it can even be curiously purgative, and onetime enemies can become fast friends. Perhaps this is because, in its essence, hatred is made of the same stuff as love; they are the two surfaces of the same pane of glass, the inside and the outside of the cup. Both love and hate are passions of existential concern, the one positive, the other negative. The first is the attraction of what is one's own; the second represents the repulsion of what is other. The two plants spring from the same root.

LOVE

This consideration of hatred as the essence of war now leads to another suggestion. Perhaps the essence of war is not hate, or at least not hate alone, but love. Is hatred of the enemy really possible to one who does not love what is his own? But even if we entertain this suggestion as remotely possible, how are we to think about these two alien spirits, love and war, together? Even as this suggestion is raised, however, it is obvious that there are historical precedents for such thinking. The ancient Greeks manifested their deepest thinking in terms of their myths, revealing through these wonderful stories and the genealogy of the gods fundamental ways in which the human mind understands the world and itself. One of the more fascinating genealogies is that of the siblings Ares, the god of war, and Aphrodite, the goddess of love. They were the children of Zeus and Hera, and in the theology of these stories this meant that love and war were closely akin. On the other hand, although they have the same parentage, mythical siblings connote not only similarity but difference, particularly if the sex is different. They represent two sides of the same reality, sharing a common source but representing it in opposing ways. Thus, for the mythical consciousness of the Greeks, war and love were to be understood as coming from the same source, though representing it in conflicting ways.

To the modern mind, the kinship of Aphrodite and Ares may seem highly inappropriate and counterintuitive. During the years of protest against the Vietnam War, the slogan "Make love, not war," was ubiquitous, and as the sentiment expressed in that slogan seems opposed in spirit to the genealogical pairing of these deities by the Greeks, it may be helpful to begin with an analysis of this antiwar epithet. Those who scribbled the protest on walls or taped it on their bumpers certainly did not intend to suggest anything so intimate as a family connection between the two activities. At the very least, they were implying that one's time is better spent in doing the one rather than the other. The deeper implication was that love was better than war, perhaps even that lovemaking was morally good and war making morally bad. In part, of course, the slogan was not only antiwar but also a parcel of the so-called sexual revolution. This suggestion leads to a further indictment: whatever spirit of prudery had eclipsed the sunlight of open sexual activity was of the same gloomy repression that generated war. A further and insidious innuendo hints that war making is the result of lovelessness, and with this there is the suggestion that warriors are those who have failed in their sexuality. Aggressiveness and belligerence are rooted in sexual repression;

alleviate such artificial restraints, and the inspiration for war will dissipate. By this declension soldiers were soldiers because they were sexually perverse.

Such reductionism may be exaggerated, of course. Not all who espoused the slogan may have believed that warriors had knots in their sex lives. But the picture suggested by the four brief words is nevertheless compelling. On the one hand, one sees an idyllic, arcadian picture of life as a cheerful meadow of pleasure and intimacy; on the other, a grey, dismal battlefield of misery. Surely one cannot be blamed for preferring the one to the other. And even if one were to admit that under extraordinary circumstances perhaps some wars were morally necessary, one would still not *relate* war to love as the Greek myths seem to do. Nevertheless, this is what we must do if we are to grasp the nature of both.

It is the capacity to love that makes the warrior; the love of one's country is no less a form of loving than the sharing of sexual intimacy with a woman. For in loving we care for and protect, perhaps even *establish,* what is our own; we *make* someone our own. In war we sacrifice our individual interests for the interests of the whole that is ours; as in love, we care for, protect, and in some cases establish our ownness. But war affirms this ownness on a truly massive scale, the very dimensions of which impress and stun the mind.

Both war and love also have the capacity to catch us up in the sweep and breadth of fated meaning. We seem no longer to be simple masters of little destinies but to be overwhelmed in meaning that is far more extensive and expansive than our own particularity can achieve. In truly deep erotic love, one is swept up in a passion that minimizes private and personal concerns, so too in war. There is the common and mutually felt sense of participating in greater and grander destinies that characterize both love and war. For these and other reasons, classical tradition has long joined the spirits of war and of eros.

In our literature many of the greatest lovers are warriors. Desdemona loves the warlike Othello because of his courage, bravery, and even savagery. Her father thought the Moor had bewitched her, since her gentility seemed an unlikely ally to Othello's valor. Yet, Shakespeare's art convinces us that theirs was a tender passion. Radames loves the slave girl Aida, and his appointment as chieftain of the Egyptian host evokes from the captive princess an inspired devotion that depends in part on his heroic nature. Tristan's love for Isolde is the love of a warrior for his beloved, in which the notions of conquest, violence, and sacrificial death are as integral to their lovemaking as the love potion. Somehow, the literary and musical arts find the connection between lover and warrior particularly poignant. Benedict woos Beatrice as a soldier, and we cannot escape the conviction that the lofty passion of these young lovers belongs as well to their military professions.

It might be thought that the authors of these great love stories have put swords in the hands and uniforms on the backs of the young lovers merely to bring about greater tension. Surely, had Aida fallen in love with an Egyptian plumber rather than the warrior Radames, the tragic anguish of her divided loyalty would not have been as artistically dramatic. But it is not merely because the artist needs obvious and dramatic tension that the lovers are soldiers; art is not that impoverished. When the Roman Antony woos the warlike Egyptian Cleopatra, their mutual respect for each other's militancy plays more than an opportunistic role. Antony woos as a soldier, as did Othello, and this characterization gives the lovers a special poignancy and tenderness. And in Antony's case, the fictive account is based on a factual love affair. The poetic art strongly supports the family connection between love and war, not only in classical literature but in modern as well. Charles Ryder, in Evelyn Waugh's *Brideshead Revisited,* not only loved the siblings Sebastian and Julia, he also loved the army. In all of these examples, one senses rather profoundly that the lover's affection for the armies is an essential part of what makes him a great lover. What art has grasped and revealed intuitively, we are seeking to understand philosophically.

There is something so elemental and primitive (in the favorable sense of that term) in both war and love that the two ideas genuinely belong together. J. Glenn Gray, in his book *The Warriors,* points out the heightened erotic sensitivity in warriors and how waging war and making love inevitably seem to coexist. Men fresh from battle return to tender and romantic relationships with special fervor and intensity. Perhaps the urge to destroy is made of the same metal as the urge to create. But in any event, there can be no denying the *fact* that erotic love flourishes on or near the battlefield; our minds conjure up these opposing deities as if they were sired from one and the same spirit. It is a peculiarity of the species that man both makes love and makes war, and it is a peculiarity of our unique understanding that the one is made intelligible in terms of the other.

War, like love, is not judged by purely moral criteria; war, like love, transcends the limits of what ought and ought not to be; war, like love, must be understood existentially. In both cases, love and war, what is predominant is the operating principle of ours versus theirs, the we-they distinction. In war and love, the sense of mineness is massive and overwhelming; and in war and love, what is achieved is a sense of meaning, what is defeated is nihilism.

This pairing of the love-war siblings suggests that perhaps in studying the sister we can discover something about the brother. Both love and war seem to have dual natures. The first kind of love is what might be called maternal, or familial, love, the love that binds us together and makes an existential unity out of psychological plurality; it is the love of "the nearest and dearest." Second is what might be called erotic love; this is a passion that seeks the beautiful for the sake of high thrall and thrill, and it often jeopardizes what is nearest and dearest. The genealogy of a love affair may be seen as representing both: when the young man first sees his beloved, he may defy all prudence and security in order to achieve her. Her beauty stuns him into abject slavery. He woos and wins. They have offspring. Now the young man has a new kind of ache and love: to protect and to treasure his sole resource of what is nearest and dearest. To be sure, the erotic is often independent of this genealogy; it is enough now simply to point out that the two loves are different.

There are similar elements in war. On the one hand is the instinct for protection and defense. What is near and dear must be guarded against all invaders. But there is also an instinct for expansion and invasion, a will to destroy the other, a lust to conquer, to make the world adhere to the principles that are one's own. This is more than the mere technical difference between offense and defense, although of course the military technology is grounded in the more existential ideas. But every warrior recognizes the twin responsibilities of his army; he must be able both to attack and to defend, to hold what is precious safely and to advance the interests of what is his own. If warriors were merely defensive, of course, there would never be a war. And if loves were merely familial, there would be no new lovers. The daughter reveres and loves her father until her young swain sweeps her off her feet; the good general knows the stoutest walls do not defend as well as an aggressive offense. The attacking army preserves the preciousness of what is sacred as much as the stalwart defender; even an expansionist army furthers what is one's own. So the deepest sense we have that love has two faces is also applicable to the twin features of the face of Mars. Zeus's children by Hera manifest their common parentage.

To say that war is like love or that it is grounded in love has been prepared by our analysis. Even the most common of interpretations recognizes that patriotism, which supports a people's willingness to war, is a kind of love. But which kind is it? Is it the maternal concern for what is precious or the erotic conquest-enslavement of the more dangerous sort? Surely love itself is not merely erotic or maternal but both, and likewise war is grounded in both. The spirit of war and of warriors is akin both to the romantic and to the sustaining affections.

One's perception of the warrior can be tested by this analysis. It is often thought by the moralist critic of war that the world's soldiers are, in their character, loveless. Certainly it is easy to see why people so readily accept such a picture: what could be more unlike love than the monstrous savagery of a successful warrior? One who destroys cities can scarcely be thought of as a loving and gentle figure. Yet, as "obvious" as this picture seems, history as well as art is more revealing. Most of the world's great warriors are indeed great family men. One need only consider such men as Robert E. Lee, Erwin Rommel, and Marc Antony to see that a love and respect for family life is an important part of their lives. Some great generals, like Julius Caesar, manifest the love not only of a paterfamilias but of an erotic adventurer as well. Soldiers, it turns out, are not lonely bachelors married only to a dubious service; they are loving fathers, doting sons, and romantic sufferers under the lash of Eros. Nor, on reflection, should this be surprising. If a great soldier represents the struggle of a nation to protect or extend its homeland and household gods, why should it be surprising that such affection for what is one's own should characterize the champions of the military art? It might be protested that this appeal to the private lives of certain great warriors is ad hoc and misleading, but such a protest is invalid. Whatever else a great military leader must have, he cannot succeed unless he stirs within the souls of his followers an awe and reverence for the nation they defend.

But what does this tell us about our inquiry into the essence of war? The first suggestion considered above understands the essence of war as hatred; now we are considering the countersuggestion that the essence of war is love. Does not this seem inconsistent? It is surely absurd to argue that war is merely hate; it is no less awesome to suggest that war is the same as love. The former is too simplistic; the latter counterintuitive. Perhaps what these two conflicting suggestions mean is that war can be understood as a kind of love-hate, that to understand the warrior is to understand ourselves as beings who can love and hate, with all that this implies. Both love and hate focus on the meaningfulness of the existence of the person hated or loved; the twin passions care about who one is rather than what one does. If we consider this as a single, existential element that makes up who we are, then war, as both loving and hating, is the violent manifestation of that care.

Surely this, or something like it, is what is meant by the curious Greek myth that makes siblings out of Ares and Aphrodite.

Before we abandon this second suggestion, that the essence of war is love or at least love-hate, mention should perhaps be made of another character- istic of war that seems to follow from this. War, at least as we know it from our own experience and from history, is a remarkably masculine endeavor. War is a male enterprise. This is not to say that women cannot and do not fight in wars, for obviously they have and do. It is, rather, to say that the making of war reveals peculiarly male characteristics. When one thinks of a warrior or a soldier, inevitably one thinks of a man, usually a young man, doing things that are peculiarly male. I am aware that some feminists would argue that this is a deeply prejudiced remark, that the judgment that war is masculine is the result of centuries of male chauvinism. These feminist critics are convinced that there is no fundamental reason women cannot and should not be placed side by side with men on the front lines. There have been, obviously, female warriors, and some, like Joan of Arc, have made impressive claims on the pages of history. I suppose in some abstract sense, pure reason can find no resource for identifying Ares as male and Aphrodite as female, that if one conceives of the human person in purely abstract, sexless ways, there is no absolute prohibition against the next generation of warriors being all women or equally male and female. But such abstractionist arguments are not very revealing of anything meaningful. In our normal understanding, which is admittedly partly traditionalist and prejudiced, the business of war is the business of males. Certainly this is true when we look upon actual, historical wars, Joan of Arc notwithstanding. In seeking to understand so complex and marvelous a phenomenon as human warfare, however, it is simply hopeless to try to carry out the inquiry without a robust sense of history and a bold affirmation of the way we think. It is not, I think, a prejudice to point out that war is masculine.

Other feminists, of course, departing from their sisters, would readily agree with this and use it as an indictment against the entire sex. War is male, and war is evil, and the inference, though specious, is obvious: masculinity is evil and femininity is good. The goddess peace is both ethically and morally superior to the god war, and if this indicts the male gender, then one must accept the consequences of speculative thought. To some extent, of course, this indictment is surely valid. Warlikeness is unpleas- ant and often wrong; the extent of its savagery is surely linked to the male vices; and concern for the well-being of the planet and the race must include considerable dissatisfaction with the crude and vulgar aspects of maleness that make us soldiers. But the vices of men cannot be separated from their virtues, and if war is horrible in part because it is masculine, then too its greatness is due in part to the male character of its history. There may indeed be a great deal of truth to be learned by studying the extent to which war is carried out as a part of the male ego, the strutting, violent, cocky, insensitive, and thoughtless drive on the part of the predatory male to conquer the lovely prize. War may indeed be a kind of rape, a peculiarly male crime and outrage. Indeed, it is surely true that masculinity, as we understand it *as we are,* plays an essential role in the fighting man. But in this inquiry we can only work with what we have, with human nature as we have inherited it, not as we would perhaps like it to be. It may be logically possible to imagine that some future war will be fought with women generals, but such a speculation is not different from imagining a world peopled only with saints. Such a world is not self-contradictory, but it is unintelligible; that is, to imagine it does not produce a logical contradiction, but neither does it provide any illumination of who we are as real beings. Each of us is a sexual being, either male or female, though we probably all partake of both sexes and some are more masculine than others; and what it means to be male, female, and androgynous is understood in part by history, custom, language, tradition, and whatever else our heritage provides for our understanding.

The very *language* of war seems to parallel the language of sexual love. One reads of Germany's *rape* of Austria, using the language of sexual violence to describe military events; but the converse is also true: the male lover is often described as having conquered his beloved. In both love and war there are penetrations, climaxes, seductions, feignings, encirclements, thrusts, embracing, allurements, mastery, submissions; we even speak of the battle of the sexes. There is something so primordial, so fundamental, about the way we think of men and women that these basic ideas seem to construct the very edifice of the twin. War, too, is fundamental. Perhaps our very natures as lovers and warriors are so original that we cannot help but think of them as being the same thing, even though different. What then, is really being suggested in the antiwar slogan "Make love, not war," as if one could only do one and not the other? How does this compare to the mythological suggestion that war and love are siblings? Philosophically, perhaps, the slogan should be "Make love *and* war."

PRIDE

It is sometimes suggested that war is the result of pride. Were men not proud, they would never go to war. This suggestion, as with the two previous ones, emphasizes the transmoral quality of the warrior consciousness. When we speak of pride, we mean a lofty sense of one's own worth, precisely beyond that which mere legality demands. If one has offended my pride, my recourse is not the law but some vague code of honor that demands some activity that is both dangerous and daring. By pride we mean something that cannot be accounted for by rights. Pride is both noble and sinful; it is accounted the first among Christian vices, the sin that brings Lucifer down from the lofty heights of heaven and changes him into Satan. Yet pride is also seen as a necessary element for any worthwhile or decent existence. Without any pride, I am a mere worm, a man unworthy of the dignity of humanity.

There can be no doubt that many wars are inspired by a sense of pride, in both its negative and its positive meanings. When we speak of national pride, we seem to mean some vague but powerful emotion that keeps the integrity of the state intact. The phrase "outraged pride" evokes a sense of some kind of value that cannot be allowed to go unchallenged. It is almost as if pride were the very worth of existence itself. And it is profoundly curious that pride is seen as both extremely evil and extremely precious. The historian Joachim Fest claims in his book on Hitler that bad history, which generates a sense of outraged pride, has probably caused more wars than all other sentiments put together. Its opposite, humility, is seen by the Christian as a virtue, but not so by the pagans. The Greeks could never have understood humility as a virtue, though they did possess their notion of sophrosyne, which shares some of the qualities of the Christian virtue. Yet even for the Christians, pride is among the most troublesome of all notions; it is as elusive as truth itself, almost defying any ready attempt to define it. Pride is problematic because its absence seems to render us worthless, whereas its possession makes us arrogant and dangerous. For the Christian, pride is the source of evil because it challenges the authority of God, but it is morally corruptive because it is selfish. If the Christian virtue is love, then that which makes us loveless, selfishness, is to be avoided. The obvious soundness of this teaching, however, does not put to rest the anguish over our understanding of pride. For a man who has no pride at all seems as incapable of love as one who has too much.

The Greek treatment of this trait is perhaps more profound. In their mythology, of course, the gods were not necessarily loving of humankind. Indeed, those who tried to advance humankind, like Prometheus, were often magnificently tortured. Zeus was a jealous god who saw any advance of man's stature as a threat against his own. Pride, in this sense, was anything that advanced man and oneself at the terrible cost of the gods' ire. But in the fifth century B.C., the problem of pride had reached an aesthetic zenith that is almost unparalleled in history. The modern notion of tragedy was born. Partly because of the sheer poetic genius of Aeschylus and Sophocles, and partly because of the refinement of the Dionysian religion, the art of tragedy became one of the most spectacular achievements of an already spectacular people. In these wonderful plays tension is developed between sophrosyne, the virtue of knowing who one is and one's place in life, and hubris, the dangerous quality of grandeur and overreaching greatness. At first, of course, these two opposing principles were seen as virtue and vice. The man of hubris overreaches himself and provokes the ire of the gods, but the man of sophrosyne knows who he is and keeps his station. Hubris, pride, is etymologically connected to the Greek word for rape, and it suggests usurpation and illicit overreaching. But this purely moralistic theology is subtly transformed under the inspiration of the great poets and the Dionysian religion until the destructive vice hubris becomes a curiously admired quality of greatness. The tragic heroes and heroines become models not of wickedness but of leadership. They are magnificent in their grandeur. When Antigone and Creon suffer their deep anguish, more than mere pity is evoked: there is an admiration for their greatness, a sense of reverence for what they reveal about man's nature. The heroes are often contrasted with the chorus, which represents the mind of the common man, the virtue of sophrosyne. But the chorus finds itself retreating from the excellence of the heroes, and in so doing exposes itself as small, frightened, unworthy, and ultimately lacking in virtue. The play becomes a contest between the merely good and the dangerously great. Hubris, then, becomes a virtue-vice, the call to greatness and meaning at the sacrifice of what is safe and secure.

One of the reasons this artistic treatment of hubris is so revered is that it is so profoundly revealing of how we think of pride. To be sure, it reaches beyond itself and hence is usurpatory and dangerous, but at the same time it brings us closer to the gods. Perhaps in our nature we are not merely servants of God, but beings destined to reach divinity. It is almost impossible for the human spirit not to admire those of hubris, not to cheer on the boldness of creative men, no matter how dangerous their boldness may be.

The Greek tragedies expose this hidden truth in a way that remains un-
equaled in power, for these tragedies reveal the essential truth about our
existence, and like the forbidden fruit in the garden of Eden, once tasted
they cannot be spit out.

In the Christian epoch, the poet Milton reveals much of this same
anomaly in his characterization of Satan in *Paradise Lost.* When Satan says
that he would rather rule in hell than serve in heaven, he becomes a kind of
hero, for we understand this rebellion as a part of our own nature. When
Eve, mortally following the example of the fallen angel, also chooses to have
knowledge beyond her given state, we both regret and applaud her act.
With Milton we ask, Can it be sin to know?

Institutions very often provide one with the ways and means of achieving
a sense of self-dignity that generates pride. This is especially true among
those disadvantaged and unfortunate in their given states. Among ghetto
youths membership in gangs often is the only way an otherwise worthless
and mean existence can be given a sense of meaning and dignity. In prisons,
especially, the dreadful spiritual nihilism afforded by the forced incarceration
can be offset only by a fierce and terrible pride taken in gang membership.
The demands made on these young men because of their membership is
often stunning. But when one sees the alternative—a broken, spiritless,
zombielike existence—the mind cannot help but wonder if the vaunting
pride is not a better way. No one can doubt that this pride, especially in the
youth, is volatile, unsettling, dangerous, and threatening. No one can deny
that such pride is often wedded to passionate hate and distortive prejudice.
But can we really prefer to eliminate this pride altogether? Above we saw
that pride is often seen as a kind of selfishness, but experience denies this. It
often is only when one has pride in one's membership in an institution that
genuine tenderness, self-sacrifice, and even love are possible. Why should
self-sacrifice, which is surely the opposite of selfishness, be carried out
unless one first cares about others? But to care about others as oneself is to
see others in terms of the self, and that is precisely what institutional
identification does. It is, to be sure, less admirable perhaps when the
institution is a street gang, more so when it is a nation. But pride in that
membership is what makes the membership matter; without that pride
perhaps not even love itself would be possible.

The notion that pride is the essence of war can be furthered by the
realization that unless there were pride, there would be no war. The
complete pacifist and the total hedonist might agree with this and together
condemn pride as the source of human evil. But in such a view man is

merely an animal whose sole purpose is to live as long as possible. Pride is precisely that virtue which denies such a view.

Thus, it is not merely the love of one's country that supports war, it is also the pride in one's country. This pride can, unfortunately, be provoked in many dubious and questionable ways. But the ground of the provocation is essential to self-understanding: being who we are matters.

FREEDOM

There is one final suggestion to consider in this matter of war's essence. The fundamental nature of war may reside in the fundamental nature of human freedom; that is, the essence of war may be freedom. If this idea can be understood in the existential sense, its truth will be made manifest.

Individual wars are, of course, "caused" by a multitude of political factors. Some wars are caused by the need of one country for the goods of another; others are caused by the sheer rapacious greed of the leaders; some wars are caused by disagreements about how a district should be governed and by whom; and a few wars are fought by men seeking freedom from tyrannical rule. Thus, it would seem that only some wars are fought for freedom and that to identify the essence of war in this way would simply be wrong. At best it might seem that the essence of a *defensive* war is the attempt to free oneself from the unwanted invasion of an enemy bent on conquest. But one cannot understand the essence of war merely by studying why people defend themselves; one must also study why some people seek to invade, conquer, and usurp others. Those who endeavor to enslave others are hardly to be seen as manifesting freedom. At the very least, these reflections should assure us that freedom is not to be understood as a political cause; it is not to be confused with liberty.

Nevertheless, the suggestion that freedom is the essence of war deserves careful consideration. What is meant by freedom? This enormous question may never be fully answered, but we can make considerable advance on it if we begin by clearing away a few false ideas. It may be helpful, then, to start our inquiry by listing several things that freedom is *not*.

1. Freedom is not liberty. As wonderful and as worthy as liberty obviously is, it should not be confused with freedom. Liberty is a political notion, implying a certain guarantee of well-defined rights to the

citizens. It is also a negative concept, defined in terms of the absence of political restraint or tyranny. Liberty, that precious commodity inherited by the citizens of democratic republics and democratic monarchies, can be lost or taken away. Freedom, however, cannot be taken away. A man unjustly imprisoned has certainly lost his liberty, but as long as he is morally right, he has not lost his freedom. Liberty seems to vary in accordance with the political order. The American colonialists wanted their liberty in 1776, but South Carolina also wanted it in 1861. Although it is certainly proper to use the term "freedom" in cases of political struggle against an oppressor, it is important to keep in mind that when we speak in philosophical exactitude, the term "liberty" should be reserved for political meaning.

2. Freedom is not dependent on choice. Very often, in quarrels over freedom versus determinism, the question is raised in terms of choice. Inevitably, such disputes rage over what are regrettably contrary-to-fact conditionals. We ask, Granted that I did x, could I have done *non-x?* If I could not have refrained from doing x, then surely I am not *free* to have done x. This question appeals to our instinct and intuition, and on one level it is certainly legitimate. But it unfortunately raises the question in ultimately unsolvable terms, for there is no way what is not the case can be used to establish what is the case. (If, in fact, I did break the law and you argue that I should be held responsible because I *could have* kept the law had I chosen, the argument relies on a logically murky notion that somehow what I did not do is possible or at least meaningful.) The argument should be reversed. Freedom does not depend on choice; rather choice depends on freedom. That is, it is not because I have a choice that I am free; rather it is because I am free that I have a choice. *Being* free is something that can be understood without imagining a contrary-to-fact situation.

3. Freedom is not merely moral responsibility. There can be no doubt that the most fundamental sense of freedom is that presupposed by moral judgments. To say "I am responsible for x" is possible only because I am free; and hence, at the very least, freedom means the capacity to be held responsible for one's actions. This is why the man in prison, although deprived of his political liberty, has not lost his freedom. It is still possible for him to be morally good or morally wicked even though the extent of his actions has been limited. Indeed, some thinkers, like Kant, go so far as to argue that a man's

will is the sole determination of his freedom, so that even if all action is restricted, the man can still be said to be free. So the moral definition of freedom is superior to the political one or the one dependent on psychological choice. But even so, freedom means more than the formal condition of morality, as I now intend to show.

If freedom is not liberty, if it is not choice, and if it is more than moral responsibility, then what is it? When I speak of freedom in its deepest sense, I must speak of what it means *to be* free. And when I do this, I am saying that what it means to be *matters*. To be indifferent to the meaning of existence is to be unfree. Freedom, therefore, is being something that matters; if we press this further, we may even suggest that to be free is to matter.

This can perhaps be clarified by considering the opposite state, slavery. What is a slave? Ultimately, a slave is one whose autonomy simply does not matter; or rather, strictly, a slave is one who has no autonomy whatsoever. What the slave *does* may matter, if he serves his master well; if he is strong and healthy, the slave may be expensive and hence of financial value. But the single most important difference between the slave and the master is simply that after both have completed their work, the worth of the slave ceases altogether, whereas the worth of the master still exists. It is possible to imagine a happy slave—indeed, many slaves may well be happier than their masters—but it is impossible to imagine a slave whose existence itself is precious, for if it were, the slave could not be a slave. This is an important point to keep in mind: slavery is an undesirable state not because one is unhappy in it but because it eclipses the light of autonomy. It is for this reason that modern thought has forbidden slavery altogether. It is possible for someone to recognize that it is better to be unhappy and free than a slave and happy, if by "happy" one means "enjoying the pleasures of life and being content." In fact, one kind of slavery is surely the bondage created by a life dedicated to pleasure and contentment. This is what is meant by Dostoyevsky's argument in "The Grand Inquisitor" in which humankind is depicted as opting for a life of assured salvation, with only a very few capable of embracing the cold steel of self-recognition that is freedom. It is also the point made by Nietzsche in part 1 of *Thus Spoke Zarathustra*, when the happily contented last man is contrasted with the suffering superman. These appeals are not mere depictions, they are arguments, for they succeed in showing us that slavery is to be shunned not because of its pain and suffering but because of what it does to our own worth. When King Lear, at the end of the play, casually announces that he "hath killed the slave that was hanging thee," the term is used as a dismissal of any concern. To care about the death of a slave is an error in judgment; it is akin to the practice of leaving vast fortunes to one's pet animals. The characterization of slaves being whipped and beaten may be historically accurate, but it is misleading. Many nonslaves suffer far worse than slaves. It is the ignominy of slavery, its debasement, its assault on one's integrity, that matters, not the physical abuse.

But if slavery consists in losing one's existential worth, then freedom must be the gaining of this precious commodity. To be sure, the derivative senses of freedom all stem from this basic notion. It is because I have existential worth—that is, it is because I matter—that I desire liberty, that I have choices, and that I am morally responsible. But the fundamental meaning of freedom is that my existence is meaningful. Those who possess political liberty, are given choices, and are held responsible, but are unaware that who they are matters, are only superficially free; on the other hand, one who through misfortune has lost political liberty, has been denied choice, and is dealt with unjustly, but nevertheless courageously maintains a sense of his own self-worth, is absolutely free. It is possible, of course, to lose this fundamental freedom, by loss of self-awareness or by bad thinking. It can also be eroded by a special kind of cowardice: the unwillingness to defend or resist erosions of the structures that help make us who we are.

There is a curious self-creating or even self-justifying quality to this. Those who defend the worth of their existence are those who, in so committing themselves, create their own self-worth. Freedom given is freedom denied. To be free is to care about it; to care about it is to be free. As puzzling as this is, it cannot be denied. As Goethe says, "Nur der verdient sich Freiheit wie das Leben, / Der täglich sich erobern muss." The idea that freedom must always be seen as a kind of self-creation is evident even in the earliest myths of humankind. Was not Eve literally creating her own guilt, and hence herself, in choosing to know of good and evil? Was not her guilt the only thing she had that made her autonomous?

But can I be free to just *be?* Surely freedom refers to *actions,* not states. Who I am is surely determined by factors beyond my control. Granted that I should, perhaps, try to be true to myself, but what "myself" means in this context is beyond my will to change or alter. This protest, however, is only partially valid. To be sure, I am fated in many ways, among them my nationality, but in affirming who I am, what is given becomes curiously self-given. I can reject or affirm how I am thrown into this world, and this fundamental realization is mine in the most original sense of the term.

Indeed, no other sense of mineness is as original; all other senses of mineness follow from this. To retreat from this awareness, to surrender this meaning to others, is capitulation of the worth of self; it is fundamental, that is, existential, slavery.

For a man to take up arms in defense of his country, then, can be seen as stemming from the more original meaning of a man affirming the worth of his own being. Not to do this is to accept slavery. Thus, it is not outrageous to suggest that the essence of war is existential freedom. If you ask an ordinary American soldier why he has joined the army, particularly in a time of crisis, he may well say that he is willing to fight for his country. When the soldier is pressed further, his willingness to fight often reveals itself as an acceptance of his being born an American, and you realize that this quality, even though not chosen, matters very much to the young warrior. To recognize this as a form of freedom is not a strain on our understanding.

We have entertained four suggestions concerning the essence of war: hatred, love, pride, and freedom. Unlike the nine existential marks that *describe* war, these suggestions are an attempt to *define* war in the essentialist sense. As the inquiry unfolds, it is obvious that these four suggestions are not mutually exclusive, even the first two, which seem at first glance to be contradictory. War is hatred, it is love, it is pride, it is freedom. To inquire into the essence of a term is to ask for the most primitive and fundamental ways in which this term can be *thought*. If the essence of war is a loving pride and a hateful freedom, this means that when we think about the meaning of war, the notions of love, hatred, freedom, and pride are necessary to make sense of the idea. Unlike terms that describe an idea and that can be verified by experience or analysis, the terms that make up an essence can be *argued* about. Thinking of war in terms of pride may be quite different from thinking of it in terms of hatred. If there is something common to these four terms, then whatever is shared in these four principles will be more fundamental still. How, though, can we "test" this fourfold definition of the essence of war against our ordinary understanding of the event?

What one chooses as an example will, of course, to some extent betray the convictions that lie behind the choice. War has many gruesome pictures from which one may elicit many principles, but for this particular discussion I should like to focus on an image not directly on the battlefield. During World War II, when the Nazis were in control of occupied Poland, the resistance fighters occasionally succeeded in causing havoc among the German conquerors. Often, in reprisal for these pathetic raids, the German command would order hostages taken from the civilian population and shot. For every German killed, the Nazis would take ten, twenty, or even fifty civilians and shoot them in the public squares. This was done, obviously, to intimidate the partisans and to deny them the support of the local populace. Nevertheless, in spite of these horrendous odds and the unspeakable horror officially carried out as policy, many partisans continued their acts of sabotage, and remarkably, many civilians continued to support their valiant and desperate countrymen by hiding them, refusing to disclose information to the police, and, when possible, feeding them from their own meager supply. Let us imagine what goes on in the minds of two people: a young partisan and a woman of a village whose husband may be taken as hostage. The partisan knows that his feeble attempts to blow up a few trucks or to derail a train will not result in the defeat of the Germans. If he is a spirited and sanguine personality, he may possibly believe that such acts of sabotage might help in the overall undermining of the government, but, cut off from all outside news and support, he is unsure of how well or badly the war is going. So what he does may simply result in having thirty of his beloved fellow villagers put to death. He certainly knows that in the absolute scale of things, a sabotaged truck is not worth thirty Polish lives. Nor is there any doubt of the sincerity of the threat; the Germans will ruthlessly carry out their brutal policy. If the partisan succeeds in blowing up the truck, he knows thirty of his countrymen will die.

So what does he do? In spite of this conviction concerning the hopelessness of his endeavor, he still continues to sabotage the Germans. Why? It is, of course, possible to dismiss his activity as insane or as frenzied by the passionate hatred of war. And there can be no doubt that hatred is a part of the explanation: the Polish youth hates the German invader; why should he not? But such an account is inadequate, if not misleading. The partisan does not think in terms of some moral calculus, weighing good against evil. He knows his act will produce greater suffering even for his own people. Perhaps he even seriously doubts whether the allies will be triumphant. Certainly in 1940 and the early parts of 1941 there was every reason to believe the Germans would prevail while the gutless democracies did little to resist. No, the impulse for the act is not a calculation of utilitarian benefit. The partisan continues to sabotage because he feels it is necessary to be true to Poland; he is convinced that being Polish matters, even more than the lives of the Polish hostages matter. This is to argue that the passions of love and hate and pride outweigh the purely moral concerns of proper behavior.

And how would we morally judge the partisan? Would we argue that his putting the lives of innocent civilians in jeopardy is simply immoral? Perhaps. But it is difficult to indict such acts as morally wrong. Perhaps one could defend the young man's acts of sabotage on the ground that wickedness, in the form of the Nazi occupation, should be defeated, or at least efforts should be taken to defeat it. But if that is the argument, then the point of freedom and the pride of a nation and the hatred of the invader and the love of a people plays a determining role. For the partisan does not kill the Germans because they are immoral, he kills them because they are German.

Let us consider the mind of the woman in the village who knows of the partisans and their activities and who has been told that her husband will be among the next group of hostages killed unless the resistance is foiled. How must she think if she refuses to tell the Nazis where the partisans are hidden? If she does tell, of course, one could argue that her love for her husband made her do it, and no one could gainsay such reasoning. But if she does *not* reveal the whereabouts of the partisans, knowing that this jeopardizes her husband, what does this malignant and cruel decision reveal? That she loves Poland more than her husband? I think not. Is it not better to say that her love for her husband as Polish and for herself as a Polish wife supports her remarkable courage? And is this not to say that who she is, as Polish, matters?

In order to make this point clearer, let us suppose that both the partisan youth and the wife of the hostage realize that the act of sabotage against the German invader will not appreciably deter the Nazi war machine, that thirty or more Polish lives will be sacrificed for a mere symbolic gesture of rebellion. And suppose, to make the situation even more existentially fraught with agony, among the thirty hostages to be shot are those who do not support the partisans and who would betray them to the Germans to save their lives. The partisan, by carrying out his act of sabotage, is therefore putting these men to death against their will and against their own assessment of what is important. Now, granting these circumstances, what would the moral observer say about the partisan's effort to sabotage the trucks? Are gestures important enough to sacrifice thirty innocent lives?

We should perhaps remind ourselves that such cases obviously did exist, that this is not an exercise in fantastical speculation. Young men actually faced such horrific decisions and made them. Perhaps no one who has not been through such anguish can truly judge them. But it seems clear that to argue against the decision of the partisan to sabotage the German trucks would be to deny something very sacred. Even a gesture can save a soul. The youth who actually blows up the trucks, and the wife of the hostage, can be understood only in terms of such existential notions as pride, love, freedom, and even hate. Even for those who would argue that the partisan is morally wrong would have to admit some value to the acts of sabotage beyond a mere emotional support. To realize that men and women will indeed do such things without becoming moral villains is to realize the true nature of war. It is, perhaps, to realize the essence of war. The principle is one that was found in our description of the nine marks: the we-they distinction matters. The very foundation of the ethical system itself presupposes the notion of the integrity and even sanctity of the self, especially as it is embodied in the we-self. Personal sacrifice, a mark of saintliness, is itself impossible without a sense of the we. Perhaps one might even go so far as to suggest that not to blow up the trucks would be immoral.

Why do we not argue that the partisan and the women should simply accept German rule as legitimate? Why do we not argue that the morally right thing is to support the only functioning government, the Nazi occupation, and to treat all violations against their commands as criminal acts, unjustifiable and immoral? Some of course may actually argue in this way. But we resist this simplistic account of authority for the simple reason that being Polish matters. It is important to note that if someone were to argue that *in Germany* a resister to the government who was blowing up trucks would be in the same situation, the counterargument would be given that the reasons would be quite different indeed. There is a danger here, of course, that one might think this kind of argument involves a slippery slope in which any act of rebellion could be justified on an appeal to the integrity of the we-self. Could not wanton revolutionaries, or even criminals, argue that *their* authenticity requires them to destroy innocent civilians on behalf of who they are. This is to misunderstand the point, and for two very important reasons: First, the slope is not that slippery. There is a huge difference between war and a revolutionary group using terrorism to bring about the downfall of a legitimate government. Second, the argument is not basically a moral one to begin with. The argumentation does not seek morally to justify the acts of the partisan (though such an argument could probably be given); it seeks to show that our ordinary understanding approves of such acts as are normally immoral on the basis of a different kind of appeal: that who one is as a member of a nation or people has an autonomy independent of our moral concern. The revolutionary terrorist may believe he, too, is acting on the basis of such principles, but that does not mean that the terrorist is correct. The example of the Polish partisan is given, rather than an abstract example, just for this point. It must be understood that the Polish example was from a real wartime situation, and the point of the example was to see the act of sabotage as an act of *war*. War is not terrorism, although some pacificists try to collapse the distinction. Also, the example was given, not to make a moral point, but to show how the passions of love, hate, and pride and the passion for freedom play an essential role in the waging of war.

The Polish partisan, then, takes what would normally be wrong and perceives it through the prism of love-hate-pride-freedom; thus refracted, such an act is understood as an act of war. From the perspective of the postbellum victors, we see the boy's hatred as intelligible, his love for Poland, his pride as a Pole, and his yearning for Polish freedom as intelligible. What makes it intelligible is how we understand war. If our perception is correct, then we must understand these passions as belonging to the essence of war.

The nine existential marks used to describe war now can be given a clearer reading. The vastness of war, the communal, historical, violent, and organized behavior, even the horror and the heroism—all are grounded in pride, hatred, love, and, most of all, existential freedom. Thus, not only on the level of war's description through the nine marks but also in understanding war's essence, the nature of war must be seen existentially, in terms of the we-they principle.

7

Judgments About War

To see war as grounded in the existential concern for the priority of the We over the They is not merely to see an abstract notion explicated in terms of existential principles, it is also to see the concrete manifestations of war rendered intelligible by the same way of thinking. We have considered the "theoretical" aspects of this view on war, but it is now required that we also interpret some of the more practical and concrete aspects in light of this speculation. The point of this is not to "show" that the theory somehow "works," for that is degrading and improper, but rather to extend the range of our understanding. War, as a phenomenon, has many aspects, and if any theoretical account of it is to be adequate, it must also illuminate the entire range of this remarkable human occurrence.

How we think about anything must have its effects on how we carry these things out in our daily lives. The theoretical descriptions of any human activity are reflected in the events themselves as they are concretely experienced. Thus, if the present theoretical account of war is accurate, it will have some significance for our judgments of actual wars. Without becoming a military handbook, our inquiry can nevertheless include what these analyses provide for our understanding of how to judge success and failure in the business of war. This is not military science, for we are not considering what tactics to use on the battlefield or what strategies to employ in the war rooms. But it *is* an attempt to understand what makes war *war* and thus an attempt to distinguish wars from pseudowars and wars fought well from those fought badly. The distinction between wars and pseudowars, however, has some immediate military values, for if a nation decides on so dangerous and risky an enterprise as warfare, it is essential that it do so with full realization of what is entailed. One of the easiest ways to be defeated in war is to misapprehend what war is.

It is a Platonic notion that in order to understand what something is, one must also consider what something is not; it is also a Platonic notion that what something *is* can be approached best by considering those instances that most obviously succeed in *being* the thing in question. Thus, we must study the greatest poets to discover what poetry is, the fastest runner to grasp what running means. It is a part of our understanding of war, therefore, that we now reflect on such questions: How are wars won and lost? What distinguishes great wars from lesser wars (aside from mere quantity)? How are wars judged? How do we distinguish wars from pseudowars? These questions have both speculative and practical significance, even though their consideration here is primarily concerned with the former.

The questions of distinguishing wars from pseudowars and success in war from failure in war are closely aligned. For often the failure of a war effort comes about because of a confusion about the phenomenon itself. Many nations have stumbled into a disastrous war by misapprehending the event that lay before it, interpreting an act of violence as a mere isolated criminal act when in fact it contained the germs of a true revolutionary war, for example. One of the most important principles that can be found in this regard is the Napoleonic-Clausewitzean doctrine of concentration of power, which has not only tactical and strategic applicability but speculative meaning as well. However, even this time-honored principle of warfare can be reexamined in terms of the we-they principle and the description of war as revealed in the nine marks. Although the prudential wisdom behind this teaching may be of greater significance to professors of military science, it nevertheless deserves our attention here for philosophical reasons.

Dribble Wars. In the description of war, we included the two marks vast and violent as necessarily belonging to our understanding of what war is. Thus, in order for an event to be a war, it must be both vast and violent. Yet, both generals on the actual battlefield and national leaders in the realm of military policy have often and dreadfully forgotten this truth, and the result has been disaster. If we were to add the third mark, communal, even more precision would be achieved and more disasters avoided. It is when a nation or even an army forgets these three marks, and hence forgets what a war *is*, that there occurs what may be called a "dribble war." To initiate the inquiry it may be helpful to approach this concept from a purely tactical point of view.

How is it possible for a well-equipped army of fifty thousand men to be defeated by an equally well-equipped army of only five thousand men? If by the phrase "equally well-equipped" we mean that there is no outrageous advantage of weaponry on one side, it might seem that such a scenario is impossible. The general commanding the larger force would have to be totally inadequate, even stupid, to allow an army one-tenth the size of his own to defeat him. One might suspect that with such odds, history would be void of any such instances. In point of fact, however, history reveals such a scenario quite often, and we must now ask why. One way, of course, in which the larger army could be destroyed by the smaller would be if the officer commanding the larger force sent to the front line only a few hundred men at a time. The five-thousand-man army would, in effect, be handling many attacks by a five-hundred-man army and hence possibly win the war quite easily. If, in other words, the fifty-thousand-man army drib-bled its resources away, the battle could be lost. Now, this is so obvious as to be assumed, and it might be thought that no time should be spent on laboring the self-evident. But let us look more closely at this principle. To be sure, no general in his right mind would, on an open field with the two hosts drawn up in classical eighteenth-century array, deploy his troops in so disastrous a manner. What happens is that very clever generals manage to use the topography of the land, the intelligence of their spies, the ignorance of the enemy, and perhaps even the slowness or hesitation of the opposing officer, to so arrange their own troops that, *in effect,* the opposing forces can only bring the full weight of their destructive power in bits and pieces. This is, of course, the whole purpose of maneuver, and history honors the few who could achieve this with brilliance. Robert E. Lee was a master of it in Virginia, and so was Napoleon almost everywhere he fought. Rommel was remarkable in such feats, and on the water, so were Nelson and Spruance. The opponents of such brilliant men were simply outclassed. They were certainly not unaware of the principle, they simply could not apply it as well, and hence they lost.

History gives us grosser examples. The Dardanelles campaign during World War I is a classic instance of a dribble campaign. Time and again during that ill-conceived campaign, the British and Australian forces threw too few divisions at entrenched Turkish soldiers, giving the enemy time to reinforce their beleaguered army. Churchill claims that had the British and Australian forces attacked in full force as originally planned, Gallipoli would not have been the tragic disaster that it became. Kitchener's decision to hold back the divisions was, for the Turkish campaign anyway, a dreadful error. Kitchener, of course, had his reasons. He was afraid that the European theater would be left too vulnerable by the shift of so many divisions southward, and perhaps he was right; but if so, the original plan was wrong, and the invasion should not have taken place. The point is, quite simply, that if the British wished to dislodge the Turks from the Dardanelles, they should have provided enough troops to do the job. Instead they opted for a dribble attack.

Contrast this with a Napoleon, for example, who had deep and profound instincts to bring in every available soldier when confronting the enemy. He would even enlist the runners, the cooks, the maintenance men, give them rifles just to add to the sheer ballast and enormity of an attack. His was the genius of knowing how and when to press the full force of all his host. Wellington, who should know, once admitted that Bonaparte's presence on the field was equal to fifty thousand extra soldiers. And his one great talent, aside from his unparalleled skill at maneuver, was his ability to bring as many and as much against the enemy as possible. It did not disturb him that some might protest he had too many men; he thought it impossible to have too many men at the right place. His skill consisted in making the opposing general use only a part of his force at any given time. In short, he knew how to use the principle of concentration of power and hence how to minimize the danger of dribble battles or dribble attacks.

One must not be simplistic about this, however. Lincoln, who had read Clausewitz carefully, knew the full significance of the concentration of power, and he chafed and protested at the delays of his early generals, especially McClellan, who would not press against the weaker enemy. But not all the delays of the Northern generals were ill advised; it is as foolish to dash in unprepared (as the Russians did in East Prussia in 1914) as it is to wait until the enemy has built his strength, as in Gallipoli. Churchill, in

World War II, was so hungry to fire in anger at the Nazis that he was led to foolish, though soul-satisfying, attacks in Greece and Cyprus. But even such foolishness pales before the other ill. Those whose instincts may occasionally lead them to unprepared ventures nevertheless stand the test of history better than those who waste their precious energies of warfare on piecemeal expenditure.

Yet all of these examples, illuminating as they might be, are of battles and campaigns within actual wars. In none of the above cases is there any doubt that the war in which these events occurred was a genuine war. A dribble campaign does not necessarily make a dribble war. But history also reveals that entire wars can be fought in such an inauthentic and ultimately disastrous way. Vietnam might be called a dribble war in this sense, not only because of the step-by-step escalation but also because the war was constantly being presented to the public *as* a nonwar. We were informed we could have both guns and butter, that no ultimate sacrifice had to be made, that it was not a war but a police action, that it was never declared by Congress, that the boys in the field were being given hot steak dinners flown in by helicopter, that the opposing forces were not really our enemy, that those who aided and abetted the enemy were not traitors. Yet, as these deceptions were daily presented to us from the official news sources in Washington, the networks nightly showed us the torn bodies and the corpses and the wounded. There seemed to be no consistency between these two pictures at all. We were told it was no great sacrifice, but when we saw the savaged bodies of our young men, what judgment was left to us? If it was not sacrifice, it must then be savagery.

To fight a war that for some reason or other is not perceived or conceived *as* a war is to fight a pseudowar, and all pseudowars are wicked. The term does not refer to the actual event but to the deep mind-set that judges the event. A war fought without the participants' attributing to it the full nine existential marks is a war that is inconsistent with the very meaning of the term "war" and hence is inauthentic, or pseudo. It may be possible to win such a conflict by sheer dint of superior weaponry and power, but even then the pseudowars have a tendency to corrode the pride of a nation and corrupt the military readiness of a people. One form of a pseudowar is a dribble war in which the inauthenticity is the result of approaching a big problem with small knives.

How we think about a war, therefore, becomes an essential characteristic of the event itself. To think badly or wrongly about a war often leads to defeat, but even if it does not, it leads to philosophical corruption and an offense against truth. The first existential mark, that war is vast, here reveals itself as spiritually important. Those who enter the arena of Ares without respect for the enormity of the endeavor are doomed either to failure on the battlefield, for want of spirit, or, even worse, to a deterioration of meaning even if the conflict is won. Just as the battlefield commander must realize the Clausewitzean doctrine of concentrating one's forces to the hilt, so the inquirer must realize that to think about the meaning of war is to think about the endeavor as necessarily huge in its import.

Many warriors and thinkers have espoused the view that the greatest threat either to comprehending war or to winning it is not to take war *seriously,* but perhaps few have manifested this critical doctrine more powerfully than William Tecumseh Sherman. He and Ulysses S. Grant both insisted that war be confronted in all of its terror and ugliness and that once initiated, the sole principle governing the commanders should be to end it as thoroughly and as quickly as possible. Grant, early in the war, expressed his personal belief that the North should prosecute the war with utmost vigor until, the South defeated, they could then embrace these wayward Americans again with affection. But it was the more articulate and reflective Sherman who, in a famous letter to Lincoln, spelled out his, and apparently Grant's, fundamental view. The South should, he argued, be thoroughly whipped, wide swaths of their land so savaged it could no longer sustain their armies, and the citizens of the rebellious states so deeply scourged that they would never again either want or be able seriously to consider taking up arms against the federal government. For Sherman, it was unconscionable to hazard young lives unless the victory was to last. It did no good to defeat an enemy who, five years later, would again rise up and start the war anew. The dreadful cost was worth it only if the enemy was so roundly beaten he ceased to be an enemy. This harsh doctrine may seem heartless, and indeed many historians do not hesitate to label Sherman and, to a lesser extent, Grant as butchers. The infamous march from Atlanta to the sea, leaving Georgia a scorched and devastated wasteland, strikes many simply as barbarism. But the point must be stressed. Especially in a civil war, the enemy is not merely the armies but a way of thinking, a social or cultural persuasion that must be excised, as a cancer, from the entire body politic. Why go to war at all unless the enemy is thoroughly destroyed? For Sherman, war was pure hell; to undertake it for any reason less than a meaningful victory was immoral.

Lincoln accepted this stern view, if for no other reason, because he had seen his first six commanders of the Army of the Potomac lacking in precisely this appreciation of the fundamental mark of war as a vast, and hence fundamentally serious, endeavor. They seemed to think that wars should be fought with the minimum of disruption, that a few easy battles or safe retreats would suffice. Especially with McClellan, the North, at least in the eastern theater, seemed willing to fight with one hand tied behind its back. Sherman's policies, though severe, in the end may seem more honorable. Unless the enemy is defeated, the war is a waste, not a noble sacrifice, of the lives of soldiers. Both he and Grant believed that when pressed with utmost vigor, the war would be over more quickly and hence, in the long run, less costly. Grant's courageous decision to pursue Lee's army, not Richmond, caused hideous casualties, but it ended the war in forty days. Sherman's reasoning echoes the truth of the first mark; to accept the grim but real meaning of war is thus essential for its victories. Contrast this with Tsar Nicholas II, who believed, in 1905, that "a nice little war" with the Japanese would help him enormously with his domestic troubles. He not only miscalculated the warrior spirit of the Japanese, but more important, he also miscalculated the nature of Ares himself. He was to make the exact same mistake, with the titanic consequences of Armageddon, only nine years later.

On Judging Wars. It is an instinctive and perhaps necessary part of our understanding to go beyond the mere awareness of an event and to seek to grasp what it means. We want to know not only that something occurs or exists but also how to think about it. It is difficult to appreciate wars, or anything else, without judging them in some way. However, as a corollary to the analysis thus far, it should be obvious that the proper way to judge a war is not morally or even militarily but existentially. It is possible, of course, to make certain moral judgments about war, and these judgments must be respected and defended. But they do not at all tell us what the meaning of the conflict is. And even if one were to consider the moral questions about particular wars (is this war moral or immoral?), the problem of indicting an entire event is formidable. One might say, for example, that Hitler and Stalin were immoral in their invasion of Poland in 1939, but surely the Poles were not immoral in trying to resist them. So, to call World War II immoral is meaningless, since one could just as easily say that World War II is probably the most moral war ever fought, meaning that the Allies had to stop Hitler. Moral indictments, like moral approvals, of wars as such are simply silly. One can certainly make moral judgments about certain people in wartime and about certain acts within a particular war; one might even go so far as to say that the initiation of a war by country *A* against country *B* is immoral, but that does not mean that the war itself is immoral. Further, even if the initiation of a war is morally dubious, it does not follow that the subsequent development of the war is morally dubious, even with regard to the aggressor. If country *A* commits an act of aggression against *B* over a small border dispute, we may indict that act as immoral. But if the act brings about a conflagration of enormous dimensions, fully unexpected by the aggressor, it does not follow that the aggressor nation forfeits all rights to defend itself against a huge and violent counteraggression. France may have been morally wrong in the severity of its punishment of Germany in 1919, but it surely had a right to defend itself against the panzers in 1940; and even Germany itself, wicked to the core, had a right to defend itself against the final invasions of its homeland in 1945.

These obvious reflections lead us to a maxim that is of considerable importance in carrying out the bewildering but essential task of judging wars: wars are not to be assessed, ranked, rated, or judged solely in terms of their beginnings. This, by the way, is true not only of wars but of almost every kind of human endeavor. A man may begin his association with a woman on purely carnal grounds, but the subsequent development of a deep and passionate commitment to marriage and family cannot be understood in terms of that initial spark of selfish lust. In Plato's *Phaedo,* Socrates informs us that it is silly to confuse conditions (events that may bring about other events) with true grounds (principles that explain the meaning of an event). Too many historians spend years of research and reams of paper trying to pinpoint the exact "cause" of the outbreak in 1914; even worse is their attempt to explain World War I in terms of the "guilt" of one nation or another. Understanding something does not consist in spotting what made it happen.

But if we should not judge a war in terms of the events that bring it about or in terms of the guilt ascribed to the aggressor, how can we judge it at all? The answer must surely lie in the existential meaning of a war, its spiritual significance, its achievement of the understanding of the we-they distinction. A war that is carried out in the absence of some of the nine marks or that is lacking in sufficient revelation of meaning, even if it is won, is less of a war than one carried out in accordance with the existential principle, even if lost. In 1939 Russia invaded Finland, a wholly unequal affair; and although the Finns officially "lost" to Russia, her valiant defense and courageous performance left the integrity of her soul intact. One should always hope, of course, that one's own nation should fight only just wars, but even a war begun on dubious grounds can become an authentic and noble endeavor. How, though, do we make such judgments?

Before we isolate the principles and the maxims, it should be helpful to begin first by actually making existential judgments about some wars, so as to reveal the method and procedures of the analysis. Most of us are familiar with the great wars in history, and thus it is advantageous and perhaps even necessary to begin with these familiar events. The two world wars that plagued the first half of the twentieth century provide us with examples of how we judge wars from an existential point of view.

The World Wars. There is a fairly common perception among Western thinkers about the two German-initiated wars of 1914 and 1939. The First World War might be called the "pacifists' war" because few events in history support the antiwar protesters as profoundly as World War I. On the other hand, World War II might be called the "moral war," since few acts of belligerence among nations equal the moral justification given to the Allies' defeat of the Nazi tyranny. When one reads an account of the First World War, one cannot help but feel the deep frustration of witnessing a carnage that surely could have been avoided; it may have been the saddest war ever fought. On the other hand, it is impossible even for the most cynical reader not to rejoice at the final defeat of the Axis powers in 1945. Even archpacifists like Bertrand Russell were moved to support our involvement in the Second World War, and reflections on our victory even today bring a sense of gratitude and pride in the courage and sacrifice borne by the combatants. And yet, it is the very morality of World War II that tends to eclipse the full meaning of that effort, just as it is the pathetic stupidity of both the diplomats and the generals in World War I that tends to distract our appreciation of the nobility of that effort.

World War I. There are essentially three ways to interpret the outbreak of the so-called Great War. First, the opposing sides simply stumbled, almost by diplomatic accident, into a war that neither side really wanted; second, the war was inevitable given what was happening in the major countries, particularly the growth in Germany and the corruption in Russia; and third, the war was the result of German aggression, inspired by its rapid rise in economic and international importance, its desire for colonies, and its fear of being hemmed in by the implacable Russians and English on either side. The first two of these views see the events that led up to the outbreak of hostilities in August as minor nonevents, none of which by itself constituted a *causus belli,* and even collectively need not have led to war without considerable misunderstanding on both parts. According to the first two views, neither the Central nor the Entente Powers wanted a wider war; both the kaiser and the tsar, cousins after all, desperately tried to contain the conflict to Austria's punishment of Serbia, and most ministers, like Foreign Minister Grey of England and unlike the warmongering Berchthold of Austria, hoped to avoid an all-out conflict. After the assassination of Archduke Ferdinand in Sarajevo, was it really possible to prevent an all-out conflict? One reason for saying the conflict *could* have been avoided is the fact that most leaders and ministers doubted it would happen. The Serbian leaders, themselves on the throne because of earlier assassinations, were not innocent lambs; Austria certainly had some legitimacy in her anger; German support of Austria, though perhaps criminally simplistic, was not unexpected; it was surely possible that the tsar and the kaiser could have reached a common understanding of what Russian mobilization *meant,* and so on. The declarations of war seemed to follow from a series of events that were grossly misinterpreted and blown out of all proportion. British waffling, as usual, seemed both to provoke and confuse. Thus, the reader of history comes away from his texts with a decided feeling of dismay rather than outrage. Was it, then, merely a series of insignificant misunderstandings, goofs, misinterpretations, and just bad luck that brought about the carnage? Granted that all sides were deeply suspicious of each other, was it not possible to clarify positions so that the actual belligerence need not have started at all? The facts seem to support this sad interpretation.

On the other hand, the facts also seem to support other interpretations. One such interpretation is the favorite among anti-Teutonic types, putting the whole blame on a Germany eager to achieve its position in world affairs and ready to accomplish this by any means whatsoever. It is true that in the first seventy-five years Germany existed as a unified state within Europe, it engaged in three of the bloodiest wars in our era: 1870, 1914, and 1939. Even if we grant that it was France that declared war in 1870 and that perhaps Germany was provoked in 1914, it is hard to escape the conclusion that a unified Germany spells disaster for Europe. On this reading, Germany always had wanted a war with France, had prepared the great Schlieffen Plan long in advance, waiting merely for the opportunity. It had developed a long and serious tradition of military preparedness, had shunned international disarmament conferences, and had openly expressed its right and destiny to have more colonies. The very fact that it was *successful* in the early stages of all three wars shows, to some, that it was the aggressor.

But it was, after all, not Germany but Russia that first mobilized, and

Russia and France combined had a much larger force than Austria and Germany combined. The facts, unfortunately, seem to permit of several interpretations. Poincaré, the president of France, who had been born in Alsace-Lorraine and who felt passionately about returning those provinces to France, was visiting Russia at the time of the Austrian ultimatum to Serbia, and what he said to the Russians has never been fully clarified. Some argue that Poincaré was the one who really wanted the war. To argue that Germany was "aggressive" in its desire to extend its influence is to argue that Britain, which was the most successful in terms of colonies and its fleet, should have been allowed to remain on top of the international hill, that in the name of peace Britain should have been allowed to rule the seas and Africa and India and whatever else it pleased to dominate.

More cosmic-minded readers of history like to suggest an even further interpretation, that the war was inevitable given the unification of Germany, the frustration of France, the aloof arrogance of the English, and the rapid deterioration and corruption of tsarist Russia. Given these spiritual forces, it seemed as if only armed conflict could result, for the spiritual forces were simply incompatible. Viewing the map of Europe after the event, there does seem to be a kind of inevitability to the story. The German Empire, ever since the end of the Napoleonic era, was gathering together such enormous spiritual energy that it seemed to threaten to spill out of its boundaries by the sheer genius of its accomplishments. In almost every field, German spirit and German mind were dominant; from the synthesizing vision of Hegel to the encompassing art of Wagner, the German people manifested an ascendancy over the rest of Europe, especially in light of the degeneration in Russia and even France. The wild man Rasputin mirrored this degeneracy no less so than the excesses of the later Roman emperors, and the sense of doomsday was felt by more than just a few. How could Russian autocracy continue in the new enlightenment of the new century? How could the explosive spirit of the German people be contained by a mere congregation of loosely organized principalities? And once they were unified, could even the world stop the bubble from bursting?

Whatever the causes of the actual decision to declare war, there can be no doubt that once it began, the war took on a power and significance of its own. I have suggested above that there is a narrowness in seeking to explain things solely by focusing on their beginnings, and this is especially true of World War I. It is possible that Germany, faced with a two-front war, invaded neutral Belgium in the sincere belief that the Schlieffen Plan was the only sound military thing to do. And indeed, there is much sense in this reasoning. But it was not the actual invasion that caused people to hate the Germans; it was the brutality of the terrorist occupation that caused the indictment of the kaiser's army. But even this is open to interpretation and wonder. There is little doubt that German forces were exceptionally cruel and vicious in Belgium, but subsequent cruelties proliferated on both sides. Modern warfare was simply revealing itself as far more gruesome than anything in the nineteenth century. That the terror backfired can scarcely be doubted, for Germany won few friends by its brutality, yet it may have impressed a few as well. Turkey seemed to see what happened in Belgium as a sign of dominance and strength, and its eventual alliance with Germany is surely due in part to respect for the stern authority and will to power found in the German advance.

The first six weeks of the war were radically different from the remaining four years. Once the war of maneuver stopped, the war of attrition took over; and it is this grinding, merciless, harrowing, and dismal history that one remembers of what came to be known as the Great War, the War of the Trenches. And it is also this war that most provokes the pacifist's indictment: wave after wave of useless, mindless slaughter; battles that changed nothing but left the landscape carpeted with corpses, into the millions of dead. This war did not seem to make any sense at all. The Central Powers were Christian nations, led by Christian princes ruling over lands that were not unduly severe or harsh; the various enemies all believed in the same God, read the same classical literature, heard the same music. The Entente Powers, though less unified, since France was a republic and Russia an autocratic tyranny, were nonetheless similarly persuaded by Christian values and tradition. The amount of land that actually changed hands during those four bitter years was so negligible as to be unnoticed on a general map. What were they fighting for? What were they fighting against? Why were they fighting at all? But they were not merely fighting, they were battling with unusual savagery, gigantic sacrifice, enormous bloodletting, senseless attrition. The pictures are wickedly grim; countless battalion after battalion marched solemnly into the soldier-eating machines only to be spit out as bones. And no one could stop it, or rather would stop it. Surely if the battle line was almost the same after four years, the waste was prodigious.

The careful reader of the various accounts of this war cannot help being astonished by the historian's evaluations. On one page, we are confronted with the assurance that the various attacks after the First Marne were simply exercises in futility, that the generals did not seem to learn anything from their earlier experiences, did not learn that another offensive, even vaster than the previous, would not achieve the breakthrough. As we read this, we cannot but wonder if all the leaders on both sides were simply demented. But a few pages later, we are also asked to imagine that, had commander x or general y only added a few more divisions, there *would* have been a breakthrough. Had the tanks been held back until they were ready, had the resources of a campaign not been withheld, had a few more thousand men persisted for just a few more days, perhaps one side would have achieved that slicing of the Gordian knot that the other campaigns had been unable to untie. But if we, a half century or even a century later, are confused by these assessments, how much more must Joffre and Ludendorff and Foch and Haig have been by the same tantalizing but frustrating uncertainty. Was it indeed criminally stupid to send millions to their deaths on hopeless new offensives? Or was it indeed genuinely possible that one of these attacks might have succeeded and the sacrifice, hence, worth the cost?

If we, protected from the agony by generations and informed by the gift of hindsight, remain confused by conflicting analyses of military historians, how can we expect from those who lived during the event any greater wisdom? And in the absence of that elusive knowledge, what are we to make of those who sent the hundreds of thousands of Europe's finest young men into the maw of relentless attrition? This question serves as a lever to lift the rock and allows us to peer underneath. What we have in World War I is a spectacle of the highest devotion, a true and wondrous commitment to the sanctity of what is one's own. These were not glory seekers, flush with the trumpet of a new adventure; these were men with sunken faces and bitter experience, men who, after four years of the most dreadful bloodletting, without much hope of instant victory, perhaps even mangled by the press of despair, nevertheless continued on with unfathomable courage. It is the very absence of a clear and moral goal that makes these awesome sacrifices the more noble. They struggled, wept, endured defeat, and even died, not for some ethical principle or even a moral necessity, but simply for their country. The dense fog of moral uncertainty that eclipsed the landscape of the war's beginning continued to occlude the very grounds of the war throughout its bloody duration. That they nevertheless fought on appears to the unspirited as supreme stupidity, but to those sensitive to the enigma of Mars, such courage is illuminating. Morally, World War I is utterly dark, but existentially, it is an unwavering source of meaning.

For a war fought so savagely and endured with such bitterness, the final results of the war—none could call it victory—were deeply confusing and curiously ineffective. Germany, the loser, retained her heartland; the victors organized an international league that could do nothing; the guilt that was supposed to fall on the vanquished actually backlashed and fell on the victors. It must be remembered that although Germany was the vanquished, it had never had a single foreign soldier on its soil: the entire carnage had taken place in Belgium, France, the Balkans, Russia—everywhere except on the territory of the defeated. Surely that is a record of some sort; it is at least an oddity. There was spite and meanness in the Versailles treaty, but it set the way for an even more horrible confrontation twenty years later. So the war that had such a dubious beginning reached its final phase in an even more inglorious and dubious end. But if wars should not be judged by their beginnings, neither should they be judged by their endings. What one must judge in the Great War is what went on in the trenches, and that was simply heroic. For in spite of the dubiety about the rightness of it all, in the end the French soldier bled for France, the German soldier for Germany, and the British soldier for Britain. What does it signify to point out to the youth dashing into harm's way that the event could have been avoided? Does it make his sacrifice any less?

But if the avoidability of the war does not lessen the bravery and courage of the individual soldiers, can the same thing be said about the long-range consequences, not of the war but of the peace? I have suggested that World War I may be the *saddest* war ever fought, and the reason for this assessment is not that so many millions had to die in seemingly senseless frontal offensives but that the political consequences of their nobility were beguiled by abstractions in the end. Consider, just for a moment, the existential meaning of this war and its consequences. Germans fought for Germany and Frenchmen for France: in this there is pride, dignity, courage, and true patriotism. But what was hewn out of the charred wood of the burned forest was a new map entirely, not made up of well-recognized and identifiable countries, but brand new concepts, institutions without history, borders that had no precedent. Two abstractionist thinkers on either side of the globe, Lenin and Wilson, were determining the atlas based on ideologies rather than traditions. Out of the ashes popped republics no one had ever heard of before, like Czechoslovakia and the Baltic republics; artificial entities like the Free City of Danzig and an artificial Poland; and much, much worse, a *republican* Germany designed by non-Germans to satisfy the victors. The war itself was fought for the sacredness of the We over the They, but the postwar political intrigues were rearranging what the We meant at all. This is not to say that any one of these decisions was corrupt or immoral, but the fact remains that *who one was* had radically changed. Paradoxically, the

greatest changes of institutional meaning occurred in those countries that
were apparently unchanged, those favored by victory. In France, the bold
but foolish believers in spirit and aggressive behavior had become frightened defenders behind a useless wall of solid defense, the Maginot Line.
The British had become appeasers, yielding and ceding and giving all to the
new enemy. And even the Americans, who had offered the ballast of their
young bodies on the side of France and Britain, had become isolationists.
People no longer thought in terms of country but of ideology. The isms took
over from the flag. For the most part, the countries that fought in World War
I were simply not the same as fought in World War II, even though they had
the same names. And the sadness of all this consists in the dread fact that
the men who died so gallantly for their countries were remembered by their
offspring in totally new institutions. Russia, Poland, Italy, Germany, Czechoslovakia, Austria, Hungary—all were entirely new nations. The war seemed
to have put a permanent end to the classical notion of a nation-state. What
remained were ideological nations, countries recognizable not in their people
but in their weltanschauungs.

Unfortunately, this too was an illusion. The rearranging of loyalties, the
reanchoring and recasting of the institutions of meaning, were soon to
collapse into a different kind of we-they distinction. Those who had fought
so nobly for their countries in 1914 came out of the war realizing that their
countries had ceased to exist, supplanted by modern, ideological governments.
They therefore had to fight again.

World War II. That single generation of peace, from 1919 to 1939, was
forced to watch it happen. Their parents had fought for countries that were
loved; the children had to fight for institutions that were *believed in.* And
there is the great but sad difference between the two wars. The Allies were
morally required to defeat the Axis, fully aware that their own timidity and
appeasement were as morally corrupt as the satanic lust for power of the
enemy. The so-called Second World War was really the *first* World War, for
it was truly global; the so-called First World War, in spite of wide-flung
allegiances, remained essentially a European affair. World War II began as a
bitter and necessary battle to save civilization, but it turned into the same
war that started out in 1914, a war between nations. The introduction and
use in 1945 of nuclear weapons has once again recast the entire bowl of the
universe of war; we cannot think about it with the same principles or the
same hopes and loyalties.

Perhaps it was because of the ideologies, not the nations. We were told that what mattered was not England or America or France, but democracy; the enemy was not Germany and Russia, but fascism, Naziism, communism. These we did not inherit; these were beliefs we adopted. They were not our native sons but our adopted parents, not the homeland of our affections but the new worlds that beckoned us as citizens of the universe. In this, we were equally beguiled, because, when it came down to the actual business of warfare, we fought as we always fought, in the uniforms of our countries. But the confusion and distraction had done its work. If in World War I we stumbled into a war because of darkness, in World War II we slithered into war blinded by light. It was only in the furnace of actual combat that these beguiling and misleading notions got straightened out and we once more returned to ourselves, fighting as countrymen for the land we loved. But by then it was almost too late.

The titanic wickedness of one man, Adolf Hitler, is the greatest distraction of the twentieth century. For it is not in the character of this loathsome man that we must seek to find an understanding of the war. There were other wicked men: Stalin, Mussolini, Tojo; and there were wickedly beguiled men, like Chamberlain and even Roosevelt, who equally deserve the blame. No, the question is not How was Hitler possible? but rather How could Germany let him be possible? Not How could Chamberlain be so weak and criminally appeasing? but How could we support and provide an atmosphere of appeasement? In World War I it may have been the secret treaties that caught the critics unaware and led to worldwide bloodshed, but in World War II it was open and clear for everyone to see. The Nazis openly declared to the world they wanted a new order, built on the Aryan superiority, and to *believe* in such a worldview was to be a Nazi; the Soviet Communists were openly declaring that the world must yield to the dictatorship of the proletariat, that the workers of the world would throw down their unnatural weapons and join up in a utopian union; the Fascists were less clear in what they offered the world, but it was no less supported by anger and determination. On the other side were the democracies, echoing the pitiful cry of Wilson, hoping that the various tyrannies would go away. Here there were no secret alliances, at least not that were secret for very long—witness the prearranged agreement between Russia and Germany once again to divide Poland—because for the most part there was no *need* of secret alliances. Everyone knew what the upcoming conflict would be about: not countries or nations or traditions, but *metaphysics*. Would those who believed in communism defeat those who believed in racial superiority? The term "we" no longer meant the Germans or the

French; it meant "believer in this or that orthodoxy." Or at least, so it seemed on the surface.

The shift from national sentiment to "belief" in an ideology as the ground for the we and the they is not entirely illusory. There were many who thought this way, and those who did were not too shy to *use* the classical institution of the state to carry out these ideological triumphs. But in appealing to the national character, the ideological wars became national wars, suggesting once again that for some magnificent reason, our allegiance to our nation ranks higher than our political persuasion.

It is in this way that we must seek to understand the phenomenon of Adolf Hitler. For the war was not, as many might suppose, a private playground for a demented Austrian housepainter; the war was fought for classical and profound reasons that have to do with belonging and identifying who one is. Therefore, the question that haunts the interpreter of history is this: How could the German people, that great and creative populace of such genius and stature, find in Adolf Hitler a leader of what the Germans thought of as *theirs?* What was it about Hitler that allowed Germans to see him as *theirs?* And the answer to this, I think, is deeply revealing. After Versailles—indeed even earlier, after Compiègne—the Germans were told that they were *guilty.* They were forced to sign the treaty condemning them as the immoral aggressors in 1914; they were burdened with massive indemnities that were paid, not by the defeated regime, since that had ceased to exist, but by the children of those who fought and died. Thus, they were paying huge debts simply because they were German. To be German was to be guilty, to be bad. The symbol of this self-imposed guilt was Weimar, and those who tried to work within the Weimar system were those who supported the view that being German was being guilty. The man who hated Weimar, who rejected Versailles, who offered to the world not a repentant and reformed naughty child but an upstart nation proud to be guilty, even to be bad, was Adolf Hitler. The world told the Germans that being German was bad. Very well; if being German is being bad, then by God we'll be as bad as we can be, because that is what being German means. Of course, "good" in this context meant "pro-Weimar" and all that it stood for—defeat, acceptance of guilt, payment of indemnities—whereas "bad" meant being German and proud of it, being anti-Weimar and antidemocracy.

The point is alarmingly simple: given the thesis of this inquiry, namely, that the we-they distinction is an essential way of understanding who we are, if one characterizes that we as guilty, shameful, naughty, and punished, one must either abandon the affection one has for that institution or find some way of accepting it without shame and guilt. But the victors of World War I had made any acceptable form of being proud of one's Germanism impossible. And so Germans found the only way they could of supporting who they were, by supporting the one man who resisted all attempts to shame the German nation. Indeed, to some extent, the ploy backfired; the Germans became proud of being the black sheep of Europe, proud of being "bad," that is, nondemocratic. Because this is what the very victors had insisted was what being German meant.

There is much that is outright troubling and even paradoxical about World War II. We think of it as Hitler's war, not Tojo's war or Mussolini's war. Yet the Japanese invasion of Manchuria predated Hitler's invasion of Poland by *eight years,* and no one dates the beginning of World War II as September 1931. Nor do they date the beginning with Italy's invasion of Ethiopia in 1935, four years before the invasion of Poland. These acts of aggression by Italy and Japan certainly helped to create an atmosphere of war. Mussolini and Tojo were allies of Hitler, they were cruel and aggressive and brutal and warlike, but their actions are not seen as starting the world war. Why not? Nor can it be argued that September 1 began the involvement of the great powers; that did not occur until 1940. It seems that the reason for spotting September 1, 1939, as the beginning of the war is that it was *German* aggression, not Italian or Japanese aggression. Why should that be? The point is, the historian is quite right in spotting 1939 as the start of World War II, but why this is so is not so obvious. (Surely May 10, 1940, is actually a better date; that was when Germany attacked a meaningful enemy.)

Another way to approach this curious paradox is to examine the war from the perspective of the Soviet Union. They, together with their allies, the Nazis, invaded Poland in 1939. This can be seen as their natural commitment to the extension of communism, just as their later invasion of Finland can be seen as an extension of the Soviet system. But, these two acts of brutal aggression are not what constitute the present-day perspective of World War II; the Russians see that war as the Great Patriotic War! Not love of communism, but love of Russia! I have noted in the second mark how Stalin appealed to the Russian (not Soviet or even Marxist) people during those grim days of 1941. And they were not fighting Nazis; they were fighting Germans. And surely the degree to which those long-suffering and incredibly brave people withstood the German assault can be traced to their loyalty to Mother Russia, not to their belief in the Soviet system. Men do *not* fight for what they *believe in* but for what they *love.* One can love a nation;

one cannot love an ideology. One may *start* a war for ideological reasons, but if it is to be won, it must appeal to the patriotic fervor of a people who identify the struggle *as their own.* This also explains the rapid fall of Marxism once the reign of terror was defeated in the coup against Gorbachev.

Consider the American involvement. We are rightly proud that we helped stop the slaughter of the victims of Naziism; we rejoice when we see the films of concentration camp survivors being set free. Many morally good things were accomplished by the Americans joining the Allied cause in the late days of 1941. But the reason we went to war was not because we thought it morally right to defeat the Nazis or the Fascists or the war party of Japan; we went to war simply because we were attacked at Pearl Harbor. Germany declared war against the United States; it was not the other way around. Again, it is the very righteousness of World War II that tends to eclipse its true meaning. We fought, not primarily because it was *right,* but because it was *ours.* If one were to argue that we fought against the evils of Tojo, Mussolini, and Hitler, then we would stand indicted of an even more insidious delay than that of England. If it was right of us to defeat the Nazis in 1941, then it was right to defeat them in 1940 when they could have been beaten more easily and when Britain so desperately needed our help. Perhaps, indeed, we *ought* to have joined forces against the enemy earlier than December 1941, but the reason we did not was simply because the war was not *ours.* The attack made it ours. And once attacked, the dispute was not moral but existential; it was we against them. It was not democracy versus tyranny, but America versus Japan and Germany.

This may seem a harsh doctrine indeed. Surely the victors were morally superior to the defeated in 1945; surely it was right and not merely patriotic to defeat such brutal and immoral foes as the Nazis and the Japanese. I agree. But the enemy was defeated because we fought as a nation, not as a moral monitor for the world. We can be proud, of course, that our nation was on the side of the right, but being on the side of the right is not what makes us a nation. The "problem" in trying to come to grips with understanding World War II is that the moral rightness of our position tends to eclipse what was really happening. The *national* (not ideological) defeat of the Germans in 1914 had left them without an identifiable national spirit; to overcome that, they appealed to a national rebirth disguised as an ideology. The reasons and causes for the various victories and defeats throughout the course of the war are not ideological but military, and the spirit behind the various armies was not ideological but national. This is what must be seen, lest an important lesson of the war be lost.

In his masterpiece, *Dr. Faustus,* the German author Thomas Mann describes the fall of Germany in remarkable terms. It was the conquest, he wrote, of machines over men, of technology over a people. Mann wrote *Dr. Faustus* in California, a German refugee fleeing from Nazi tyranny. His books were among those burned by the Nazi book-burners, and he was no friend to Hitler and his regime. Yet, as German, he could not fail to sense profoundly the terrible loss that his country was going through. Morally, of course, he supported the Allies, to which he had expatriated; but spiritually he wept at the loss of German lives and national unity. What he says contains some truth, though to deny the Allies also had spirit and great leadership is ridiculous. One reason the Allies defeated Japan and Germany *was* simply that they had better machines, a deeper economic resource for the production of countless airplanes, tanks, guns, and new weapons. It was in its own way a copy of World War I, a war of attrition, a gradual wearing down of those vital resources necessary to carry on a major war. We did not win merely because we had good soldiers, greater patriotism, and braver men. We also won because we had more money and materials and the will to use them. Historians point out correctly that Hitler also made some huge mistakes, chief of which was Barbarossa. But even the ill-advised attack on Russia in June of 1941 possibly could have been successful had the economic productivity of Speer's Germany provided enough machines. What is incredible is not that Germany lost but that it came so very close to winning. And one of the main reasons it almost won, with all the odds against it, was that it had a terrific patriotism among its anti-Nazi soldiers.

Consider for a moment the following speculation. Imagine, if this is possible, Hitler without the Holocaust, that is, Hitler without the concentration camps. Imagine merely a man who unified a beaten and distraught nation into a powerful and feared nation, a man who put the idle to work and restored the economy and managed through military genius to defeat completely his earlier foes. He had defeated all of France, most of European Russia, all of the Baltic nations, and had Britain in desperate straits. If we judge him on these lights alone, he would doubtless go down in history as a man equal to Napoleon Bonaparte or Julius Caesar, among the world's great conquerors. No world-conquering hero is ever a nice man, and the list of the heroes who did conquer worlds is a list of violent and often unscrupulous men. But they remain among the great. Yet, Hitler is not so remembered. Why?

Surely he *would* have been remembered as great, even though he finally lost. After all, Bonaparte also lost in the end. Russia and Waterloo were dismal failures, but Napoleon's position in history as a great man is intact. But Hitler is remembered, not as the man who actually conquered Europe — which he *did* — but as the man who sponsored the concentration camps. Were it not for his hatred for the Jews, the Gypsies, and all other non-Aryans, he would certainly be remembered as a man of considerable achievement and even greatness. He is, instead, remembered mainly as a thoroughly wicked man. This *moral* judgment is correct, and history is unerring in its assessment. But it is also a distraction. For after the smoke had cleared and the rubble was pushed off of European streets and the wounds began to heal, the world's warriors were as they had been in 1914, men of patriotic inspiration, not ideological persuasion. Even the Communist heroes are seen as Russian heroes.

A point must be made here concerning the historical impact of the concentration camps and the death camps. The grisly and repulsive pictures one sees of these feral camps are often presented as pictures representing the horrors of war. There is, for example, some famous postwar film footage that shows a bulldozer pushing hundreds of emaciated cadavers into huge pits, but this horrific film is often accompanied by protests of the horror of war. History needs its lens cleaned. The war was fought to put an end to these camps. The elimination of the Jews in Germany and in German-occupied lands was a *domestic* policy of the Nazi regime. They would have carried it out, perhaps even more effectively, *without* the war. It was not the warrior who made the camps possible, but the gestapo, that is, the internal police of a corrupt government. To lump the inhumane savagery of the camps together with the cruel brutality of war-suffering is blatant perversion of truth and meaning. Hitler was admittedly pressed to speed up the process of the "final solution" when the Allies invaded Normandy and the Russians reversed the tide in eastern Europe, but there is no doubt that, strictly speaking, these gruesome decisions had nothing to do with war; they were a result of what might loosely be called the "ideology" of Nazi Germany. Pacifists who use images of death camps to ensure their support of all antiwar sentiment are dissemblers. It was not war but Nazi ideology that caused the camps. Or perhaps a better comment is that such camps were not the result of any true policy at all but the result of the madness of their leaders.

Consider the two so-called ideologies of Naziism and fascism. Aside from a few lunatic fringe groups, are these ideologies alive today? Did Naziism last one minute past the death of Hitler? Aside from its obvious racism, can anyone articulate today the principles of these beliefs? Were there ever any principles? When Marx died or Lenin died or Stalin died, people still knew what communism was; there were others to take over. But who took over from Hitler and Mussolini? Today we do not fear for democracy but for the United States or for France or for Canada. And until recently, we feared, not the ideology of communism, but the very real nation, deeply patriotic and traditional, known as Russia, *not* the USSR. Surely those who would make judgments about World War II must look beyond the wickedness of Hitler and the moral rightness of the Allies and see what really happened: it was a war among nations, in which the stronger alliance was victorious. If we insist on reading World War II as a war among ideologies, then, I fear, we must judge the war as lost. After all, the stated political reason for England and France declaring war on Germany was to keep Poland democratic. And surely that, until recently, was not achieved. The Russians, I believe, have the right name for it: it is the Great Patriotic War. To see it in ideological terms is deeply distortive.

There are some puzzling aspects to the enemies in the war and they deserve reflection. One is the curious policy of the Japanese. They, after all, were the earliest of the belligerents; they were also the last. Their war lasted from the invasion of Manchuria in 1931 to the signing of the peace treaty aboard the *Missouri* in 1945, a full fifteen years. Germany was at war only six years, America only four. Japan's goal, of course, was to become the eastern version of nineteenth-century Britain: a naval power far in excess of its natural wealth and population. Japan found China not a very formidable foe when it came to modern warfare. (Even today, China's billions do not constitute a deadly aggressive danger, in spite of the Pentagon's concerns.) There were many British military bases and colonies Japan coveted, such as Singapore. But its true natural enemy was Russia. Why did Japan decide to take on the United States? This was a country it could never hope to defeat, whereas, with Germany's help, Russia might well have been defeated, faced as the Russians would have been with their own two-front war. By bombing Pearl Harbor, Japan brought the dreadful economic might of the United States against Germany as well as itself, a most unfortunate occurrence for Japan. When Churchill heard of the attack at Pearl, he leaned back and sighed happily, "We have won the war!" Surely it was a bitter blow to Japan's number one ally, Germany. So why did Japan do it?

Or consider Germany's curious attitude toward her two fronts, east and west. Surely anyone could see that Russia was far more threatening than the hesitant West. During the war, Germany had twice as many divisions on the eastern front as on the western front, even after June 6, 1944. Yet all the venom of Hitler's remarkable hatred was turned against the West. It was westward that he directed all his new weaponry, sending up first the V-1 and then the V-2 and finally the jet fighters against the West, not the East. Did he not realize where the greater threat came from? In fact, his own attempt to develop an atomic bomb was designed to be used against the West, not Moscow. These are deeply troubling military issues that deserve to be mentioned, even though they do not appear to have ready answers.

It should also be mentioned, by the way, that Barbarossa may not have been quite as foolish as it looks on paper. Hitler could have invaded England, but had he done so, then he would have had the Red Army at his back, with no possibility of shifting huge numbers of divisions east. He may well have felt, and possibly with justification, that once an invasion of England began, Stalin would not hesitate to take advantage of the lowered defenses on the eastern front. As it was, Britain, alone at the time, could not seriously launch a land invasion in the West, so an attack against the East was either then or never. And indeed, difficult as it was, Barbarossa may well have succeeded in the long run had America remained neutral. So once again, it was the foolishness of the Japanese attack against Pearl that made the invasion of Russia so terribly fatal.

These are but military speculations, of course. They trouble the mind because they seem to be errors of such a gross kind as not to make much sense. However, I should like to suggest that the deeper error that lay behind these military blunders is the very error I am suggesting beclouds the contemporary historian looking back on the event. Both Germany and Japan continued to see the war as an ideological conflict rather than a patriotic one. I am suggesting that Germany and Japan, had they seen the war as nationalistic efforts rather than as metaphysical attempts to develop "new orders" in their respective spheres, may have won. Germany may have won the war; it was the Nazis who lost it, just as it was the nation of Russia, rather than the Red Army, that finally defeated them. For in the last analysis, the reading of the Second World War reveals the truth contained in this interpretation: men do not fight primarily for justice but for meaning. And meaning cannot be achieved solely by metaphysics or weltanschauungs but by inherited affection for what is one's own.

Strategically and tactically, then, those who do not understand the essence of war are very likely to lose it. All nations at war make military blunders, some enormous and stupid, but none is as fatal as misunderstanding the nature of war itself. The Americans' unsuccess in Vietnam, a mere relative failure, was nevertheless due in major part to their forgetting what war really is; their victory in World War II was due in large part to their remembering what war is. War is a vast, sacrificial, and heroic contest in which the difference between the *we* and the *they* is fully tested. Anything less than that invites disaster.

The above pages represent the kind of judgments one makes about wars. They are, for the most part, *not* moral judgments but military, historical, and existential judgments. I have focused on the two world wars and Vietnam as concrete examples. It is now imperative to consider the broader question, How are existential judgments made about wars?

1. The first point is surely noncontroversial. As we have already noted, man in his essence is a historical being, which means he cannot divorce his self-understanding from the major historical events that alter his world. And so it is proper and necessary to consider such questions as, What were the historical effects of the major wars? Once again, the question is not Were the wars moral or immoral? but rather What did the results of the war produce for the meaning of mankind? For all its hideous and seemingly senseless attrition, the First World War was fought for absolutely classical reasons: to protect the nations. In the sense that this is the reason the men fought, it was a glorious endeavor. But in the sense that this is the criterion one should use in judging the result, that war was a disaster, since the institutions that were loved with enough passion to inspire enormous sacrifice simply failed those who defended them. This does not mean the war itself was stupid or immoral; it merely means that history played a cruel trick on those who bravely died. The same can be said of World War II; we were told we were fighting for and against ideologies, but we were not. In this sense, the second war was better than the first, because the emerging nations were true nations and not mere ideological stepping-stones to world orders. So one way of judging a war existentially is to interpret the *results* of the war in terms of the questions of meaning.

2. However, a war is not restricted in its meaning solely by its outcome. It is also necessary to judge a war in terms of the kind of effort and the nature of the inspiring principles that support the we-they principle. In this case, the first war was superior to the second and both were superior to Vietnam. The true existential test of a war is the amount of meaning that it throws on the institutions that both win and lose. When the effort of a war reveals the commitment and devotion of a

people for what is theirs, it is a genuine and worthwhile war, whether won or lost. Men do not need success in order to qualify them as worthy adherents to what is their own. In this sense, all pseudowars or dribble wars are existentially weak.

3. Finally, wars must be judged by the extent to which they demand of all men the final allegiance to what is theirs. If there is a criterion in distinguishing "good" wars from "bad," the principle is simple: any military action or decision that exceeds the need for self-realization is cruelty, and any hesitation on the part of a nation or a soldier to carry out what is necessary to retain the integrity of what is one's own is either existential stupidity or, worse, existential cowardice. This principle, stated blandly and in the abstract, seems formally cold and perhaps even glib. Who is to determine what is "essential," or "necessary"? Hindsight (history) is always easier than foresight (statesmanship). But difficulty in actually carrying out a principle does not negate or invalidate that principle.

Our study of history, then, provides a concrete exemplification of how we think about actual wars. I have tried to show in the *interpretation* of actual wars and the isolation of the principles that govern those interpretations how, in this concrete art, history, which rests on the a priori modality of telling stories, the we-they principle actually works. But it also works in another humanistic discipline, literature. And here I do not mean the countless masterpieces about war, from *The Iliad* to *Dr. Faustus*. Rather, I mean how literature reveals to us our humanity in terms of our primordial understanding of what it means to be loyal. Great writers, no less than great generals or great military historians, reveal to us through their art the primacy of the we-they principle.

Consider the final cantos of Dante's *Inferno*, the more favored and popular half of his *Divine Comedy*. In the *Inferno*, Dante depicts the various levels of hell, often showing us highly imaginative tortures for the various kinds of sin and crime. The deeper one goes into the levels of hell, the worse are the crimes. In this way, whether one is a Christian or a believer in postterrestrial existence hardly matters; we can appreciate the indictments made of the various human crimes. They are ranked.

At the very bottom of hell, on the lowest possible level, Dante describes an ice-bound lake, from which the torso of Satan rises in maleficent majesty. Satan has three faces, each of which is gnawing on the frozen souls of three infamous people from history. If we are to understand the grand metaphor, these three men are supposed to represent what is worst in human depravity. But they are not murderers, rapists, thieves, cheats, liars; apparently their crime is far, far worse than any of these. This, after all, is the bottom of hell. Who are these three? They are the world's most famous traitors: Judas Iscariot, the betrayer of Christ, and Brutus and Cassius, the traitors to Caesar. Thus, to betray what is one's own, to be treacherous to what and to whom one belongs, is, in the vision of the great Italian poet, the supreme wrong. Note, too, the kind of suffering to which these hapless three are submitted: the world is cold, dark, lonely, and hopeless. There is no warmth at all, not the hell of tradition, which is flaming and hot, but a hell reserved for the frozen spirit, the lifeless decadence of total immobility. Treachery and betrayal: for Dante we think of such things as sins of darkness and ice, worse even than murder.

Why does Dante make such a metaphor, such an image? One may, of course, disagree with Dante. For some, cruelty is worse than treachery; for others, indecency or unkindness or selfishness may be worse. But Dante seems to represent a universality in human sentiment; that is why he is regarded as a great poet; that is what it *means* to be a great poet: that he speaks universally. Yet, why should treachery of the sort represented by Judas and Cassius and maybe even Brutus (save that Shakespeare is much kinder to Brutus than is Dante) strikes us as so formidable a vice? It is not because the *results* of their actions are so devastating or because the amount of suffering generated by their acts is so great (simple foolishness probably results in more suffering than any other vice), but because to be unfaithful to what is one's own eclipses the very meaning of those who perpetrate these insidious acts. Treachery and betrayal offend us not only because they are wrong but also because they are ugly. In much of the various descriptions of torture that Dante presents in his descent, a certain amount of sympathy and compassion can be felt for the sinners caught in their eternal punishment; but for the traitors there is none. This is revealed through the brilliant descriptions of the cold:

> ... thus low,
> Blue-pinched and shrined in ice the spirits stood,
> Moving their teeth in shrill note like the stork.
> His face each downward held; their mouth the cold,
> Their eyes expressed the dolour of their heart.
>   (Canto 32; Cary translation)

They are cut off from all warmth of human understanding and feeling. The poet's brilliance in this magnificent image reveals immediately what we understand by the wickedness of the treacherous: they have sundered themselves from their home, from what is theirs. The icy loneliness seems to fit our understanding of what it means to betray. Is Dante right? Is this, the cruel divorce from what is one's own, the truly worst state that a soul can achieve? Perhaps in the rapture of his magnificent poetry, we might believe him; and poetry is capable of revealing truth.

But if the worst state a soul can achieve is treachery, then we must think again about what it means to be loyal, to belong, to share. For sharing is the one thing that seems impossible for a Cassius and a Judas, since their offense is against sharing altogether. This is not to say that one cannot ever decide to change one's allegiance; Judas could have decided that Christ was wrong, was offending Judaism as he understood it, and then could honestly have broken with his master, regretfully parting company with him. This we could understand and perhaps even admire. But Judas betrayed the one who loved him, and so the poet depicts him as forever frozen, chilled, cold, and without any sense of belonging. The image reveals.

Yet surely loyalty is a cause of war. In fact, we use the word "true" in a peculiarly revealing sense in such cases. We speak of loyalty as being true to what is one's own. But "being true" is what is meant by authenticity. By being true to what is one's own, we realize ourselves; by being false to what is one's own, we become traitors and wind up on the frozen lake. Thus, even Dante, who is not strictly a war poet as is Homer, shows us a compelling truth about ourselves. We seem to understand that our existence is meaningless if we are false to what is our own. Being morally right is not always enough; we must also be true to who we are. Being against suffering is not enough; we must also endure it if we are to ensure the meaningfulness of our existence. Dante knew this several centuries ago, and so did Socrates in the *Euthyphro*. There is no such thing as a good and meaningful life without loyalty to what is one's own. If this is true, then once again we see that men do not fight for what is morally right but simply for what is necessary for meaning.

Lest one assume I have chosen only examples that make my case, consider this obvious truth: for the thousands of years that men have lived together in various societies, it has almost *never* been the case that one nation went to war against another for purely moral reasons. Consider our own situation today. We know of atrocities in other nations, and we care deeply about the victims, but we do not go to war. We know of cruelty, of racism, of corruption, and even of murders committed on behalf of ideologies or religion, and yet we do not go to war to stop these things. What then *do* we go to war for? We fight for how we talk; we fight for what side of the street we drive on or for the kinds of clothes we wear. And that is simply the terrible truth. We cannot escape it. We may be staggered by its implications, or stunned into outrage or speechlessness by the truth of it, but we cannot escape the *fact*. Men do not fight for what is morally right but for what is theirs. In the preceding chapters, I have tried to avoid the instinct to *lament* this curiosity and have tried instead to understand it. And I submit that as long as we look at war either as a purely *moral* event or as an event sponsored merely by personal gain, none of it makes any sense at all. But a true thinker does not throw out a whole history of truth merely because his principles are inadequate to explain it; rather, he reexamines his principles. I submit that the existential principle of the we-they can and does explain it, and can even be defended.

8

Peace

Having reached a definition of war based on existential principles, it would be unbefitting—indeed outrageous—simply to assume that peace is nothing more than the absence of war. Not only would this be an insult to the nobility of peace, it also would forfeit any respect for the nature of our inquiry. We must think through to the essence of peace with as much critical concern as has been shown in the inquiry into war. For peace is not merely a negative notion, understood solely in terms of what is not happening. Peace has a positive, existential meaning as well, and in the turmoil of the debate over peace and war, it is rarely raised and even more seldom addressed with any seriousness. If we assume that there is an existential meaning to war, as I have suggested in the foregoing chapters, and if we provisionally shelve the naïve view of peace as a utopian innocence in which everyone is simply good by nature, we must now consider the question, What is the existential meaning to peace? That is, how are we to think of the notion of "being at peace" in terms of our meaning? Does the we-they principle cease during a time of peace? If peace is more than a mere absence of war, then what does it mean?

The difficulty with this question is exacerbated by the historical fact that extended periods of peace are far less frequent than war, that the historian often must interpret periods in which there was no actual fighting as lulls between the serious matters of war, that by "peace" is meant the preparation for, or the reaction after, another war. There have, however, been a few periods of peace, and even during times of war the notion is not absent. Indeed, for those fighting, peace may be the single most dominating thought. Surely, then, in spite of the historical prejudice in favor of war, it should be possible to think about peace in a meaningful and positive way.

Yet, this remark about history may allow us a wedge into the question. When did the truly great periods of peace exist? If we can go beyond the mere political contingencies, we may ask, What is the nature of such times? And what clue can we garner about this historical observation if we are to harness not only the principles of war but of peace as well? It seems obvious that the longest and most effective periods of peace have been those which followed a great victory or the conquest of a major part of the world by a single victorious power. One thinks immediately of the Pax Romana, the period in which the Roman legions dominated the world and so threatened the other powers with their might that sheer respect for Rome's awesome military strength forced a universal peace. Or we think of the Pax ·Brittanica, the post-Napoleonic period of relative peace more or less dominated by the British navy; and perhaps we even think, if only for a moment, of the fleeting Pax Americana that followed the explosion over Hiroshima. In other words, historical instances of meaningful peace seem to be the result of conquest. Clausewitz defined peace as the ultimate goal of war, and of course, if we are to understand it in these terms, peace always means an imposed peace, one achieved by the victors over the vanquished.

The question we must ask, in all seriousness, is this: Does this historical fact suggest that there really is no other true meaning to peace than that achieved by conquest? There is a temptation to accept this as a cruel but undeniable truth, for there is considerable evidence to support the idea, as long as we consider only the factual understanding of history. But, even if we accept it in some sense, there can be no doubt that "peace" simply does not mean the same as "conquest" and that this historical point in no way relieves us of the task of digging more deeply into the meaning of peace. A clue can here be taken from the military themselves; even the generals and conquerors make a distinction between an *armistice* and a *peace*, in which the former means a mere cessation of hostilities, whereas the latter means a formal agreement in which the ready tendency and will toward violence has been replaced by a willingness to respect each other's sovereignty and autonomy. And in this context we make even further distinctions, one of which is paramount: the difference between a negotiated peace and an unconditional peace, or surrender. The latter implies that the defeated no longer has any say in the matter; the former implies that the cessation of hostilities can be mutually agreed upon without the complete and total submission of one power to the other.

It may be objected that to approach the notion of "peace" by these indirect and even military notions is distortive. But the greater fear is not that we will achieve an overly "militaristic" or even "political" notion of peace, but that it will be completely abstract and meaningless. We must begin on the experiential and familiar level, and that level is the one implied by history: peace occurs when the victor establishes an order that is preferable to the dangers inherent in resisting it.

Let us, then, begin by considering, even if counterintuitively, the meaning of peace accomplished in the extreme cases and seen solely from perspective of the victor. What, then, is meant, to the victor, by the Carthaginian peace? Of course, Rome completely annihilated Carthage, as Greece had annihilated Troy. Leaving aside whether we judge such harshness as acceptable, what does it *mean?* For the Romans, at least, it meant there was no more Carthage, and that meant there was no more threat, that Rome continued intact. An enormous feeling of security must surely follow such a triumph; no longer is the threat of total annihilation by the enemy a constant danger. Not only Cato but also most Romans may well have felt that there simply could not coexist a power like Carthage and a power like Rome, that either Carthage must be destroyed or Rome would be destroyed. And hence, along with a feeling of security, the conquest of Carthage must have instilled a sense of relief. There must also have been the gratitude to the fates or to the gods or to their armies that it was a peace dictated by Rome and not a peace dictated by Carthage, that is, that *their* culture would continue on and affect history.

(And here a purely formal point must be made. Let us suppose that the results had been otherwise, that Carthage and not Rome had been victorious. Carthage may have had many good elements in its culture that were forever lost. Roman law, still the greatest contribution of that nation and still with us in our tradition, would have been replaced by whatever Carthage would have handed down to us. Might it have been better? Perhaps the Carthaginian tradition would have been morally superior to the Roman. That is possible to suggest. But even so, it would not have been *our* tradition. We cannot be disinterested in the victory of Rome over Carthage, because we *are* Roman by inheritance. Granted that we would have been Carthaginian by inheritance had the results been otherwise, but there is no way we can understand the meaning of that. Hence, it is *our* victory, whether moral or not. It is impossible to read history in the abstract like that: I must affirm the triumph of Rome over Carthage simply because it is mine. That, however, does *not* stop me from making the moral judgment that the Carthaginian peace may have been immoral in its severity. The two judgments are *different.*)

To return to the main theme: peace, for the Romans, meant security and relief, and possibly gratitude. It also meant rejoicing in being Roman. Even if some Romans may have blanched at the severity of the punishment, it would have been existentially impossible for a Roman to have preferred the Carthaginians to have won. A further point should perhaps be made: in the case of a Carthaginian peace, surely there is considerable pleasure taken in the idea that we, the Romans, defeated them in a Roman way — that is, that being Roman not only *would* continue but also, because of the victory, *ought* to continue. For in seeing the triumph of Rome over Carthage, the Roman could not help but feel that his nation was *superior.* Whatever it is about Roman culture that produced the superior armies and commanders simply deserves to outlast the inferior Carthaginian culture. There is, if you will, a sense of fate or destiny in such sentiment: to the victor belongs not only the spoils but the place in history.

However, all these elements, security, relief, gratitude, and historical superiority, are all present in the nation at war as well; that is, these are the sentiments that prod us on to victory simply because they are desirable and their lack is regrettable. Thus, it might be possible to claim that, existentially, a Carthaginian peace is in fact a mere extension of warrior consciousness and does not reveal anything peculiarly *peaceful.* But Rome had enemies other than Carthage; it defeated many powers it did not annihilate, like Egypt, Greece, and Palestine. These nations it conquered but let remain autonomous, even letting them retain their own peculiar local law and provincial governments. In these cases, once defeated, the enemy became a part of the Roman Empire. It was still the case that Roman authority was the ground of the peace, but the continued existence of the non-Roman nation not only was permitted but was even seen as a benefit to Rome. Although superiority was retained, there was the further notion that the existence of the Other (the They) had a value. This, I think, suggests not only security, as in the Carthaginian peace, but self-confidence. Not only does being Roman matter, but being Roman among others matters. Rome feels no need to annihilate the other nations, so she is secure; indeed, she feels the paternalistic neighborliness enhances her true worth. Thus, self-confidence requires the possibility of the autonomous existence of the Other, a dimension lacking in the raw need for security.

But it is possible now to advance with this concept. Surely there are times in which peace is achieved, not by annihilation or even by conquering, but by mutual agreement. The nations struggling in the First World War, for example, wanted victory and, after the first half year, wanted some accommodating peace that seemed always just out of reach; but they were not committed to an annihilation of their enemy as a people. They hoped to achieve some kind of agreement in which all sides could coexist. Now, this idea may well first come from a realization of one's limitations: that it is impossible to eradicate an entire people even if one wanted to. But surely many statesmen genuinely felt then and feel now that there is something intrinsically worthwhile about having neighbors with cultures other than one's own. This goes beyond self-confidence; it also entails a care for the existential worth of the Other. Thus, peace in this third stage implies a willingness to respect not only one's own autonomy but the right, and indeed delight, for there to be others who have their own autonomy. This third peace includes the essential elements of the first two, security and self-confidence, and adds the respect for alternative cultures.

An interesting historical point can be made to support this distinction. In the Second World War, during the period of its ascendancy, the German Reich maintained an absolute Carthaginian attitude toward the Jews, a harsh, *almost* Carthaginian attitude toward the Poles, a merely paternalistic attitude toward their defeated neighbors the French, and possibly an even coexistential attitude toward the never-defeated English. The reasons for these differences are perverse, but they do show the differing notions of what "peace" can mean and indeed did mean as recently as 1940. Hitler wanted to wipe out the Jews entirely, wanted the Poles only as slaves, but would leave the French as vassals, superior to the Poles, and actually desired a shared regency with the British. In all these cases, the Nazis thought of their desired ends as differing kinds of "peace."

But there is a fourth level of peace. This is when a nation not only desires coexistence but is willing to sacrifice some or even all of its autonomy for the sheer avoidance of belligerence. In the case of a nation that is willing to sacrifice some but not all of its autonomy, one can see the beginnings of a destructive peace; in the case of a willingness to forfeit all of its autonomy, one sees nihilism. We see these two models exemplified in Chamberlain's Britain and the unfortunate Czechs in 1938. Czechoslovakia may have found it politically and militarily hopeless to resist the Munich agreement on its own, but it still could have resisted. The bitterness felt by the Czechoslovakian government was a nihilistic one; they had capitulated completely, perforce, and the meaning of that ignominy was as powerful, or more so, in their final defeat as was the threat of military power. Perhaps historians are too generous to the 1938 Czech government; granted the major blame is on Chamberlain's Britain, but *some* resentment can be felt toward a nation that gave up its own existence, without a shot, for the sake of an abstract peace.

But in this genealogy from Carthaginian to Czechoslovakian, or "Chamberlainian," peace, the development is not universally benign. At some point, peace ceases to be the desired or enviable quality that it at first seems. Why? What is it that is lacking in the fourth level? Surely what happens in this development is that the very reasons for peace in the Roman senses are somehow lost in the later stages. So we must retrace the steps. In the third step, there remains a robust sense of one's own worth; coexistence is possible only because what is one's own still matters as a supreme value. But in the fourth stage, what is one's own becomes sacrificed, not for a nation or a people, but for an abstraction. For "peace," conceived independently of the worth of autonomy, is nihilistic.

This development suggests that "peace" has two entirely different meanings, the one authentic and legitimate, the other nihilistic and illegitimate. The first sense of peace includes all the elements of the first three stages: security, self-confidence, and respect, perhaps even affection, for the autonomy of other nations. The second sense of "peace" is the notion that peace can somehow be meaningful without the worth of what is one's own, that is, that a continued nonbelligerence is *intrinsically* worthwhile and that this continued nonbelligerence simply outweighs whatever value there is in what is one's own.

It is the third step in this story of peace that, I believe, is the true essence of peace. As such, it is *always* desirable. It is morally superior to the first two steps, but since it includes the essential values of both, it is no less existentially desirable. The fourth step is *always* undesirable, and, paradoxically, usually causes war in spite of the sacrifice. How, then, are we to understand peace *existentially* the way this inquiry has sought to understand war? War is understood in terms of the we-they principle, in which the We represents the existential meaningfulness of who we are and the They represents the threat of what is alien. But are all who are *other*, or alien, necessarily a *threat*? It seems possible that one might consider what is alien as interesting and nonthreatening, of value *because* they are other. This is to think of what is ours in relation to what is alien in terms of a we-ye principle, where "ye" means "others as nonthreatening neighbors." In the we-ye relation, neither the we *nor* the ye is in any way overlooked or demoted; the differences are not dismissed but celebrated. I have used the archaic form of the second person plural to emphasize that by the term "ye" is meant not merely other people but others "as a *different* people." The integrity of the we is sustained, indeed enhanced, by the juxtaposition, rather than the opposition, in face of the ye. Just as male becomes more masculine in the face of the female, and the female more feminine in the face of the male, so the we becomes more "ours" and the ye becomes more "theirs" in this counterfacing of the we with the ye.

The we-they principle is fundamentally warlike, for the we is threatened by the they. Through war, as a means of achieving peace, the they is defeated so as to allow a ye. (But the we-ye principle is *not* a mere derivative of the we-they principle. It is possible, and indeed desirable, to establish a we-ye modality without the grim necessity of war at all.) In history, the we-ye can, of course, degenerate into a confrontational modality that alters into a we-they. But it is the skill of statesmen, together with the wisdom provided by true historians, to keep that from occurring. The possibility of the we-they must always reside as a fundamental presupposition assumed in the we-ye; but conversely, the we-ye also resides as a fundamental possibility in the we-they. A Carthaginian peace is an inauthentic we-they because the possibility of we-ye is not a part of the existential structure of what such a peace means. A Chamberlainian peace is an inauthentic we-ye because the possibility of the we-they is not contained in what such a peace means. Thus, the two extremes of peace, Carthaginian and Chamberlainian, are existentially inauthentic, since the opposing possibilities of we-ye and we-they are not entailed.

To conceive of peace as illuminated by the existential we-ye principle *in no way* sacrifices the autonomy of either the we or the ye, nor does it render the possibility of changing into we-they unacceptable. The popular phrase "living together as brothers" is therefore misleading, for brothers are not only of the same family but also of the same gender. "Living together as brother and sister" might be more apt, since a male sibling can never "become" a female sibling. Even the phrase "living together as neighbors" is not as good, since a male neighbor may take his female neighbor as wife and hence lose the distinctness. We-ye flourishes *on* the differences. The threat of losing what is one's own is too fundamental a fear to be disregarded or sacrificed on the elusive altar of world-sameness. The world is what it is because different peoples matter *as* different, and any "peace" that seeks to undermine that difference inevitably awakens the sleeping modality of we-they.

But why should we-ye become we-us? Peace is the positive existential modality of sharing the world without surrendering autonomy. To confuse "peace" with "reductionism" is the guarantee of war. But what must be presupposed in order for there to be such a thing as we-ye? The ultimate presupposition is that for us, the we matters, and for the other, the ye matters. In other words, the we-ye is possible only because both "we" and "ye" care about their autonomy. If either of these autonomous ways of being are *in any way* threatened, the we-ye becomes we-they. The threat can be either from outside or from an insufficiently existential understanding of who one is from within. Thus, to continue to care about who we are is actually a support for the integrity of the we-ye and hence also implies a respect for the autonomy of the other. Hence, the genuine threat to peace, to the we-ye, is the failure to let who we are *and* who ye are *matter.*

Peace is always between nations, just as war is between nations. Thus, if one nation ceases to be an autonomous nation, there can *be* no peace. Just as, in moral terms, it is impossible for anyone to have respect for others unless one first has respect for one's own self, so in international terms it is impossible for there to be a true peace without the sense of a nation's own worth. But this means that the state of coexisting in nonbelligerence is *not* the supreme value; it is dependent on the more fundamental principle that one's *own* matters. The true sense of peace consists, therefore, in letting others be, but only if both the security and self-confidence of one's own nation is first assured. The third step in the story of peace is a major advance over step one and step two because it allows others to enjoy the worth of who one is and, in doing this, is a deepening and enrichment of oneself.

And surely this corresponds to one's normal, everyday sense of peace. We enjoy peace, not merely because we do not have to fight but because the wealth of other cultures can be enjoyed. In peace, we can visit other nations, share other cultures, learn other traditions. But to recognize and even respect others does not imply relativism; on the contrary, a genuine peace is possible only if the robust sense of one's own is retained.

Does this mean that only armed, militarily prepared nations, supremely committed to autonomy, *can* enjoy peace? Surely this is true. This is true, first, in the *practical* sense. Deny, by conquest, another nation of its sense of worth, and you surely sow the seeds of resentment and another war. Witness the peace treaty against the German nation after World War I. On the other hand, compare the attitude of the victors in World War II. One of the most brilliant moves of MacArthur was surely letting the Japanese keep their emperor. For frail and disarmed as he was after the peace treaty, he was still the same man who was emperor of the Japanese: they were still a people. So, on the level of simple practicality, respect for the autonomy of oneself and others is essential. But theoretically the point is even more obvious. How can I respect others unless I first respect myself? How can there be peace unless there are nations at all?

But as obvious as these observations may be, they have not as yet focused on an existential understanding of peace. We have seen that peace is we-ye and war is we-they. This distinction is thought of in different ways for the nation at war and the nation at peace. We have seen that, in peacetime, we ourselves respect the fundamental right of meaning that another nation has. But of course, we do this in war as well. The difference is that in peace we see this affirmation as a part of our own meaning, nonthreatened by the other. This is to rejoice that we are we and ye are ye. War and peace are equally fundamental: war focuses on the triumph of the we *over* the they; peace, the triumph of the we *with* the ye. Hence, the autonomy of the we-meaning is paramount. Since this paramount meaning of the we is *presupposed* in war and peace, it is fundamental, presupposed in both we-ye and we-they. But this does not mean that peace is reduced to war, for with peace a new and further concept is developed, that of the autonomous ye. We now celebrate the fact that others can have the same affirmation of what is their own.

With this definition, peace is seen as entirely consistent with the meaning of war. It has its own special meaning, established by the journey through the first three stages of our genealogy: it gives security, self-confidence, and affirms universality of belonging. The meaningful peace exists only because of the willingness and readiness of each nation to assert its own independence and autonomy, so that meaningful and lasting peace can be accomplished only by the continuing respect of the warrior as an essential part of one's nation. To think in this way is to be a man of peace, for it establishes an existential worth in being at peace that is lacking in being at war. The man of peace, however, must always remain a reluctant warrior, ready to defend his home and nation should the we-ye develop into the threat of the we-they.

The man of peace, however, cannot be a pacifist. For a pacifist denies the very existential foundation of true, or authentic, peace: the worth and meaning of a we. Having sketched out the existential meaning of a man of peace, we are now required by the tide of the inquiry to consider the enemy to both true peace and war. Who is the pacifist? How are we to understand him?

THE PACIFIST

Who is the pacifist? Obviously he is one who rejects war, one who maintains that war is an unacceptable form of human behavior, that war is immoral. There is surely no thoughtful person who has not, at some time in his life, wondered if the suffering and cruelty found in all wars is simply too enormous to justify any organized belligerence at all. And because of this, even those who support the idea of war under certain conditions, find themselves instinctively thinking of a pacifist as one who espouses essentially moral ideas and who should, perhaps, be regarded with no little degree of sympathy and compassion, if not approval. Usually the image is one of a delicate conscience, sensitive to the suffering of others, perhaps even saintly; we imagine someone like St. Francis of Assisi or Gandhi or even Christ.

Not all pacifists are alike, however, and much that is suggested by this fanciful image is distortive. Distinctions must be made. We must make sure that the private pacifist is not to be thought of in the same way as the distortive pacifist or even the absolute pacifist. Exactly what are the grounds of one's pacifism? Are they all equal? There seem to be four major divisions among those who resist war: the private, the distortive, the absolute, and the deceptive pacifist. Within these major groups are important subdivisions. It is only after he has been so dissected that the figure can be analyzed truthfully.

The Private Pacifist. This is one who simply cannot take the life of another human being. He makes no universal claim that war is immoral, nor does he censure others for being able to kill. He may often be willing to serve in noncombatant roles, but he feels genuinely convinced that his nature is not up to the huge demands of taking another's life. Just as some people are cursed with vertigo and know themselves well enough to avoid looking out of high windows or walking near the edge of cliffs, so the private pacifist confesses a quirk to his character: he simply cannot kill. What is important about this type is that he makes no moral claim, but simply a private one. With such a one, even the combatant can feel sympathy. Many of these noncombatants not only serve their country in services that do not entail actual fighting, they at times achieve genuine heroism as medics, runners, correspondents, and chaplains. A few even overcome their reluctance on the battlefield. Although it is impossible for a concerned society to universalize such behavior, it is usually the case that in a wide and generous society such men are accepted without much dissent. We may feel that they are deficient in some way, but since they refuse to base their reluctance on universal moral claims, they are accepted as being without threat.

There is another kind of private pacifist, however, far less noble and enviable than the first, and that is the coward. To be a pacifist is not necessarily to be a coward, of course; often, to defend one's deepest principles against the mob, even if these principles are misguided, requires a high degree of courage. But there are many who espouse antiwar sentiments simply because they are afraid. To be afraid is no fault, but to submit to fear is a vice. In periods of frenzied public debate this cowardice is often proudly proclaimed, and is wedded to a kind of cynicism against the lofty and noble spirits of patriotism. (The public debate is further muddied, of course, by warmongers and glory seekers, who often do more to further the cynical pacifist than any appeal to peace.) It is crucially important to distinguish the cynical and craven pacifist from those more firmly grounded in genuine sentiments. For it must sadly be admitted that cowardice has a powerful appeal on the mind; it attracts us not only because of our fear but also because of its cynical suggestion of superior prudence. "All you crazy people can go ahead and kill one another; you obviously enjoy it; but my fellow cowards and I will stay at home and delight in our hedonism!" There is an attraction to this, partly in its deliberate cleverness in converting ostensible vices into sensible virtues. Like the sensitive private pacifist, the cowardly private pacifist makes no universal claim; but whereas the former quietly accepts his uniqueness, the latter offends us with the coupling of his arrogance with his cravenness. Not all cowardly pacifists, of course, do this; many will hide behind the formal arguments of any antiwar position in order to cloak their own timorousness, of which they may be personally ashamed. But such a frightened weakling may indeed have the germs of salvation, for if there is shame, there is the possibility of overcoming it. It is the public coward who offends precisely because he also lures.

The Distortive Pacifist. Even the man of peace admits some wars simply ought not to be fought. But there is a special kind of mind that presents a formidable opponent in the public arena of martial disputation. He admits that in certain cases he and his country should fight against a threatening foe, but in arguing against a particular war, he uses pacifist principles. The very fact that he maintains he is not a universal pacifist makes his position seem more rational, yet he argues against specific wars simply because they are violent. Indifferent to revolutionary or terrorist violence, the distortive pacifist presents a stunning display of feigned sincerity and dazzling contradiction. On the level of his sentiment he appears antiviolent, but on the level of his interests he supports some local violence. It is he who uses and abuses the term "antiwar," and he triumphs in the confusion. For what does it mean to be "antiwar"? If it means preferring peace to war, then we are all antiwar, and the term has no meaning. Perhaps it means being against this or that war. But to be against a specific war requires specific reasons; without adopting pacifist principles, one cannot be against a war simply because it is a war. Many say, for example, they believe it was right to fight against Hitler but believe all subsequent wars have been illegitimate. The distortive pacifist hops from moral to prudential reasoning with the aplomb of a wanton child; he seeks support from those who think from the spleen rather than the mind, but also gains among those who recognize the need of self-defense.

Within the category of the distortive pacifist, one must distinguish between the genuine relativist and the merely cautious, and so I submit the distinction between the distortive pacifist as such and the merely cautionary peace lover; the latter is suspicious of the warmongers and the saber rattlers and is a healthy specimen within the body politic, but the former wins his applause because of obfuscation and confusion. And here it must be emphasized what makes the distortive pacifist so objectionable: he appeals to his own morally superior position on the grounds that peace is preferable to war, at the same time admitting abstractly that a nation has a right to defend itself, but refuses to admit that a given threat is ever sufficiently dangerous to his country. He then lumps all who support a war effort as warmongers and militants, castigating them as morally inferior. Unlike the cautionary peace lover who merely hesitates to engage in any ferocity unless absolutely required by the needs of honor, the distortive pacifist straddles both camps, borrowing from the absolute pacifist the aura of high morality while enjoying equally the respect given to one who recognizes the integrity of honor. He calls himself antiwar but also defends the right of protective belligerence. He refuses to argue against this or that war, for that makes him morally precise; he *argues* against war as such in order to win the approval of pacifists, but he does not mean it.

It is the confusion that such a man causes that is so reprehensible. It is difficult enough to think correctly during an issue as volatile as war, and any obfuscation of principles is regrettable. The distortive pacifist has neither the personal dignity of a private pacifist nor the bold commitment of an absolute pacifist; neither does he possess the careful patience of a moral critic who may oppose a particular war on nonpacifist grounds. Since his position is essentially inconsistent, he can flourish only by confusion, and at this he excels.

The Absolute Pacifist. There are those for whom any violence at all is simply inconsistent with the proper calling of the human person. To them, the spectacle of vast hordes of armed men clashing on a blood-drenched field is totally repugnant and counter to all moral understanding. War, for the absolute pacifist, is simply immoral; it is wrong, wicked, evil, ugly, and irrational. The absolute pacifist, therefore, must be confronted directly, and that means in terms of his principles. Not, as with the private pacifist, in terms of his character, nor, as with the distortive pacifist, with his unevenness and inconsistency, but with his mind. We may call the first weak, the second confused, but with the third, we must boldly assert his position and judge him wrong: he is a teacher of false doctrine. But as in the case of the other kinds of pacifists, there are, in fact, two variants, and both must be considered. The first is deficient in his principles, the second in his imagination.

What is the rational basis for absolute pacifism? It is simply this: that life, particularly human life, is precious. In essence, if the pacifist is correct in this principle, then he is likewise correct in his indictment of all war. But if he is incorrect, then he is wrong in his moral attitude as well. But surely the principle, in all its simplicity, is appealing. Is not life precious indeed? Of course, it is not life but life lived well that is precious, not the mere elongation of life or its duration, but the excellence of life, the quality of living, that which makes life meaningful. It is not a moral requirement to live; it is simply a moral requirement to live a good life. It is not required that we go into the analysis of this; it has been articulated with great brilliance from Socrates through Schopenhauer to Heidegger. But it *is* important to realize that the pacifist profoundly repudiates this entire philosophical tradition. For the pacifist, *nothing* is sufficient to provoke violence, not even the threat of greater violence. And it is important to realize what this view entails. Many noble people, including war heroes, may well believe it is better to be killed than to kill, that it is nobler to sacrifice one's life for the sake of another. But that is not what the absolute pacifist believes. His principle is that life is sacred; therefore, even his *own* cannot be sacrificed. He will submit to anything—cruelty, torture, insult, slavery, obscenity, ignobility, and defilement—just to live a few hours longer. He himself will not take life, though he cannot stop others from taking lives. He would rather see his children raped, his family tortured, his culture eclipsed, his friends defiled, his own pacifistic religion destroyed, than lift a finger in violence against another. This is surely not cowardice, as it might be in the first classification, or confusion, as it might be in the second; it is simply false. And because it is a view based on principle, it is hideously universal. Unlike the private pacifist who cannot take another life, the absolute pacifist condemns all who would protect their own. He does not see that to allow a vicious murderer to fulfill his lustful pleasures—when death or the threat of death alone would stop him—is to condone the crime; he does not see that to refuse to shoot an invader is to support the invasion. When this is pointed out to him, the absolute pacifist accepts the horrors of his principle just because it is an absolute principle. Thus, there is no weakness in his character, no cowardice, no confusion, just profound error. There remains the confusion, of course, that to take no steps against the violence of others supports the violent, but the absolute pacifist dismisses this as less important than the commitment he makes to his principle. Thus, the only way to confront him is to deny his principle. This kind of pacifism, then, is simply the result of bad thinking; it must be rejected with the same authority with which we reject the absolute hedonist or the violator of *modus ponens:* he is not relatively wrong but absolutely wrong.

There is another kind of absolute pacifist. He begins, not so much with the affirmative principle that life is sacred, but with the negative one that there is no cruelty as unacceptable as war. He looks about and sees that the product of war is death, and just as he would indict the murderer, he indicts all who would bring about the phenomenon of wholesale murder, war. He may, indeed, when pressed, admit that his principle is the same as the man's described above, that life alone is sacred; but that is merely a response necessitated by the demands of consistency. Basically he does not see life as supremely sacred but rather death as supremely evil, and as a morally sensitive person, he cannot imagine any injury as severe as death or any wrong as grievous as killing another. At first glance, this may not seem very different from the position taken by the absolute pacifist described above, but in fact the error is quite otherwise, for the deficiency of this perspective lies in the imagination. Such a person is simply incapable of *imagining* how dreadful true slavery can be; he cannot imagine how outrageous it is to endure the permanent insult of having no respect as a nation; he cannot imagine a life so miserable and destitute that death is a boon of release. This is why such a person very often enjoys the best of life's amenities; such views most often come from the well-heeled and comfortable. It is they who rarely have to endure much, who need not suffer the scourge of the unacceptable or the ignominy of the stateless, who often fear death beyond all reason. Not knowing how dreadful it is to be defeated, they invite defeat. They protest they would rather live under the heel of a dictator or inhuman regime than risk not living at all. "Better Red than dead" represents this way of thinking, which is often due to the simple inability of the imagination to present to oneself a sufficiently precise picture of what it would be like to be "Red." Often, those who espouse such "unimaginative pacifism" are precisely those who will change their minds radically when confronted with the true savagery of the wickedness of the tyrant or the inhuman ideology. Thus, a man who piously laments war will suddenly discover a concentration camp, witness the enormous inhumanity of it, and suddenly support the war effort. Although such conversions are to be greeted with relief, it is irritating that so many others are able to imagine these ills without having to experience them directly, and one cannot help but wonder why the onetime pacifist is so unimaginative. The roots of this error are often found to be an unwillingness to admit that evil exists and the sluggishness that comes from a comfortable existence. In many ways, an ignorance of evil is the greatest evil; those who cannot believe that supreme wickedness is possible often find themselves supporting the forces that bring that wickedness about. There is a kinship between the unimaginative pacifist and the antipunishment social theorist. The belief that all boys are really good boys, save for bad environment, is similar to the belief that no state of existence is as bad as death or that no political concern is great enough to go to war over. And this, I think, is the main reason thoughtful people feel uncomfortable in the presence of an absolute pacifist: the pacifist is unwilling to care profoundly enough about what is our own. If this lack of caring is due to an unfertile imagination, it is all the more unpalatable.

The Deceptive Pacifist. We now turn to a more sinister individual. There are some who publicly argue against war, who support peace marches, disruptions of the civil order, and resistance to governmental authority — all in the name of peace — but who, underneath, are simply revolutionaries. In undermining the authority of a state, the deceptive pacifist has as his goal not the cessation of a war or the diminution of a nation's military strength, but the collapse of the system entirely. These may be few in number, and the response to them may be the same as the response to any saboteur. History has always recognized the fact that there are wolves in sheeps' clothing, and occasionally the sheeplike outfit may simply be pacifism. But the threat here is far more serious. We know how to think about the conscious deceiver, the spy, the traitor; we have laws against them and do not hesitate to judge them harshly. But their influence is greater than their own criminality, for they make possible the self-deceptive pacifist, the saddest and most pathetic and perhaps the most dangerous of them all. Here we speak of the sincere, honest, gullible, and essentially stupid man who, ostensibly working for peace, itself a noble enterprise, finds himself almost unconsciously working against what is his own. He corrupts his own nobility by letting his hatred for war become a hatred for his own country, which might make war. Thus, the deceptive pacifist is not merely a menace to his country for espousing treason, he is in one form also a menace to his own mind. It is an easy course to follow: to start with the sensitive and even worthy concern for peace and to let it corrode into the rust of nihilism. It is a dangerous descent, from a hatred of war, to the hatred of the machinery of war, to a hatred of the state that supports the military, to a hate of the country, and finally to a hatred of oneself as a member of that country. One can perhaps have a vestige of admiration for a foreign spy who infiltrates his enemy's land and stirs up antiwar sentiment so as to make his own country ultimately victorious. We may admire the courage and even loyalty of this foreign traitor, since that is the task of spies. But we can have only pity for one who allows his legitimate interests in peace to corrode his own loyalty so that he becomes a traitor to what is his own.

Thankfully, of course, the self-deceptive pacifists are probably not that numerous, although the number of actual deceivers, conscious of their own treason and even proud of it, may be more numerous than we would like to believe. Nevertheless, it is self-deceptive pacifism that most distresses the mind, for it seems to sound the depths of all pacifists: it is the corruption of loyalty to what is one's own. And this, I think, is the real anguish we feel about all pacifists: they have no loyalty to what is their own. They are, at bottom, men without a country, profoundly alone, for they cannot affirm what is their own, inspired perhaps by a worthy ideal, that of peace, but paying for that ideal with an unmeasurable price, their home. Perhaps no tragedy is as dreadful as that which portrays the man who has, unwittingly perhaps, destroyed what is his own, as does Othello or Creon.

We recognize, then, four major categories of pacifists: (1) the private pacifist, who is either overly sensitive or simply cowardly; (2) the distortive pacifist, who argues against specific wars with principles that really argue against war as such; (3) the absolute pacifist, who maintains the false doctrine of the total sacredness of life and hence forfeits the good life, or who is lacking in imagination and cannot conceive of evil or the true nature of slavery; and (4) the deceptive pacifist, who is either an enemy of the people in his deceit or is self-deceived, and who destroys his own for an ideal that is impossible without his own. Some of these are more pitiful than dangerous, but all are essentially wrong and, in two cases, are complete menaces to thought and freedom. The essence of pacifism is shown to be a lack of reverence for what is one's own. However, there is a fifth kind of pacifism that does not belong in this list, because it rests on completely different principles, but it should be considered here because of its seeming kinship with the others.

The Nuclear Pacifist. There are those who argue that all four of the traditional pacifists are indeed corrupt and unacceptable, and who would agree with the indictment of them that is presented above. But they would argue that the existence of nuclear weapons completely alters the picture. For now the question is not the moral one of supporting violence or the existential one of supporting what is one's own. Rather, the argument is that the entire human race is in jeopardy and that no one has the right to threaten the species. It may be correct, they argue, to point out that one should fight against a tyrant or a foreign invader, but it cannot be right or even existentially meaningful to hazard the entire globe with nuclear incineration. This gives rise to a radically different kind of pacifist, the nuclear pacifist, who defends his antiwar position with reference to the ultimate threat, global suicide.

According to this way of thinking, 1945 has driven a wedge into the course of history, forever disjoining the past from the present and future. Those who live after 1945 simply must *think* differently than those who lived before 1945. What makes this new kind of thinking imperative is an argument that has curious force and persuasion and needs to be analyzed.

The argument has four premises, one of which is a factual claim, one a moral imperative, and two predictive scenarios. The argument is as follows:

1. We now possess enough nuclear armament to destroy the entire planet and with it all of humankind.
2. An all-out nuclear war between superpowers would in fact result in the total destruction of humankind.
3. Any war, even a nonnuclear war, ultimately involves the super-powers and enhances the possibility of (2).
4. It is unthinkable and unspeakable to bring about the total annihila-tion of the planet and the human species, and as a corollary, it is morally wrong to do that which threatens the annihilation of human-kind or which makes the annihilation more likely.

Each of these four premises is, in some way, vulnerable. Nevertheless, the argument is used by many otherwise nonpacifists to argue that the develop-ment of nuclear weapons has completely altered our moral understanding to the point that although all pre-1945 pacifists may have been deficient, it is now morally imperative to indict all war, not only nuclear war, because of the threat it brings to the human species. This produces a "new" kind of pacifist, the nuclear pacifist. The issue is, of course, complex. For example, the veracity of (1) can be disputed by the layman only by appeal to various experts, who themselves disagree. Granted that the majority support the claim, but there are many who do not. The layman, of course, believes the expert with whom he is in agreement. Or consider briefly the two scenarios: they have no more authority than any other suggestion of probable or even possible happenings. As for (4), the moral imperative, it may be believed by many, but it seems to come from nowhere. There is no imperative against a risky individual existence; why should there be one against the race as such? To prohibit *any* action that may imperil the race may entail an indictment of any and every social system that allows individual creativity and genius. Do we forbid all private research lest it stumble across a lethal strain of disease? Do we forbid space travel altogether if there appears to be the likelihood of counteraggression from aliens? We may argue that it would be prohibited (by ordinary moral principles) to imperil any large numbers of people (much less the entire race) if we were *certain* of the results of our actions, but of course no human activity is ever that certain, especially not the premises that support this curious argument.

The proper place, however, for the analysis of this argument in detail is elsewhere; it is enough to mention merely that none of the four premises that support the nuclear pacifist is invulnerable to critique. What is deserving of our attention here is not the validity or invalidity of the argument but what is entailed by the meaning. Let us assume, if not complete validity, at least considerable persuasion by the argument. This means, then, that modern (post-1945) humanity is prohibited from sharing precisely in those courageous and sacrificial acts that are necessary for human meaning. If the argument is valid, no man can join up with others to struggle against a tyrant, and no nation can resist an invasion from another. Those who violate this principle cannot be punished, since only by arming oneself against an invader can a determined invader be stopped. It is now considered *wrong* to love one's country as one's own, precisely because that love supports the idea of a nation, and the idea of a nation supports the idea of a war. That all nations might live in spontaneous brotherhood without the need for armies but with a mutual respect for the various independent autonomies is simply denying historical and psychological reality. And even if it were possible for there to be an agreement among extant nations never to go to war again, what should happen if a single leader in a single nation in some future time decided to expand? There are countless suggestions of this sort that appall the mind and reveal that we do not favor such possibilities, but nonetheless the attraction of the argument stands.

The most disturbing characteristic of this argument and of the nuclear pacifist generally is the cruel wedge it drives between us and our forefathers. It is no longer possible, according to this view, for us even to *think* like those who have come before us and whose boldness and courage created our history. Our children cannot stir to the magnificence of Henry V's speech at Agincourt or fill their hearts with patriotism in hearing Churchill's vow to fight the enemy on the beaches and the streets. We ourselves can no longer share the sentiments of Washington or Lee or Patton; we must forever be divorced from the Shakespearean Caesar, from Sophocles' Antigone or Homer's Achilles, for under the guise of this persuasion, all patriotism, all spirited triumph of men at arms, all heroes, and all martial sacrifice are grounded in sentiments that are wicked, false, and immoral. We must cluck in sad deprecation and superior wisdom at all who believe in being able to fight and die for something. And this ugliness is a very real threat, for the public now senses in the nuclear pacifist not only a hatred of war but a hatred of history. It is not only that we should scorn all warlikeness, we should also scorn the noble heroes of the past. For the reasoning is clear, *their values are no longer ours.* The nuclear pacifist inevitably finds himself a historical nihilist. History can be read only as an interesting but sad specimen of immoral events, a chronicle that offers no values but only information.

The year 1945 does indeed offer a wedge for many people, forever sundering the two species of history. The date threatens to replace that of the birth of Christ as the watershed for measuring events: Before Hiroshima and After Hiroshima. A.H. implies the new value system, with emphasis on pacifism, submission, simple hedonism, and the dread of nuclear annihilation. B.H. implies the old value system, with violence, savagery, nobility, and bloodletting honor. For if the argument is valid, how can we maintain any reverence for those virtues that unite men to fight against a foreign enemy? If the argument is valid, surely a reverence for the great men of history is misprized. New heroes, gentler, kindlier, surrendering, prudent, and fearful, must be created; new epics and tragedies in which the hero is praised not for his valor but for his meekness must be written. Or at the very least, the old ones must be reevaluated or recast, as Nathum Tate rewrote the ending of *King Lear,* making it into a comedy. Lest this seem a fantastic suggestion, one need only reflect that such gruesome reexamination is being done right now. Many students come to the great heroic classics uneasy and suspicious of their glorification of war and recognize that such bygone values no longer apply in a nuclear age.

Reverence for history is among the first values to suffer in any revolutionary period, of course, but this is unique because it rests on a certain kind of moralist argument. The threatening of the entire species has become a new kind of real possibility with the development of our horrible new weapons, and with this technological development (one can hardly call it an advance), there is a natural concomitant development of moral standards. The nuclear pacifist is a special and peculiar phenomenon, for he argues that the technology has literally revolutionized the ethical vocabulary. Since there is a "new evil," the destruction of the entire species, there must be new ways of thinking about what ought and ought not to be done.

There are no "new" moral principles, and usually those who argue that there are, whether in the nuclear age or in any other, are simply championing variants of a different form of immorality. There have been different forms of fear and psychological terrorism throughout history to distract us from our freedom and our integrity. The nuclear pacifist is simply another in a long line of those who would persuade us that we must submit to blackmail and surrender our freedoms lest we be killed. But the appeal in the public consciousness cannot be denied, and the blackmail and threat of the nuclear pacifist cannot be dismissed as trivial merely because it is wrong. It is important for us to realize just what the ransom money is, however. To avoid the possibility of the "new evil" of threatening the entire species, we must surrender all martial piety and commitment to the male and heroic virtues, must sever all true linkage with our tradition, and must even forfeit all sentiment that puts the warrior in a good light.

Many, if not most, people will simply not accept the blackmail, and unless the entire population of the globe accepts it, the payment is forfeit. It is the twin insult of rejecting our tradition and relying on naïveté that so upsets us, I think, about the nuclear pacifist in particular and all pacifists in general. It is simply too high a price to surrender our historical values merely on an empty hope that can be realized only if everyone suddenly becomes saintly. The contemporary appeal of pacifism may be intensified by the threat of global destruction, but its essence has not changed. In the first description of the modern pacifist, he was recognized as essentially a moral man, perhaps naïve and overly gentle, but still moral or at least moralistic. But on deeper analysis we see that "moral" is simply an improper adjective. Why is it any more noble to submit to fear and blackmail than to stand up to the threatener? Why is concern for one's own death more worthy than concern for one's dignity? Why is the pacifist who upsets the social order in his attempt to bring about unilateral disarmament any more enviable than a young man willing to offer his life for his culture, tradition, and country? It is not necessary to doubt the sincerity of either of them or the depth of their convictions and commitments. Yet if both can be admired for their devotion to their causes, why is the pacifist always instinctively seen as morally on a loftier plane than his warrior fellow? The answer to this obviously lies in the earlier recognition in this work of the paradoxical nature of war: we cannot look cheerfully into the face of Mars. At least, however, geared with the present arguments, one should resist the overly ready tendency to grant to the pacifist critic the natural halo. At bottom, the pacifist is a nihilist, in all of his guises. When the true light of thought is cast on these two young men, the warrior can be more admired than the pacifist.

In criticizing the pacifist, however, we must not confuse the issue by also criticizing the lovers of peace. In that vast dialectic between the sacrificial warrior and the stable man of peace, there is simply no reason for acerbic or unfriendly animosity. The point remains, war is a paradox; what is not so obvious is that peace is also a paradox; indeed, the warrior and the peace lover (though definitely *not* the pacifist) are mutually involved in the same paradox. The only true way to achieve peace is to understand this paradox, to understand that peace is based on a reverence for the human need to belong to what is ours as opposed to what is theirs. Peace, then, is possible only if pacifism is rejected. (This might be called the peace paradox; it is no more misological than the paradox of war.) Thus, it must be emphasized that the *paradox* is between the genuine man of peace and the genuine sacrificial warrior; the paradox is *not* between the pacifist and the warmonger, for both of them are simply wrong. In order to have a philosophically meaningful paradox, both claimants of the dispute must be fundamentally right. Our concern for peace is surely fundamentally right; our concern for the integrity of what is our own is likewise right: hence the paradox. But the pacifist and the warmonger are both wrong, so there is no paradox there at all; there is simply confusion.

Having arrived at an existential definition of peace and having isolated the pacifist, this inquiry might appear to have reached its natural conclusion, and so it has, in a purely formal sense. But these reflections on peace do not occur in a vacuum, and the cruel and vivid fact is that today we still live and probably always shall live under the threat of a nuclear holocaust. Strictly speaking, that should not really change anything, since we are dealing with fundamental ideas. But as a matter of fact, these considerations do add to our difficulty in seeking to understand the nature of a meaningful peace. Thus, we are not quite finished with our analysis, since it is not enough to talk about a "meaningful" peace; we must also talk about a *nuclear peace.*

Let us assume that the above several paragraphs are true: peace can exist only when total commitment to the autonomy of one's own nation is a paramount concern. Let us also recognize that all sane men dread a nuclear holocaust as a supreme evil, to be avoided by all means save that of denying the prior sentence. How are we to think about this? The following are observations that seem to follow from the above analysis.

1. The concept that the only acceptable behavior among nations is a total and continuous peace, that such an unbroken peace is the supreme desideratum, is fatal. For a commitment to a complete and total peace means that at no time can any nation assert its own interests or values to maintain itself as an autonomous nation. The counterargument, that a nation might sacrifice its uniqueness or autonomy for the sake of a world peace, is to misunderstand what peace *means.* True peace is possible *only* if the we-they principle is respected. Furthermore, the idea that no nation can struggle for its own authenticity or independence, because such uses of military

power manifest a step away from peace, is simply bad thinking. It does not seem to me that a small nation going to war in order to achieve some semblance of respect for its own values necessarily entails an all-out nuclear holocaust. Perhaps such small struggles throughout the world are actually beneficial, for they keep the world political body alive with change and with openings for hope. Indeed, even the idea of the superpowers involved with certain wars for their own interests is not necessarily an antipeace event, since peace depends on the authenticity of one's own. It is far more likely that an actual nuclear confrontation with the two superpowers will happen if no wars are fought on the level of "conventional" weaponry. Mankind does not function well in the greenhouse of abstraction.

2. The disjunction assumed by some who perceive this question simplistically is that one must always assume that there are only two choices: nuclear confrontation or submission. This notion must be resisted at all costs. Surely no simplistic idea is more deadly than this, because in the last analysis it tends to make any notion of sympathy for what is one's own an impediment to peace. But peace can be achieved only when the sense of what is one's own continues to matter, and to matter greatly. Indeed, the concept that one must see this problem in terms of the dreadful decision between submission and nuclear madness should be replaced with an understanding of what it means to be a state at all. We must recognize two things: retention of our own values is an absolute commitment, but avoidance of a nuclear holocaust is also an absolute value. By these principles the two values are conjoined rather than disjoined.

3. Contained wars, whether nonnuclear or even using nuclear weapons on a limited basis, should not be seen as an absolute evil. Those of us who care very much about avoiding a nuclear confrontation are simply different from those who merely lament the possibility with a wringing of hands. To forgo those values is to submit to the nihilistic point of view that the nuclear weapons confront us with only two alternatives. We must remain human beings, and we must retain patriotism in order for there to be peace. But peace entails the willingness to defend oneself against tyranny; otherwise peace comes to be identified with capitulation. A Carthaginian peace is *not* the only kind of peace possible; it is indeed only an embryonic notion of peace.

4. The slogan "Peace at any price," therefore, represents the greatest

promise of a nuclear war: first, because it promotes an opportunity for blackmail and would-be aggressors, but second, and more important, because it sponsors an atmosphere and a way of thinking that undermines the very meaning of peace itself, respect between nations. To urge capitulation rather than warfare when basic institutions are threatened is to deny the very meaning of peace, since peace can occur only when there are autonomous nations. Such pacifistic thinking also creates a totally false view of what it means to be a human being, for it sets up as the supreme value the continued existence of individual lives only, denying the truth that we are not isolated beings without institutional meaning.

5. Therefore, the great question of our day is not the question of peace *or* war, but rather the avoidance of a nuclear holocaust as well as a nihilistic capitulation. By recognizing the true *meanings* of war *and* peace, the proper misunderstanding of this profound truth can be realized. To forget these fundamental meanings invites both nihilism and nuclear war.

I have tried to show in the first chapters of this work that the proper way to understand war is to grasp the fundamental character of the human species: we are beings for whom our meaning is the fundamental and indeed only ultimate concern. In war, the question is always that of they against us. What I have tried to show is that the we-they distinction, assumed in such ordinary and everyday understanding, is, in fact, a profound principle that can be articulated only by existential language. Everyone knows that in war "we" fight against "them," but it is not obvious just what this distinction is about. I have tried to show that the we-they distinction is as fundamental as thought itself, that it is a distinction and indeed a *principle* based on how we must think of ourselves as meaningful. This makes war an essential part of who we are, but it does not make any individual war inevitable or necessary. I have *described* war in terms of the nine existential marks; I have then *defined* war in terms of the four suggestions concerning war's essence. In both the description and the definition, I have tried to show that the key principle always turns out to be the we-they principle and that this principle has existential rather than moral significance. Finally, I have tried to show that this analysis of war as an existential notion is supported by actual wars, by how we understand the warrior and the pacifist. I have ended the analysis with a discussion of the existential meaning of peace. Throughout this work I have often made use of the adage, Men do not fight for justice or private gain; they fight for meaning. With the inclusion of this final chapter, I would now add that men concern themselves with peace for the same reason. Peace is of value, not because it is just or privately advantageous, but because it is a source of our meaning. But so understood, a meaningful peace cannot be a pacifistic one.

There are, I suppose, some inevitable "political" ideas that follow from this analysis, but they are not my concern. I have endeavored to do only one thing, to make clear a concept. I have tried to make the phenomenon of war intelligible by spotting and isolating the principles that make it an aspect of how we seek to lead meaningful lives. The spirit against which I have argued throughout this work is nihilism. This inquiry into the meaning of war, as philosophical, concerns only its truth. Not sated with propositional certainty, we mortal fools learn much about the wonder of our finitude when we look within and ask why we go to war. If the answer is, Because who we are, as a people, matters, it must also be said that because of who we are, the uncovering of our own truth matters for its own sake. Both of these realizations astound those who are convinced that only untroubled lives should be led and only certainty of verified knowledge should satisfy our inquiry. We are more complex than that, and often it is in our darkest and most wretched ways that we find what is most precious, like the jewel in the mud: things like truth for its own sake and the esteem for who we are, regardless of how grim the truth and how frail our efforts. Perhaps Plato is right: the lovers of truth must be selected only from those who first manifest the sacrificial spirit of the warrior.

Works Cited

Auden, W. H. *W. H. Auden: Collected Poems.* Edited by Edward Mendelson. New York: Random House, 1968.

Burke, Edmund. *A Philosophical Enquiry into the Origin of Our Ideas of the Sublime and Beautiful.* London: Vernor and Hood, F. and C. Rivington and J. Nunn, 1798.

Clausewitz, Carl von. *On War.* Translated by Peter Pavet and Michael Howard. Princeton: Princeton University Press, 1984.

Dante Alighieri. *Divine Comedy.* Translated by H. F. Cary. Garden City, N.Y.: Doubleday, 1946.

Fest, Joachim. *Hitler.* New York: Random House, 1975.

Gelven, Michael. *A Commentary on Heidegger's "Being and Time."* DeKalb: Northern Illinois University Press, 1989.

———. *Spirit and Existence.* Notre Dame, Ind.: University of Notre Dame Press, 1990.

Gray, J. Glenn. *The Warriors: Reflections on Men in Battle.* New York: Harcourt, Brace, 1959.

Heidegger, Martin. *Being and Time.* Translated by John McQuarrie and Edward Robinson. New York: Harper and Row, 1962.

Hume, David. *A Treatise on Human Nature.* New York: E. P. Dutton, 1911.

Kant, Immanuel. *Groundwork of the Metaphysics of Morals.* Translated by H. J. Paton. Hutchinson's University Library, 1958.

Mauldin, Bill. *Up Front.* New York: H. Holt, 1945.

Nietzsche, Friedrich. *The Birth of Tragedy* and *The Genealogy of Morals.* Translated by Francis Golffing. Garden City, N.Y.: Doubleday Anchor, 1956.

———. *Thus Spoke Zarathustra.* Translated by Walter Kaufmann. Harmondsworth, Middlesex: Penguin, 1978.

Schopenhauer, Arthur. *The World as Will and Representation.* Translated by E.F.J. Payne. Mineola, N.Y.: Dover Publications, 1958.

Sun Tzu. *The Art of War.* Translated by Samuel B. Griffith. Oxford: Clarendon Press, 1963.